AVAILABLE

The programs described in this book are available on disk for your IBM PC (and most compatibles). They have been written in C and you will need to have a C compiler. (The author used Lattice C$^{(TM)}$ and Turbo C$^{(TM)}$.)

Order the Program Disk <u>today</u> priced £12.65 including VAT/$20.80 from your computer store, bookseller, or by using the order form below.

Ammeraal: **Programs and Data Structures in C** – Program Disk

Please send me .... copies of the Ammeraal: Programs and Data Structures in C – Program Disk at **£12.65 including VAT/$20.80** each

0 471 91834 2

D1511182

If you have any queries about the compatibility of your hardware configuration, please contact:

Helen Ramsey
John Wiley & Sons Limited
Baffins Lane
Chichester
West Sussex
PO19 1UD
England

Customer Service Department
John Wiley and Sons Limited
Shripney Road
Bognor Regis
West Sussex
PO22 9SA
England

Programs and
Data Structures in C

Programs and Data Structures in C

Leendert Ammeraal

Hogeschool Utrecht
The Netherlands

JOHN WILEY & SONS
Chichester · New York · Brisbane · Toronto · Singapore

Reprinted June 1988
Reprinted with corrections November 1988

Library of Congress Cataloguing in Publication Data:
Ammeraal, L. (Leendert)
  Programs and data structures in C/Leendert Ammeraal.
  p.   cm.
  Bibliography: p.
  Includes index.
  ISBN 0-471-91751-6
  1. C (Computer program language)   I. Title.
QA76.73.C15A47 1987
005.13'3-dc19   87-22184
CIP

British Library Cataloguing in Publication Data:
Ammeraal, L.
  Programs and data structures in C.
  1. C (Computer program language)
  I. Title
  005.13'3   QA76.73.C15

  ISBN 0 471 91751 6

Printed and bound in Great Britain by Anchor Press Ltd, Tiptree, Essex

Contents

Preface   vii

1 Programming Style, Iteration and Recursion **1**
   1.1 Introduction   1
   1.2 Using a Sentinel in Linear Search   3
   1.3 Using a Sentinel in Comparisons.   4
   1.4 Global Variables and Side Effects   6
   1.5 An Introduction to Recursion   10
   1.6 Elimination of Recursion   11
   1.7 Euclid's Algorithm for the Greatest Common Divisor   15
   1.8 Horner's Rule.   17
   1.9 Radix Conversion   19
   1.10 Powers with Integer Exponents   22

2 Array and File Manipulation **31**
   2.1 Straight Sorting Methods.   31
   2.2 Quicksort   35
   2.3 Sorting Strings of Variable Length.   38
   2.4 Sorting a File.   41
   2.5 Binary Search   50
   2.6 Hashing   54

3 Some Combinatorial Algorithms **61**
   3.1 A Variable Number of Nested Loops.   61
   3.2 Permutations   64
   3.3 Combinations.   69
   3.4 The Knapsack Problem.   71
   3.5 Dynamic Programming.   74

4 Linear Lists **79**
   4.1 Introduction   79
   4.2 Manipulating Linear Lists   80
   4.3 Linear Lists and Variable-length Strings   85
   4.4 Stacks and Queues   89
   4.5 Circular, Doubly Linked Lists   92

5 Binary Trees. **101**
   5.1 Basic Operations on Binary Search Trees 101
   5.2 Perfectly Balanced Binary Trees. 106
   5.3 Addresses of Pointers and Node Deletion 113

6 B-trees **123**
   6.1 Building and Searching a B-tree. 123
   6.2 Deleting Nodes in a B-tree 135
   6.3 B-trees on Disk 139

7 Tries **149**
   7.1 Introduction 149
   7.2 A Demonstration Program 151

8 Graphs **159**
   8.1 Directed and Undirected Graphs. 159
   8.2 Graph Representations. 160
   8.3 Topological Sorting; Detecting Cycles 161
   8.4 Activity Networks; Critical Path Method 166

9 Fundamentals of Interpreters and Compilers **175**
   9.1 Syntax Diagrams for a Very Simple Language. 175
   9.2 A Source-text Interpreter. 179
   9.3 Conversion from Infix to Postfix 181
   9.4 A Postfix Interpreter. 185
   9.5 Object Program and Run-time System 188
   9.6 A VSL Compiler 190

Appendix A: Some Pitfalls for Beginning C Programmers **195**

Appendix B: Program Index by Chapter. **199**

Bibliography **203**

Index **205**

Preface

There are several good books that discuss algorithms and data structures using either Pascal or some fictitious language. Instead, I use the C language for this purpose, and although I feel no need to apologize, let me briefly explain this choice.

Many years ago, authors who wanted to publish algorithms in a real programming language had to choose between a practical language, Fortran, which was not very suitable for that purpose, and a nice language (Algol 60), which was somewhat unpractical. Wirth's publication of Pascal in 1968 was a major step forward. Not only did this language offer new facilities for dynamic data structures but very soon efficient compilers and good textbooks for this language became available. However, Pascal has some serious shortcomings, such as, for example, the lack of facilities for random file-access, for bit operations and for separate compilation of procedures and functions. Every Pascal implementor has invented his own language extensions, at the cost of portability, and, consequently, Pascal cannot possibly be a practical successor to Fortran. Though for beginners it is possibly the best language that is currently available, there are a few aspects of Pascal which make it not an ideal language for teaching. To mention just one thing, my students are always inclined to test if a character is a newline-character *after* it has been read instead of using *eoln* beforehand, as Pascal requires, and it is a pity that we have to spend so much time teaching language peculiarities like the fact that a newline-character should become available as a space-character. As I have no experience in teaching the C language to absolute beginners, I would be reluctant to recommend it for a first introduction to programming, but as for students who have some familiarity with Pascal, my experiences in teaching C have been very positive. In C we find just the things we need, neither more, nor less. It is very practical, and, contrary to what people often think, C programs can be reasonably readable, provided that we pay some attention to this aspect; for example, by indenting in the same way as is customary in Pascal programming. C is a good language, both in practice and in (advanced) teaching, because:

(1) It is suitable for expressing all kinds of algorithms, and, as in mathematics, it does not require lengthy phrases to express something that can be said in a few words or symbols.
(2) It is supported by many efficient compilers, which all accept the same programs without any problems.
(3) It is used by a large proportion of the programming community all over the world.

C has some well-known pitfalls, which are briefly discussed in Appendix A. Knowing and understanding them will almost certainly prevent you from getting into trouble if the C language is new for you (especially if Pascal has always been your favourite language!).

When studying some intricate algorithm most students will appreciate having a ready-to-run version at their disposal, so that theoretical and experimental analysis may go hand in hand. This would not be possible with rudimentary sketches of algorithms and with 'programming details left as an exercise'. Incidentally, we should not use the term 'programming details' with any contempt. In novels, not only the idea behind a story but also the written story itself is interesting, and in computer science it would be no good if we could only *talk* about algorithms without being able to express them correctly and efficiently in a real program. This book avoids any algorithmic vagueness by presenting complete programs, in which the student can insert his or her own output statements if this should be helpful in seeing what the algorithm does. Besides, it is very instructive to investigate experimentally how a program's running time depends on its input. As in physics, experiments are useful both to confirm theoretical results and to stimulate new theoretical investigations.

You will find many useful algorithms in this book. Almost all of them are related to what advanced professional programmers need in practice. Instead of mentioning some of these algorithms here I would rather refer to the table of contents. Depending on the purpose for which the book is used, Chapter 9 might be studied very early, even before Chapter 2, since it does not use dynamic data structures and it is not very difficult. I placed it at the end because otherwise the important subjects of linear lists and binary trees would have been delayed, and, once dealing with trees, the chosen order of the subjects in Chapters 6, 7, and 8 is the most logical one. It may also be noted that Chapter 8 does not depend on Chapters 5, 6, and 7, so this might be given priority, too, if desired, especially since it will be easier than some programs in these three preceding chapters.

I have not attempted to be 'complete' in any sense, and you may miss some algorithms occurring in other textbooks. Incidentally, this is why I did not use the word *algorithm* in the title. However useful a cookbook of 'standard algorithms' may be, our capability to invent new algorithms will be at least as important, because there will always be new programming problems. This explains why I emphasize the *development* of algorithms, possibly giving the impression that I invented them myself, which with most of them was not the case. Most algorithms in this book (not the programs themselves) can be found in books by other authors, such as those mentioned (and implicitly recommended) in the Bibliography.

Although still a minority, there are institutions where the C language is used in teaching. Students learn this language surprisingly quickly, as I know from experience, so there may be time left for the subject of programming itself. I hope that this book will be accepted as a reasonable textbook for this purpose; of course, any suggestions for improvements will be welcome.

L. Ammeraal

CHAPTER 1

Programming Style, Iteration and Recursion

1.1 INTRODUCTION

When learning a programming language we study many examples and, if we do it the right way, we solve many small programming problems as exercises, so as soon as we are familiar with a programming language we know what programming is about. However, after this it may be desirable to improve our programming skill. Mastering a programming language is a prerequisite for advanced programming, so its importance should not be underestimated, but it is not sufficient. In the process of learning a language the examples and exercises are subordinate to the language elements under discussion. In this book it is the other way round. The reader is now assumed to be familiar with the C language, as explained in *C for Programmers*, published by John Wiley & Sons, and in many other books. When solving a programming problem we will not only be interested in an *algorithm*, that is, a solution expressed in more or less abstract terms, but we also want a ready-to-run C program or a C function that can be used as a tool in any application program. For most algorithms that we will be discussing it would not be practicable to express them in everyday English, so we need a formal language anyway. In mathematics it is extremely convenient that we can use the single symbol $\leq$ for the phrase 'less than or equal to'. In the same way, many compact notations of the C language, possibly considered confusing or 'cryptic' for the uninitiated, provide us with a convenient means to express algorithms. In the early days of computing many people used Algol 60 to publish algorithms, and had to convert them to (some old version of) Fortran to run the resulting programs efficiently. We are now in a much better position, since as soon as we have expressed algorithms in C we can run them efficiently on a great variety of computers.

There are many misconceptions about programming style. Sometimes people say that because of the speed of present-day computers we should not emphasize the aspect of program efficiency any longer but rather focus on program readability. However well intended, such general statements are confusing and misleading. We may as well argue that the increased speed of computers and their increased memory sizes give rise to our solving larger programming problems, so that program efficiency is now more important than it used to be.

Besides simply measuring a program's running time, using either a watch or an 'internal clock', we can approach the subject of efficiency from an analytic angle. For many

1

programs the running time $T(n)$ is a function of the input size n. For example, a certain program to sort a sequence of n numbers, that is, a program to place these numbers in increasing order, may have a running time

$$T(n) = cn^2$$

where c is a constant. Although the value of c is not irrelevant, the fact that this running time is a quadratic function of the input size n is usually considered far more important. We therefore use the so-called '*big-oh*' notation, and say that, in our example, the running time $T(n)$ is $O(n^2)$. In general, we say that $T(n)$ is $O(f(n))$ if there are nonnegative constants c and n_0 such that $T(n) \leq cf(n)$ whenever $n \geq n_0$. According to this definition, the fact that '$T(n)$ is $O(n^2)$' implies that '$T(n)$ is $O(n^3)$', but the latter is a weaker statement than the former, and in cases like this it customary to ignore such weaker statements. We also use the terms *growth rate* and *time complexity* for the function $f(n)$ used in the notation $O(f(n))$. In Chapter 2 we will see that there are sorting algorithms with time complexity $n\log n$ instead of n^2. It will be clear that this is an enormous improvement, provided that the length n of the sequence to be sorted is large. With present-day computers we can more easily accommodate such large sequences than we could, say, twenty years ago, so considerations of efficiency (or *complexity*, as computer scientists would rather say) are at least as important with fast modern computers as they used to be with the slower ones of the past.

This discussion about efficiency is not meant to imply that the other aspect mentioned, namely program *readability*, should be of minor importance. Illegible programs will more often contain inaccuracies and stupidities than programs that we can read and understand, and it will be more costly to write and maintain them, so it is wise to favour program readability. However, there are two aspects of readability that many people seem to overlook. First, whether or not a C program is as readable as it should be can be judged only by those who are thoroughly familiar with the C language (and preferably with some other languages as well), and though there are a good many C programmers around today, there are also many computer users who have never used C themselves and whose opinions about the readability of C programs are therefore of little significance. Second, some algorithms, even when expressed in the best 'algorithmic language' possible, are too intricate to be fully understood quickly by every student and programmer. It may then be helpful to resort to the computer and first experiment a little with the algorithm under consideration. Such experiments may remove any suspicions about its correctness, and, especially if it runs faster than we had expected, encourage us to analyse it. The possibility of experimenting is created by discussing complete programs in a real programming language.

It is a good idea to discuss such concepts as efficiency and readability in the framework of concrete examples (not confined to sorting problems), and to be cautious with very general statements. Preferably, such examples should be more or less related to what we need in practice. However, not everyone needs the same things and, besides, unpractical examples may be very suitable to illustrate important concepts, so some programs and functions in the following sections are presented only to illustrate useful programming principles. Others, however, may well be suitable for real applications in their literal form.

1.2   USING A SENTINEL IN LINEAR SEARCH

Some well-known solutions of certain programming problems are sometimes called *techniques* or *tricks*. The term 'technique' is too pompous for many little inventions, worthless from a scientific point of view, but nonetheless of some practical value. So for reasons of modesty, we shall use the term *trick*, in spite of its unfortunate connotations: our tricks are not meant to confuse or amuse (although they sometimes do, hopefully the latter more often than the former).

Here is a well-known trick. Suppose that we are given the array *a* and the integer variable *x*, declared in

```
int a[N], x, i;
```

We now want to search array *a* for the value of *x*, or, more precisely, we want the smallest of all subscript values i ($< N$), if any, for which the value of $a[i]$ is equal to *x*. If, on the other hand, all *N* array elements differ from *x*, the variable *i* is to obtain the value *N*. Here is the first solution:

```
i = 0;
while (i < N  &&  a[i] != x) i++;
```

It is clear that the variable *i* will obtain the desired value if some array element $a[i]$ is equal to *x*, for the first such element will cause the loop to stop just when the variable *i* has the desired value. If all array elements differ from *x*, the loop stops when *i* obtains the value *N*, and then *i* again has the correct final value. Note that & & is a 'conditional' and-operator. The second operand $a[i]! = x$ is evaluated only if the first evaluates to 1 (which means *true*). When *i* becomes equal to *N*, if that should happen, there will be no evaluation of a comparison $a[i]! = x$. Thanks to the 'conditional' behaviour of & &, only existing array elements $a[0]$, $a[1]$, ..., $a[N-1]$ (not $a[N]$) will be used in this comparison. By the way, this is not an extremely important point, for if it had been a problem we could simply have appended an extra element to array *a*. We shall in fact do so in the following discussion, although for a completely different reason.)

Correct as the above solution is, it is not the most efficient if *N* is large. The while loop contains two tests for loop termination, but, with a little trick, one will do. We extend the array with one element, and write

```
int a[N+1], x, i;
...
a[N] = x; i = 0;
while (x != a[i]) i++;
```

The three dots ... stand for some portion of program text, where the variables *x*, and the first *N* elements of array *a* obtain their values. If *x* is equal to one of these *N* array elements it is clear that the loop stops with the correct value of *i*. Should *x* be different from each of them, then the loop stops with the correct value $i = N$, since then the element $a[N]$, which we have added, will stop the loop. After all, we have assigned the value *x* to that array element ourselves. This while-loop is shorter and faster than the former, since there is now no test $i < N$ in it. The artificial array element $a[N]$, equal to the value we are looking for, is called a *sentinel*. Because of this artificial array element, we may regard this method as somewhat 'unnatural' or 'tricky', so we may call it a *trick*. At the same time, the method is very useful. This trick should be used whenever we use *linear search* (assuming speed to be an important factor, which is normally the case). It applies not only to arrays but also to linear lists, as we will see in Section 4.2.

1.3   USING A SENTINEL IN COMPARISONS

Suppose that we are given the two integer arrays a and b and the integers i, j, n, and that we have to decide whether or not the two subsequences

$$a[i], \ a[i+1], \ \ldots, \ a[i+n-1]$$

and

$$b[j], \ b[j+1], \ \ldots, \ b[j+n-1]$$

are identical. We begin with comparing $a[i]$ and $b[j]$; if they are equal, we proceed with $a[i+1]$ and $b[j+1]$, otherwise we stop, since the subsequences are not identical if at least one of the elementary comparisons fails. In this problem we can again benefit from the idea of using sentinels at the end of the subsequences. If it is certain that there are the (possibly artificial) elements $a[i+n]$ and $b[j+n]$, which are guaranteed to be unequal, then in the loop we have only to test for equality of array elements, not bothering about the number of elements to be tested. We shall assume that both $a[i+n]$ and $b[j+n]$ are existing array elements. Since they may be equal, we have to make them unequal ourselves. Of course, this is allowed only if eventually they have their original values again. The following function performs the desired comparison:

```
int equalseq(p, q, n) int *p, *q, n;
{ int temp, *qn;
  qn = q + n; temp = *qn; *qn = *(p+n) + 1;
                 /* Now sentinel q[n] differs from p[n] */
  while (*p++ == *q++) ;
  *qn = temp;    /* Restore old q[n]                     */
  return q > qn;
}
```

Note the extremely compact while loop:

```
while (*p++ == *q++) ;
```

This may be hard to read, but readability, however desirable, may be less important than speed. The following explanation will make this while-loop clear.

The unary operators * and ++ have the same precedence, and, as they associate from right to left, $*p++$ means the same as $*(p++)$. Since we have written $p++$ (not $++p$), the old pointer value p is used to obtain the integer value $*p$; then the pointer value p is incremented. It may also be necessary to explain the statement

```
return q > qn;
```

If all n array elements are equal, the loop stops by comparing the two sentinels, which we have made unequal to each other. Even in this final comparison, which certainly fails, the pointer q is incremented, so it will exceed the value of qn. On the other hand, q will not be greater than qn if an earlier comparison fails; if only the final given integers, called $a[i+n-1]$ and $b[j+n-1]$ outside function $equalseq$, are different form each other, then q will have qn as its final value. So we have $q > qn$ if the subsequences are identical and $q \leq qn$ if they are different.

It is most instructive to write a program which demonstrates the function $equalseq$. Such an exercise offers a good opportunity to use pointers in connection with arrays. For example, the address of $a[i]$ is written as the pointer expression $a+i$, which is an alternative for $\&a[i]$. Another point: it is always good practice to make a program reasonably general and robust. In this example, generality means that dynamic memory allocation (using $malloc$) is to be preferred to the more traditional array declaration with some fixed dimension. As to robustness, we should take care that the program does not crash if invalid values of i, j, n are really entered. We shall also demonstrate how to check that a number is entered when this should be the case; in other words, we shall display the message $Invalid\ character$ if, say, a letter is entered instead of an integer. Recall that the value returned by the function $scanf$ tells us how many items have been successfully read. Instead of testing this returned value at various places in the main program, we do this only once in our function $readint$.

```
/* COMPARE.C: This program compares two subsequences of
              integer arrays.
*/
#define NULL 0
main()
{ int na, nb, i, j, n, *a, *b; char *malloc();
  printf("Sequence lengths na and nb: ");
  na = readint(); nb = readint();
  a = (int *) malloc((na+1) * sizeof(int));
  b = (int *) malloc((nb+1) * sizeof(int));
  /* na + 1, nb + 1  to accommodate sentinels */
  if (a == NULL || b == NULL)
  { printf("Not enough memory"); exit(1);
  }
  printf("Enter a[0], a[1], ..., a[na-1]:\n");
  for (i=0; i<na; i++) a[i] = readint();
  printf("Enter b[0], b[1], ..., b[nb-1]:\n");
  for (j=0; j<nb; j++) b[j] = readint();
  do
  { printf(
    "\nEnter i, j, n, to compare the subsequences\n");
    printf("a[i], a[i+1], ..., a[i+n-1]  and\n");
    printf(
    "b[j], b[j+1], ..., b[j+n-1]  with each other.\n");
    printf("(Restrictions: i + n <= %d\n", na);
    printf("               j + n <= %d\n", nb);
    printf("               i >= 0, j >= 0, n >= 0):\n");
    i = readint(); j = readint(); n = readint();
  } while (i + n > na || j + n > nb ||
           i < 0 || j < 0 || n < 0);
  printf("The two subsequences are%s identical!\n",
  equalseq(a+i, b+j, n) ? "" : " not");
}

int readint()
```

```
{ int x;
  if (scanf("%d", &x) < 1)
  { printf("Invalid character"); exit(1);
  }
  return x;
}


/* The function  equalseq, defined above,  */
/* is to be inserted here                   */
```

In C the notations $a[i]$ and $*(a+i)$ are equivalent, so although a is a pointer variable, we may use the notation $a[i]$, as this program shows.

1.4   GLOBAL VARIABLES AND SIDE EFFECTS

Suppose that we want to read some integers from the keyboard, to compute their sum. The integers are entered in their normal decimal form and they are separated by any number of white-space characters, that is, spaces, tabs and newline characters. After the final integer, any nonnumeric string, such as *STOP, END, QUIT, EXIT*, should be allowed to signal the end of the input sequence. As mentioned in Section 1.3, if numbers are expected in the input, the value returned by the function *scanf* tells us how many numbers have been successfully read, so it is zero if some nonnumeric string is entered instead of a number. (The function value returned by *scanf* should not be confused with the actual values of the numbers that are read; the latter values are delivered through the arguments.) Here is a program which detects the end of the number sequence in this way:

```
/* SUM.C: Compute the sum of a sequence of integers */

main()
{ int i, s=0;
  while (scanf("%d", &i) > 0) s += i;
  printf("\nThe sum is: %d\n", s);
}
```

This is a good program to introduce a somewhat controversial point. These days, many young people learn the Pascal language, where they have to distinguish between procedures and functions. They are often taught the following rules of thumb:

(1) The only thing a function should do is return a value; it should perform no input or output operations. For the latter, procedures rather than functions ought to be used. Functions should have only value parameters (without *var*).
(2) Neither procedures nor functions should access any global variables; they should deal with parameters and local variables only.

These rules of thumb are very instructive in elementary programming lessons. Without them, beginners might be inclined to declare all variables at the global level and to use only parameterless procedures; in other words, they might adopt the BASIC style of programming. When we learn chess, we first have to master the elementary rules of the game. After this, it is a good idea to become familiar with some rules of thumb for the first moves. These rules are very useful recipes for beginners. More advanced chess players, though familiar with all elementary rules, know that there are very important exceptions to them. They are in a position to judge for themselves what is good style and what is not. With programming, things are similar. At first sight, it seems that the above rules for Pascal do not apply to C, since in the latter there is no distinction between procedures and functions. However, we can conceptually make this distinction, that is, use a particular C function consistently either like a Pascal procedure or a Pascal function. In this way, we can still observe the above rules (1) and (2), if we wish. Anyone who switches from Pascal to C is inclined to make that conceptual distinction. For example, many people, including myself, have a tendency to use *scanf* in the same way as the Pascal procedures *read* and *readln*, ignoring any returned value. However, as the above program SUM.C shows, this returned value is extremely useful: it enables us to detect easily that no integer could be read, which means that the user has given the agreed signal (some nonnumeric string) for end of input. This way of using *scanf* as a genuine function rather than as a 'procedure', is against the above rule of thumb (1) in two respects. First, it performs input and second, it passes information back through its parameters. (Although, formally, all parameters in C are value parameters, the pointer concept of C enables us to achieve the effect of passing information from a function back to its caller through parameters.) As in chess, we need not feel guilty about violating elementary rules of thumb, nor is the C language to blame for this. Even though in C, if we wanted, we could make a sharp distinction between procedures and functions, we won't! Incidentally, C functions that do not return a value are called *void*. We can only use them in the same way as we use procedures in Pascal. More interesting, however, are functions that do return values, and the fact that we can either use or ignore these values is a very elegant language aspect.

Rule of thumb (2) dissuades us from using global variables. This rule is more important than rule (1), and it is often wise to observe it. Here is a very elementary example. The program is clumsy in several respects, but it illustrates clearly what we are talking about.

```
/* SIDE1.C: First program to demonstrate side effects
*/
int n;

main()
{ int i, x;
  printf("Enter n: "); scanf("%d", &n);
  printf("Enter %d integers to be squared\n", n);
  for (i=0; i<n; i++)
  { scanf("%d", &x);
    printf("Its square is: %d\n", square(x));
  }
}

int square(x) int x;
{ n = x * x;
  return n;
}
```

The variable *n* is global (or external). Its value is used in the for-loop, but, unfortunately, it is destroyed in the function *square*, which means that the program will not terminate correctly. We say that the runction *square* has the side effect of affecting the global variable *n*. In large programs errors like this one may be extremely hard to find.

There is another problem with side effects, due to the unspecified order in which operands of an expression are evaluated. The following program illustrates this:

```
/* SIDE2.C: Second program to demonstrate side effects
*/
int i=5;

main()
{ printf("%d", f() + g());
}

int f()
{ return ++i;
}

int g()
{ return i *= 10;
}
```

If in the expression $f()+g()$ the first operand $f()$ is evaluated prior to the evaluation of the second operand $g()$, the program computes $6+60$, but if function g is evaluated first, the result is $51+50$. Another odd point is that $f()+g()$ will differ from $g()+f()$. With bad habits, sometimes the best thing to do is to abolish them radically. Those who smoke too much know that the only good remedy is stop smoking completely. In the same way we might consider forbidding any use of global variables. However, that would be unwise. After all, there is no scientific proof that global variables are bad for our health. Our rule of thumb (2), however useful, is not worth promoting to an absolute law. If we use global variables wisely, and only exceptionally, they may be very useful and not dangerous at all. Thanks to the fact that C allows us to split up a program into several modules (each of which is a file), we can restrict the scope of global variables to the file where they are defined. We then add the keyword *static*, as, for example, in

```
static int Xcursor, Ycursor;

left(step) int step;
{ removecursor(); Xcursor -= step; drawcursor();
}

right(step) int step;
{ removecursor(); Xcursor += step; drawcursor();
}
```

In this example all functions (such as *left* and *right*) defined in the same file as the variables *Xcursor* and *Ycursor* have access to these variables, but functions in other files (belonging to the same program!) have not. Thus, we prevent these variable from being altered by unauthorized users, and still use them as 'global' variables in the above file.

However, we will go further than using *static* external variables, that is, we will exceptionally permit ourselves to use variables that are really public domain; as these external variables are not static, they are accessible in all the files that constitute the program. In the first place, global variables are not dangerous at all as long as we only *use* their values, without altering them. If we do alter them we may consider them dangerous, not 'harmful', as some other authors do. A sharp knife may be dangerous, especially for children, but we would exaggerate if we called it harmful. Let us again borrow an example from computer graphics. My book *Computer Graphics for the IBM PC* discusses the implementation of the functions *move* and *draw*, on which another graphics book, namely *Programming Principles in Computer Graphics*, is based. For example, to draw triangle ABC, we write

```
move(xA, yA); draw(xB, yB); draw(xC, yC); draw(xA, yA);
```

However, if a video display is used the function *draw* can do more than only draw line segments. It consults the global variable *drawmode*, whose initial ('default') value is 1, which means 'draw positively'. Instead, we can assign the value -1 to it, which means 'draw negatively'. With this value of *drawmode*, the function *draw* can erase anything drawn previously, that is, instead of lighting pixels, it darkens them. Finally, with *drawmode* = 0, the state of the pixels on the specified line segment is inverted. A graphics package called GRPACK.C contains the functions *move* and *draw* (and a good many others), and it also contains the definition

```
int drawmode = 1;
```

The module GRPACK.C is compiled only once, after which we can link the resulting object module GRPACK.OBJ together with any program for graphics applications. User's programs which only draw line segments (as in the second graphics book mentioned above) need not use the variable *drawmode*. In other programs, where line segments are to be erased, we can write, for example,

```
extern int drawmode;

erase(x, y) float x, y;
{ int old_drawmode = drawmode;
  drawmode = -1;
  draw(x, y);
  drawmode = old_drawmode;
}
```

In this way, we can erase line segments only occasionally, and restore the global variable *drawmode* to its old value -1, 0, 1, whichever applies. If, on the other hand, a great many line segments are to be erased and the original drawing mode need not be restored, it is sufficient to perform the assignment statement

```
drawmode = -1;
```

only once. Until further notice, all subsequent calls *draw*(x, y) will then darken the pixels involved.

This concludes our brief excursion into computer graphics, to illustrate that global variables may be useful. When writing large programs consisting of a great many functions we frequently have to choose between using either global variables or arguments combined with local variables. It is wise to make the second choice as a rule and the first only exceptionally.

1.5 AN INTRODUCTION TO RECURSION

A function that calls itself is called *recursive*. Recursion maybe *indirect*. For example, function *f* may call function *g*, which in turn calls *f*. In Chapter 9 we shall encounter quite useful applications of indirect recursion, but let us first deal with direct recursion, where only one function is involved. Program RECUR1.C, though useless for practical purposes, is instructive because of its simplicity:

```
/* RECUR1.C: First example of recursion
*/
main()
{ p(4);
}

p(n) int n;
{ if (n>0) { p(n-2); printf("%3d", n); p(n-1); }
}
```

What does this program print? In spite of the very limited program size, this question turns out to be difficult for anyone who is unfamiliar with recursion. There are two ways to analyse programs of this type, and we characterize these with the terms *top-down* and *bottom-up*. Using the top-down method, we begin with the call $p(4)$ in the main program. The important point is that we immediately focus our attention on the three resulting actions, namely

```
p(2); printf("%3d", 4); p(3);
```

Thus, we have already found that the number 4 will occur somewhere in the output. Note that this method of program analysis is different from the usual one, where we follow the actions step by step in full detail. Here we have determined that the number 4 will be printed, although we have not yet fully analysed the consequences of the call $p(2)$, which takes place earlier. We shall do so now, and sketch a tree of everything that happens, (see Fig. 1.1).

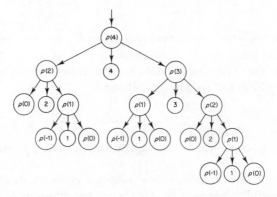

Fig. 1.1. Tree to analyse program RECUR1.C

In Fig. 1.1 we have simply written 4 instead of *printf* (*"%3d"*, 4); and so on. The tree does not branch further than the *leaves* $p(0)$ and $p(-1)$, because these calls have no effect at all. The other leaves, denoting calls of *printf*, show the following output of the program:

```
  2   1   4   1   3   2   1
```

This method of analysis is not free from duplicated work. For example, the tree contains three identical subtrees that show the effect of the call $p(1)$. This observation leads to the 'bottom-up' approach. After seeing that $p(n)$ is effective only if n is positive, we begin with $p(1)$, even though this call does not occur in the program, and we can easily see that it results in printing the value 1. We then use this result in the second step, where we the examine effect of $p(2)$, and so on:

$p(1)$:   1
$p(2)$: $p(0)$ 2 $p(1)$,   that is,   2   1
$p(3)$: $p(1)$ 3 $p(2)$,   that is,   1   3   2   1
$p(4)$: $p(2)$ 4 $p(3)$,   that is,   2   1   4   1   3   2   1

Although in this example this bottom-up method is more efficient than the top-down method, it may be more difficult to use, as program RECUR2.C shows.

```
/* RECUR2.C: Second example of recursion
*/
main()
{ p(80);
}

p(n) int n;
{ if (n>0) { p(n-40); printf("%3d", n); p(n-20); }
}
```

In this case the top-down method works as smoothly as before, but the bottom-up approach is feasible only if we discover that the analysis of $p(20)$, $p(40)$, $p(60)$, $p(80)$ is all we need. Without this knowledge, we would have to have to go a long way, beginning with $p(1)$, then $p(2)$, and so on, until $p(80)$. Still, this possibility is fundamentally important, as we will see in Section 3.5.

1.6   ELIMINATION OF RECURSION

In the programs of Section 1.5 function p calls itself recursively twice. Recursive functions that call themselves more than once are sometimes called *genuinely recursive*, to emphasize that usually we cannot easily replace them with equivalent nonrecursive functions. This is different in program TAIL.C, which reads an unknown number of integers and prints their sum:

```
/* TAIL.C: Tail recursion
*/
int s=0;
```

```
main()
{ addnumbers();
  printf("\nThe sum is: %d\n", s);
}

addnumbers()   /* Recursive version */
{ int x;
  if (scanf("%d", &x) > 0) { s += x; addnumbers(); }
}
```

This is an example of *tail recursion*. There is only one recursive call, which is placed at the end of the function *addnumbers*. This call is not much different from a jump to the beginning of the function. We can therefore replace the above function *addnumbers* with the following iterative version:

```
addnumbers()      /* Nonrecursive version */
{ int x;
  while (scanf("%d", &x) > 0) s += x;
}
```

With regard to efficiency, the latter version is to be preferred. If there are a very great many numbers to be read, the recursive version may cause *stack overflow*. Since, in principle, a function may be used anywhere in the program its return address, that is, the place to which it is to return, has to be stored somewhere. Because of the possibility of recursion, the only safe place to store it is a stack. The last item pushed on a stack is the first to be popped from it, which is just what we want. In addition to return addresses, local variables, such as *x* in our example, are also placed on the stack. Since the stack size is limited to, say, several thousands of memory locations there may be a problem if the same function is recursively called a great many times. Note that such problems will not occur if entering and quitting the function takes place alternately, no matter how often this occurs. The undesirable situation of stack overflow occurs only if the 'recursion depth' exceeds a certain value. Let us try to be more precise.

We define the *recursion depth* of a function at a certain moment as the number of times that, from the beginning of program execution, this function has been called minus the number of times that it has returned to its caller. At any moment, each function has its own recursion depth. There is a simple way of measuring experimentally the maximum recursion depth of a function, which is based on using two global variables, *depth* and *maxdepth*. For example, we can find the maximum recursion depth of a certain function f as follows:

```
int depth=0, maxdepth=0;

int f(x) int x;
{ if (++depth > maxdepth) maxdepth = depth;

  ...    /* Contents of recursive function f */

  depth--;
}
```

At the end of the main program we only have to print the value of *maxdepth* to know the maximum recursion depth that has occurred. (Note that the value of *depth* will then be 0 again!)

We now go back to the general case and to a more theoretical approach. Immediately after program start the function *main* has recursion depth 1 and all other functions have recursion depth 0. If we number the functions 1, 2, ..., k, then the amount of stack space used at a certain moment is equal to the sum

$$s = d_1 n_1 + d_2 n_2 + \ldots + d_k n_k$$

where d_i is the recursion depth and n_i is the amount of stack space involved by a single call of the ith function. The value of n_i includes space needed for the return address, all local variable parameters and possibly the value to be returned, if any. Then, clearly, stack overflow will occur when the value of s exceeds some maximum stack size. We see that our second version of *addnumbers*, which is nonrecursive, is absolutely safe, whereas the first, recursive, version may cause stack overflow.

Incidentally, even with the second function *addnumbers*, program TAIL.C would not be an example of good programming style, since the use of the global variable s is not justified here. (See also the discussion about rule of thumb (2) in Section 1.4. However, it illustrates clearly that in certain cases we can replace recursion with iteration in a straightforward way. Speaking of rules of thumb, we can now add:

(3) A recursive function should call itself more than once, otherwise we should replace recursion with iteration.

Again, this is only a rule of thumb, not an exact law. Even if a recursive function calls itself only once, the elimination of recursion may be harder than in our last example. Also, a recursive function may be shorter and, in compiled form, occupy less memory than an equivalent iterative version. If at the same time the recursive version has no real disadvantages it would be silly to obey rule (3) just because someone told us to do so. However, in many cases rule (3) applies. A well-known example of recursion is the computation of n-factorial, written:

$$n! = 1 \times 2 \times \ldots \times n$$

We can also write this definition of $n!$ as follows:

$$n! = 1 \qquad \text{if } n = 0 \text{ or } n = 1$$
$$n! = n \cdot (n-1)! \qquad \text{if } n > 1$$

A translation of the latter definition to a recursive C function is straightforward. Already 8! does not fit into a 16-bit integer, so we use type double for reasons of generality:

```
double factorial(n) int n;      /* Recursive version */
{ return n > 1 ? n * factorial(n-1) : 1.0;
}
```

The returned value is 1.0 if n is equal to 0 or to 1; for any n greater than 1 the value $n*factorial(n-1)$ is returned, in accordance with our second definition of $n!$. Note that the function assumes n to be zero or positive. If n is negative, the function *factorial* will simply return the value 1.0, whereas our mathemetical definition of $n!$ does not include this case. We could have checked if n is nonnegative, but that takes time. We often have to make the choice whether or not to include some time-consuming check in a function, only for the benefit of those who do not use that function properly. Most professionals are not fond of such tests: it is not fair that the wise should pay for the unwise. (Incidentally, the absence of some run-time checks in C makes it doubtful if this language ought to be used in very elementary programming courses.)

Resuming our discussion about recursion, we see that in the function *factorial* the recursive call occurs only once. Indeed, this is a typical case where we should consider eliminating recursion, that is, replacing the above function *factorial* with:

```
double factorial(n) int n;   /* Nonrecursive version */
{ double product=1.0;
  while (n > 1) product *= n--;
  return product;
}
```

Compared with our previous example, *addnumbers*, it is less straightforward to derive the nonrecursive function *factorial* from the recursive one. Since it is most unlikely that we will compute $n!$ for very large values of n (and we are wise enough not to use negative values of $n!$), we do not expect the recursive version to cause stack overflow, so why replace it with a nonrecursive version? Well, besides the risk of stack overflow, recursive functions also may have the disadvantage of being somewhat slower than their iterative counterparts. We may expect recursive calls to take somewhat more time than looping in a while statement. Program TIME.C compares the performance of the two versions of *factorial*.

```
/* TIME.C: Computing time used by a recursive function
      'factorial', compared with the time needed by an
      equivalent nonrecursive version.
*/
#include <time.h>

main()
{ long int t0, t1;
  int n, k, i, dt;
  double f, recfac(), itfac();
  printf("Enter the value of n, to compute n! :");
  scanf("%d", &n);
  printf(
  "How many times do you want %d! to be computed? :", n);
  scanf("%d", &k);

  time(&t0);
  for (i=0; i<k; i++) f = recfac(n);
  time(&t1); dt = t1 - t0;
  printf(
  "Recursion: %d! = %1.0f   time = %d s\n", n, f, dt);

  time(&t0);
  for (i=0; i<k; i++) f = itfac(n);
```

```
   time(&t1); dt = t1 - t0;
   printf(
   "Iteration: %d! = %1.0f    time = %d s\n", n, f, dt);
}

double recfac(n) int n;        /* Recursive version  */
{ return n > 1 ? n * recfac(n-1) : 1.0;
}

double itfac(n) int n;         /* Nonrecursive version */
{ double product=1.0;
  while (n > 1) product *= n--;
  return product;
}
```

The following results were obtained on an IBM PC:

```
Enter the value of n, to compute n! : 7
How many times do you want 7! to be computed? : 30000
Recursion: 7! = 5040    time = 343 s
Iteration: 7! = 5040    time = 334 s
```

On a simple microcomputer, floating-point arithmetic usually takes more time than anything else. In an experiment with integer versions of our recursive and iterative function the time needed to compute the same result (7!), again 30 000 times, was only 22 and 15 s, respectively. We see from these figures that much depends on the circumstances. With the integer program version the recursive function takes considerably more time than the iterative one, but with the floating-point program version the difference in computing time is relatively small. If speed is at stake, it is much more rewarding to replace floating-point with integer arithmetic (if possible) than to replace recursion with iteration!

1.7   EUCLID'S ALGORITHM FOR THE GREATEST COMMON DIVISOR

If x and y are integers, not both zero, we say that their *greatest common divisor*, $gcd(x, y)$, is the largest integer which evenly divides both x and y. For example,

$$gcd(1000, 600) = 200$$
$$gcd(-70, 90) = 10$$
$$gcd(0, 12) = 12$$

It is clear from this definition that for any pair x, y, we have

$$gcd(x, y) = gcd(y, x) \qquad (1)$$

If d evenly divides the two positive integers x and y, then it also evenly divides the two integers $x - y$ and y, and vice versa. This means that we have

$$gcd(x, y) = gcd(x-y, y) \qquad (2)$$

which, if $x > y$, means a simplification. If we only add the obvious fact

$$gcd(x, 0) = x \qquad (3)$$

we have a simple means to compute the gcd of any two positive integers. For example, we have

$$gcd(1900, 700) = gcd(1200, 700)$$

We apply rule (2) once more, and write

$$gcd(1200, 700) = gcd(500, 700)$$

As in the right-hand side the first argument is now less than the second, we use rule (1):

$$gcd(500, 700) = gcd(700, 500)$$

We now continue in the same way, each time applying either rule (2) or rule (1):

$$gcd(700, 500) = gcd(200, 500)$$
$$= gcd(500, 200)$$
$$= gcd(300, 200)$$
$$= gcd(100, 200)$$
$$= gcd(200, 100)$$
$$= gcd(100, 100)$$
$$= gcd(0, 100)$$
$$= gcd(100, 0)$$

Applying rule (3), we obtain the desired result, 100, so we have found

$$gcd(1900, 700) = 100$$

If the difference between y and x is large, it is much more efficient to use the operator % instead of $-$. (Recall that $x \% y$ is the resulting remainder if x is evenly divided by y; for example, 1900 % 700 is equal to 500.) Since the remainder $x \% y$ is certainly less than y, we do not use

$$gcd(x, y) = gcd(x\%y, y)$$

followed by rule (1), as two separate steps, but we combine these into a single rule:

$$gcd(x, y) = gcd(y, x\%y) \qquad (4)$$

In our example, we now find the answer in only five steps:

$$gcd(1900, 700) = gcd(700, 500)$$
$$= gcd(500, 200)$$

$$= gcd(200, \ 100)$$
$$= gcd(100, \ 0)$$
$$= 100$$

Surprisingly, we need not require that initially x be larger than y, since rule (4) will achieve this in the first step, if necessary. Not only by rule (1), but also by rule (4) we find

$$gcd(700, \ 1900) = gcd(1900, \ 700)$$

since 700 % 1900 gives 700.

This way of computing a gcd is called *Euclid's algorithm*. Here is our first version of it, written as a recursive C function:

```
int gcd(x, y) int x, y;
{ return y ? gcd(y, x % y)  : x;
}
```

Since we are not dealing with floating-point arithmetic this time, we may expect an iterative version to be noticeably faster. It is also more suitable to include a provision for negative numbers: according to our definition at the beginning of this section, $gcd(x, y)$ must be positive. Here is our final version:

```
/* EUCLID.C: Euclid's algorithm */
int gcd(x, y) int x, y;
{ int r;
   if (x < 0) x = -x;
   if (y < 0) y = -y;
   while (y) { r = x % y; x = y; y = r; }
   return x;
}
```

Even though the latter version performs two extra tests ($x < 0$, $y < 0$), it took only about 70% of the time used by the former.

1.8   HORNER'S RULE

Suppose that we are given the seven numbers

$$x, \ a_0, \ a_1, \ a_2, \ a_3, \ a_4, \ a_5$$

and that we have to compute the polynomial

$$P_5(x) = a_5 x^5 + a_4 x^4 + a_3 x^3 + a_2 x^2 + a_1 x + a_0$$

The most obvious way to do this is to compute the individual terms of $P_5(x)$ and to add them up. However, it is much more efficient to apply *Horner's rule*, which, in this instance, says that $P_5(x)$ can be computed as follows:

$$P_5(x) = ((((a_5 x + a_4)x + a_3)x + a_2)x + a_1)x + a_0$$

Thanks to Horner's rule, only five multiplications and five additions are needed in this example. In general, we have to perform only n multiplications and n additions to compute a polynomial of degree n. Besides speed, Horner's rule also offers elegance and simplicity, and it may also increase numerical accuracy. Here is a C function for $P_n(x)$, based on Horner's rule:

```
double P(x, a, n) double x, *a; int n;
{ double s = a[n];
  while (--n >= 0) s = s * x + a[n];
  return s;
}
```

Recall that instead of *a in

$$double\ x,\ *a;$$

we could have written $a[]$, with the same meaning.

It is a good exercise to write a recursive version as well:

```
double P(x, a, n) double x, *a; int n;
{ return n ? P(x, a+1, n-1) * x + *a : *a;
}
```

An example will make this clear. Let us use the following main program to compute $(25 \times 0.5 + 15) \times 0.5 + 5$:

```
main()
{ static double a[3] = {5, 15, 25};
  double P(), x = 0.5;
  printf("%f", P(x, a, 2));
}
```

Parameter n of function P is the nonzero value 2, so the recursive call $P(x, a+1, n-1)$ is performed. Since argument a is a pointer to $a[0]$, that is, to 5, the expression $a+1$ denotes a pointer to $a[1]$. In an obvious symbolic notation we have:

$$P(0.5,\ \{5,\ 15,\ 25\},\ 2) = P(0.5,\ \{15,\ 25\},\ 1) * 0.5 + 5$$

where

$$P(0.5,\ \{15,\ 25\},\ 1) = P(0.5,\ \{25\},\ 0) * 0.5 + 15$$

where

$$P(0.5,\ \{25\},\ 0) = 25$$

Thus, we have

$$P(0.5,\ \{5,\ 15,\ 25\},\ 2) = (25 \times 0.5 + 15) \times 0.5 + 5 = 18.75$$

Once again, this exercise shows the power of recursion. The latter (recursive) version uses only 74 bytes of object code (on an IBM PC, with Lattice C, version 3.0), whereas the former (iterative) version uses 128 bytes. In a program similar to TIME.C in Section

1.6, it turned out that our last example used 49 s when computed 10 000 times, for either version. So the recursive version is considerably shorter and not slower than its iterative counterpart. There is still the question about the stack, but it is most unlikely that with this application there should ever be any trouble. So the exercise of writing a recursive function for Horner's rule has yielded something quite useful!

1.9 RADIX CONVERSION

When, not necessarily in the C language, we are writing an input routine for integers we have to accept a sequence of characters, mainly consisting of decimal digits, and we want to assemble these to an integer in the internal format of the computer. This is often called 'conversion from decimal to binary', since, internally, integers are usually in binary format. Thus reading an integer implies a conversion from radix 10 to radix 2. Actually, if the input routine is written in a high-level programming language, the fact that 'internally' radix 2 is used is not essential. After all, we usually perform arithmetic operations $(+, -, *, /, \%)$ on integers without bothering about their internal representation, and this is not different in an input routine. (The only reason to be aware of the internal format is the possibility of 'integer overflow', a term used if the number entered is too large to fit into that format.)

Let us use an example to discuss how to use the decimal digits in the order they are given. The integer 5482 is entered as the four digits 5, 4, 8, 2. When only the first digit, 5, has been read, we do not know yet that it is to be multiplied by 1000. Therefore, instead of using the conventional form

$$5482 = 5\times10^3+4\times10^2+8\times10+2,$$

we use Horner's rule:

$$5482 = ((5\times10+4)\times10+8)\times10+2$$

Successively, the numbers 5, 54, 548, 5482 are computed in this way. Function RDINT.C shows the program text for this.

```
/* RDINT.C: Function to read an integer
            (preliminary version)
*/
#include <stdio.h>
#include <ctype.h>
int rdint()
{ int i, neg, d;
  char ch;
  do ch = getchar(); while (isspace(ch));
  /* We have now skipped any leading blanks */
  neg = ch == '-';
  if (neg || ch == '+') ch = getchar();
  if (!isdigit(ch)) {printf("Invalid number"); exit(1);}
  i = ch - '0';
  while (ch = getchar(), isdigit(ch))
  { d = ch - '0';
    i = 10 * i + d;
  }
  ungetc(ch, stdin);
  return neg ? -i : i;
}
```

We begin with skipping any leading white-space characters (spaces, newline characters and tabs). Then we admit a plus or a minus sign with the usual meaning. After these leading characters, if any, we require a digit to follow; if not, we display an error message and stop program execution. The first character (say, '5') is then converted to the integer (5), by subtracting the character '0' from it. With this initial value, i, the while-loop is entered, where we apply Horner's rule. The above version does not include a test for integer overflow.

We now wish to include such a test; if integer overflow should take place, we shall simply display an error message and stop program execution. (Of course, in practice we may replace this with a more sophisticated action, such as asking the user to retry.) Here we need some knowledge of the way integers are represented internally. Let us assume them to be stored in 2's complement notation. We shall use 16-bit integers as an example in the discussion, but our function will actually be more general and work properly for other lengths as well. Then (in the discussion) the largest positive integer is 32 767, written in binary as

$$0111\ 1111\ 1111\ 1111$$

If we add 1 to this, we have

$$1000\ 0000\ 0000\ 0000$$

which is the 2's complement notation for $-32\,768$. We see that the unsigned number 32 768 and the negative number $-32\,768$ have the same internal format. Similarly, both the unsigned number 32 769 and the negative number $-32\,767$ have the internal format

$$1000\ 0000\ 0000\ 0001$$

and so on, until, finally, both the unsigned number 65535 and the negative number -1 have the internal format

$$1111\ 1111\ 1111\ 1111$$

In general, any unsigned number $i(32\,768 \le i < 65\,536)$ has the same internal format as the negative number $i - 65\,536$. In the above function, we multiply i by 10 and then add a digit $d(0 \le d \le 9)$. This may cause i to grow too large, so we have to include a check here. However, it does not make sense to test if i is greater than 32 767, because as long as we are dealing with type int this test would fail. It is more likely that on overflow the value of i should be negative, as follows from the above discussion, so we are tempted to include the line

```
if (i < 0) { printf("Too large"); exit(1); }
```

However, this is not correct either. After multiplying i by 10, its theoretical value may grow even larger than 65 535. Then only the 16 rightmost bits of this number are used, which may result in some positive integer! For example, if we enter 80 000, the resulting internal value will be $80\,000 - 65\,536 = 14\,464$, which is not negative. We shall therefore be more careful, and perform the multiplication by 10 in a number of small steps. Instead of

```
i = 10 * i + d,
```

we use

```
i0 = i;
i <<= 1;     /*    i  =   2 * i0      */
i <<= 1;     /*    i  =   4 * i0      */
i += i0      /*    i  =   5 * i0      */
i <<= 1;     /*    i  =  10 * i0      */
i += d;      /*    i  =  10 * i + d   */
```

We will test for overflow after each of these elementary steps:

```c
/* READINT.C: Function to read an integer, including
              a test for integer overflow
*/
#include <stdio.h>
#include <ctype.h>
int readint()
{ int i, i0, neg, d, k;
  char ch;
  do ch = getchar(); while (isspace(ch));
  /* We have now skipped any leading blanks */
  neg = ch == '-';
  if (neg || ch == '+') ch = getchar();
  if (!isdigit(ch)) {printf("Invalid number"); exit(1);}
  i = ch - '0';
  while (ch = getchar(), isdigit(ch))
  { d = ch - '0'; i0=i;
    for (k=0; k<5; k++)
    { if (k == 2) i += i0; else
      if (k == 4) i += d; else i <<= 1;
      if (i < 0) {printf("Too large"); exit(1);}
    }
  }
  ungetc(ch, stdin);
  return neg ? -i : i;
}
```

Note that we did not base this function on a fixed word length of, say, 16 bits, or, equivalently, on some maximum integer value (as *maxint* in Pascal). With such a value and with floating-point variables, the test for integer overflow would have been trivial, but the above solution does the job more efficiently.

After discussing an input routine for integers, with conversion from decimal to binary, we now want to deal with the inverse operation. We will convert integers from the binary to the decimal format in an output routine for integers. Again we can use Horner's rule. (As before, the external format, with radix 10, is more essential in our algorithm than the internal binary format.) For example, since

$$5482 = ((5 \times 10 + 4) \times 10 + 8) \times 10 + 2$$

we can obtain the rightmost digit 2 as the remainder $5482 \% 10$. We also use the truncated quotient $5482/10 = 548$. Since

$$548 = (5 \times 10 + 4) \times 10 + 8$$

we proceed by computing 548 % 10 = 8, 548/10 = 54, and so on, until the quotient is 0. In this way we obtain the decimal digits of the given integer from right to left, but we need them from left to right. We therefore first store the digits in an array, and print them only when they all have been calculated. This also provides us with the possibility of printing leading spaces, using a given field width w. The following function enables us to use $printint(w, x)$ instead of $printf("\%wd", x)$, where w stands for some positive integer:

```
/* PRINTINT.C: Function to print an integer x with a
              given field width w
*/
#include <stdio.h>

printint(w, x) int w, x;
{ int n = 0, i, negint = x < 0;
  char digs[30];
  if (negint) x = -x;
  do
  { digs[n++] = '0' + x % 10;
    x /= 10;
  } while (x);
  i = w - n;
  if (negint) i--;
  while (i-- > 0) putchar(' ');
  if (negint) putchar('-');
  for (i = n-1; i >= 0; i--) putchar(digs[i]);
}
```

Both $printint(w, x)$ and $printf("\%wd", x)$ use more than w positions if needed. Note that our function $printint$ is more general than the standard function $printf$ in the sense that it accepts any positive integer expression for w. In other words, with $printint$ the field width need not be static as with $printf$ but it may be determined dynamically.

1.10   POWERS WITH INTEGER EXPONENTS

There are only four basic arithmetic operations, namely addition, subtraction, multiplication and division, in which any other arithmetic tasks have to be expressed. We need not always do that ourselves. However, internally, at the machine level, only the four operations mentioned will take place. The C language offers a set of mathematical standard functions, including the function *pow*, which raises a number to a given power. For floating-point numbers x and y, where x is positive, we have

$$pow(x, y) = x^y$$

If this function had not been available, we could have defined:

```
#include <math.h>

double pow(x, y) double x, y;
{ return exp(y * log(x));
}
```

Both this version and the standard function *pow* expect a floating-point exponent *y*. However, in many applications the given exponent is an integer, which means that the power in question can also be computed by repeated multiplication. Although, for integer *n*, we can compute x^n as

$$pow(x, \ (double)n)$$

there are three reasons for developing a special power function for this important special case:

(1) We want to admit negative values of *x* (or the value 0 if *n* is positive).
(2) We may find a faster algorithm.
(3) It is an instructive programming exercise.

Here is our first attempt:

```
double power1(x, n) double x; int n;
{ return n > 0 ? x * power1(x, n-1) :
         n < 0 ? 1.0/power1(x, -n)   : 1.0;
}
```

We wish to admit negative exponents *n*, but, unfortunately, the test if *n* is negative is performed a great many times if *n* is large, whereas only one such a test is actually needed. This is sometimes another drawback of recursive functions. It is due to the fact that the function is called both externally and internally. If we insist on using recursion the only way to avoid this drawback is using two functions, namely a nonrecursive one, *power2*, for the external user and a recursive one, *pw*, for internal use only:

```
double power2(x, n) double x; int n;
{ double pw();
  return n >= 0 ? pw(x, n) : 1.0/pw(x, -n);
}

static double pw(x, n) double x; int n;
{ return n ? x * pw(x, n-1) : 1.0;
}
```

(In cases like this, the nonrecursive function, available to the user, is sometimes called a *driver* function.) With an iterative solution we have no such problems:

```
double power3(x, n) double x; int n;
{ double p = x;
  int negexp = n < 0;
  if (n == 0) return 1.0;
  if (negexp) n = -n;
  while (--n) p *= x;
  return negexp ? 1.0/p : p;
}
```

For the exponent values $-3 \leq n \leq 3$, this function is quite good because it does not perform any unnecessary multiplications. If $n = 4$ we see that three multiplications are carried out:

$$x^4 = x \cdot x \cdot x \cdot x$$

If we had to compute this by hand we would no doubt use

$$x^4 = (x^2)^2$$

which involves only two multiplications, and *power*3 will be very inefficient for large values of *n*. As we have seen in previous sections, floating-point operations are very time-consuming, so we have to find a faster solution. The following relationship provides a basis for this:

$$x^n = \begin{cases} 1/(x^{-n}) & \text{if } n < 0 \\ 1 & \text{if } n = 0 \\ x & \text{if } n = 1 \\ (x^h)^2 & \text{if } n \text{ is greater than 1 and even} \\ (x^h)^2 \cdot x & \text{if } n \text{ is greater than 1 and odd} \end{cases}$$

(where *h* is the truncated quotient *n*/2)

Again, we begin with a recursive version:

```
double power4(x, n) double x; int n;
{ if (n < 2)
  return (n == 0 ? 1.0 :
          n == 1 ? x : 1.0/power4(x, -n)); else
  { double y=power4(x, (n >> 1));
    y = y * y;
    return n & 1 ? y * x : y;
  }
}
```

Recall that ≫ means *shift right* and that & means *bitwise and*, so we have

```
(n >> 1)  ==  (n / 2),
(n & 1)   ==  (n % 2).
```

Function *power*4 computes x^{100} as follows:

$$\begin{aligned} x^{100} &= (x^{50})^2 && \text{where} \\ x^{50} &= (x^{25})^2 && \text{where} \\ x^{25} &= (x12)^2 \cdot x && \text{where} \\ x^{12} &= (x^6)^2 && \text{where} \\ x^6 &= (x^3)^2 && \text{where} \\ x^3 &= x^2 \cdot x && \text{where} \\ x^2 &= x \cdot x \end{aligned}$$

This means that only eight instead of 99 floating-point multiplications will take place in this example.

Converting *power*4 to a nonrecursive version is not as straightforward as converting *power2* to *power3* was. In our example, with $n = 100$, we used the sequence 100, 50, 25, 12, 6, 3, 1, but actually we need the reverse sequence 1, 3, 6, 12, 25, 50, 100. We could, of course, build the original (decreasing) sequence, store it in an integer array and then use it in the reverse order, but, fortunately, there is a more efficient and elegant way. If we write the given exponent 100 in binary we find the desired numbers 1, 3, ... as bit sequences, starting from the left:

$$100 = 1\ 1\ 0\ 0\ 1\ 0\ 0$$
$$50 = 1\ 1\ 0\ 0\ 1\ 0$$
$$25 = 1\ 1\ 0\ 0\ 1$$
$$12 = 1\ 1\ 0\ 0$$
$$6 = 1\ 1\ 0$$
$$3 = 1\ 1$$
$$1 = 1$$

So we can find the numbers 1, 3, 6, 12, 25, 50, 100 by using only the first i bits ($i = 1, 2, \ldots, 7$) of 1100100, the binary representation of the given exponent 100. Actually, we do not want these seven numbers themselves; the only thing we must know is whether they are odd or even, so we are only interested in their least significant bits. This means that it is exactly the bit sequence 1100100 that we need. Starting from the left, for each bit we encounter, we have to square our intermediate result, say y, unconditionally, and multiply it by x if and only if the bit encountered is 1. If we take this literally, we have to begin with $y = 1$, so that, for the leftmost 1-bit of the bit sequence, we compute 1 . 1 . x. Although this may be considered elegant it is not efficient. Since we know that the leftmost bit is 1, we need not test it and we can start straightaway with $y = x$. These considerations lead to the following nonrecursive version:

```
double power5(x, n) double x; int n;
{ int twopower = 1, negexp = n < 0;
  double y = x;
  if (n == 0) return 1.0;
  if (negexp) n = -n;
  while (twopower <= n) twopower <<= 1;
  twopower >>= 1;
  /* Now twopower is equal to the largest power of 2 */
  /* that is not larger than n                       */
  while (twopower >>= 1)
  { y *= y;
     if (n & twopower) y *= x;
  }
  return negexp ? 1.0/y : y;
}
```

The first while loop in this function begins with *twopower* $= 1$, and shifts this to the left until it is greater than n. In our example we have $n = 1100100$ (written in binary), so this loop ends with *twopower* $= 10000000 = 2^7$. Then the statement

```
twopower >>= 1;
```

changes this into *twopower* $= 1000000 = 2^6$. Since we need not examine the leftmost bit of n (which is certainly 1), we shift *twopower* once again one position to the right in

```
while (twopower >>= 1)
```

before we use it in the bitwise AND operation (n & *twopower*).So the first time, we have *twopower* $= 100000 = 2^5$ in this operation, and we obtain the result of 1100100 & 100000, which is 100000. As this is nonzero, the statement

```
y *= x;
```

is executed, so y is multiplied by x. Prior to this, the statement

```
y *= y;
```

is executed, so when the inner part of the while loop has been executed once, we have $y = x^3$. Then, in the while test, *twopower* is again shifted one position to the right and so on. The loop stops when *twopower* becomes zero. The easiest way to verify the termination of the loop is to see what happens if $n = 1$ (instead of 100). In that case the value of *twopower* changes from 1 to 0 in the first test of the while loop, which is just what we need.

In our example $n = 100$, that is, with the bit sequence 1100100, we used the subsequences 1, 11, 110, 1100, 11001, 110010, 1100100, because the corresponding exponents 1, 3, 6, 12, 25, 50, 100 were used in the recursive function *power*4. This forced us to start from the left in that bit sequence, hence our initial computation of the largest power of 2 not greater than n. However, in decomposing an integer into its binary representation it is more natural to start from the right. This is similar to what we did in the function *printint* in Section 1.9, where we computed the decimal digits of an integer to be printed. As we did there, we can again apply Horner's rule, but instead of dividing by 10 we now divide the given integer by 2, use the remainder, and proceed with the quotient, until the latter becomes zero. For example, for the number 100, written in binary 1100100, this method would yield the bits 0, 0, 1, 0, 0, 1, 1, that is, the bits in the positions 0, 1, 2, 3, 4, 5, 6, in that order. (As usual, we are counting the bit positions from the right, starting with 0). What we actually need, however, are not the positions 2, 5, 6 of the one-bits, but rather 2^2, 2^5, 2^6, since we have

$$2^2+2^5+2^6 = 4+32+64 = 100$$

This is interesting, for we can compute x^4, x^{32}, x^{64} quickly by repeated squaring, and we have

$$x^{100} = x^4 \cdot x^{32} \cdot x^{64}$$

The best way to use this is to compute $y = x^4$ by squaring x^2, that is, in two multiplications, and then successively compute x^8, x^{16}, x^{32}, x^{64}, but use only x^{32} and x^{64} as multiplication factors to compute the final value $y = x^{100}$. We have been using eight multiplications, as in our previous function *power*5. Here is our final function to compute x^n:

```
/* POWER6.C: Raising x to the power n */
double power6(x, n) double x; int n;
{ int negexp = n < 0;
  double y;
  if (n == 0) return 1.0;
  if (negexp) n = -n;
  while (!(n & 1)) { x *= x; n >>= 1; }
  y = x;
  while (n >>= 1)
  { x *= x;
    if (n & 1) y *= x;
  }
  return negexp ? 1.0/y : y;
}
```

The first while-loop squares x until the first 1-bit from the right is found. The last square thus computed is assigned to y. If, instead, we had always started with $y = 1.0$ we would have needed only one while-loop, but that would have led to an extra multiplication with a factor 1.0. Both *power*5 and *power*6 are based on the binary representation of the exponent n. They require the same number of floating-point multiplications, namely the truncated 2-logarithm of n plus the number of 1-bits in it excluding the leftmost. We can also say that we delete the leading 1 in the binary representation of n and then use the length of the remaining bit sequence plus the number of 1-bits in this sequence. In our example, the first 1 in 1100100 is followed by six bits, two of which are 1, so we need $6 + 2 = 8$ multiplications. We should not have the illusion that this 'binary' method of power evaluation should be optimal. There are cases where we can do better, as, for example in the case $n = 15$. Since 15 is written 1111 in binary, our functions *power*5 and *power*6 would use $3 + 3 = 6$ multiplications, but only 5 are actually needed:

$$2^5 = (2^2)^2 \times 2 \qquad \text{(3 multiplications)}$$
$$2^{15} = 2^5 \times 2^5 \times 2^5 \qquad \text{(2 multiplications)}$$

This is only a theoretical remark, however. In general, it would be an extremely time-consuming task to find the least number of multiplications that are absolutely necessary for an exponentiation (even though such a task would be done with integers only)!

An experiment with the above six power functions showed that *power*4, *power*5 and *power*6 are much faster than *power*1, *power*2 and *power*3. Of course, this is what we should have expected, since in *power*4, *power*5 and *power*6 the number of multiplications is reduced dramatically by squaring intermediate results. It also turned out that there is very little difference in the speed of the three functions *power*1, *power*2 and *power*3. Similarly, *power*4 is almost as fast as *power*5, which in turn is about as fast as *power*6, so in this example, it is hardly worthwhile to switch from recursion to iteration for reasons of efficiency. This illustrates that our rule of thumb (3) in Section 1.6 should not be taken too literally. Still, this rule may be useful in other cases. After all, in this section we have dealt with floating-point multiplication, which is a very time-consuming operation compared with recursive function calls. Replacing recursion with iteration is more likely to really speed things up in applications with only integer arithmetic. More importantly, with recursion we always have to think of stack overflow, which is not the case with iteration. As to the standard function *pow*, used in the form *pow*(x, (*double*)n), this turned out to take about 20% more time than *power*4, *power*5 and *power*6. This is quite reasonable compared with using $exp(n * log(x))$, which took almost twice as much time as *pow*.

EXERCISES

1.1 What is the output of the programs P1A.C and P1B.C, listed below?

```
/* P1A.C */
main()
{ f(6);
}
f(n) int n;
{ if (n > 0) { f(n-3); printf("%3d", n); f(n-2); }
}


/* P1B.C */
main()
{ f(10000);
}
f(n) int n;
{ if (n > 0)
    { f(n/10-100); printf("%6d\n", n); f(n/5-200);
    }
}
```

1.2 Replace the following recursive functions *f*, *g*, and *h* with (more or less) equivalent nonrecursive ones. In each case, compare the amount of memory space and computing time used by the two versions.

```
#include <stdio.h>
f()
{ if (getchar() == ' ') f();
}

g(n) int n;   /* You may assume:  n < 100  */
{ int i;
  if (n > 0)
    { scanf("%d", &i); g(n-1); printf("%d\n", i);
    }
}

int h(n) int n;
{ return n < 0 ? 0 :
      n == 0 ? 1 : h(n-1) + h(n-2);
}
```

1.3 Write a function with an integer argument, which returns the sum of the decimal digits of the argument. Compare a recursive and an iterative solution of this problem.

1.4 Write a program which reads a sequence of floating-point numbers and prints the sum of the 1st, 3rd, 6th, 10th, 15th, ... element of this sequence. Interpret any nonnumeric character as the end of the input sequence.

1.5 Write a program which reads a decimal digit d. Print all positive integers x less than 100 that have the characteristic that d occurs in the decimal representations of both x and the square of x.

1.6 Write a function with a floating-point argument x and an integer argument n, which returns the following approximation of e^x:

$$1+x+\frac{x^2}{2!}+\frac{x^3}{3!}\;\cdots\;+\frac{x^n}{n!}$$

1.7 Write the function *prime*, which has one (positive) integer argument n. The function returns 1 if n is a prime number (2, 3, 5, 7, 11, ...) and 0 if it is not.

1.8 Write a program which reads a positive integer and writes this as a product of primes. For example:

$$120 = 2\times2\times2\times3\times5$$

1.9 Write the function *trunc* with a floating-point argument x and a positive integer argument n. The function returns a floating-point value equal to x except for all fractional decimal positions after the nth, which are zero. For example

$$trunc(-3.14159, 3) = -3.141$$

1.10 Write your own function *floor*1, similar to the standard function *floor*. It has one floating-point argument x. The floating-point value to be returned is obtained by truncating x. Use double-precision floating-point numbers, which may have a greater precision than long integers, so you cannot simply write:

```
double floor1(x) double x;
{ return (double) (long) x;
}
```

1.11 Write your own function *cos*1, so that it can be used instead of the standard function *cos*. Use the following properties of the cosine function:

$$\cos x = 1-\frac{x^2}{2!}+\frac{x^4}{4!}-\frac{x^6}{6!}+\;\cdots \tag{1}$$

$$\cos x = \cos(x-2k\pi)\quad(k\text{ integer}) \tag{2}$$

$$\cos x = -\cos(\pi-x) \tag{3}$$

$$\cos x = 2\cos^2(x/2)-1 \tag{4}$$

With (2)–(4) you can reduce the argument of the function *cos*1 to a value in some small domain, which will cause series (1) to converge more rapidly.

1.12 Write the parameterless function *rdflo*, which reads a number from the keyboard and returns this as a floating-point function value. The function is to read integers and floating-point numbers in the usual notation, so that the two statements

```
scanf("%f", &x);
x = rdflo();
```

accept the same numerical input.In case of any leading nonnumeric character *rdflo* is to display a clear error message and to stop program execution. (In that case *scanf* would return the function value 0.) The function *rdflo* is to read character by character, using *getchar*.

1.13 Write the function *printflo* to print a floating-point number, so that we can write

```
printflo(w, d, x)
```

instead of

```
printf("%w.df", x)
```

where *w* and *d* are unsigned integer constants (or, in the former call, any integer expressions). As usual, they denote the field width and the number of decimals after the period, respectively. The expression *x* has floating-point type. Use *putchar* as the only output facility in this function.

CHAPTER 2

Array and File Manipulation

In many applications we have to rearrange sets of objects in a specific order. An example of such a set is the data we would need to compile a telephone directory. Here each object is a 'record' consisting of three components, i.e. a name, an address and a telephone number. The process of placing objects in a specific order is called *sorting*. In the case of a telephone directory, the objects are sorted in alphabetic order of the names, so that with a given name the corresponding telephone number can easily be found. We say that the name is used as a *key*. In general, we sort records in such a way that their keys will be in ascending order. As long as we are dealing with sorting methods themselves, rather than with their applications, we may as well use very simple objects such as numbers, which are, so to speak, their own keys.

2.1 STRAIGHT SORTING METHODS

Let us use an example to discuss a simple sorting method. If the sequence

$$109 \quad 75 \quad 200 \quad 25 \quad 38 \quad 19 \quad 150 \quad 11 \quad 20$$

is to be sorted it is a good idea to exchange the least integer, 11, with the first, 109. We then obtain the new sequence

$$\underline{11} \quad 75 \quad 200 \quad 25 \quad 38 \quad 19 \quad 150 \quad 109 \quad 20$$
O.K.

The first element of the sequence is now O.K., so we still have to deal only with the remaining elements. We now apply the same procedure to the subsequence that starts at the second integer, 75. Thus we select its least element, 19, and exchange it with 75, which gives:

$$\underline{11} \quad \underline{19} \quad 200 \quad 25 \quad 38 \quad 75 \quad 150 \quad 109 \quad 20$$
O.K.

We then proceed with the subsequence starting at the third element, 200, and so on,

31

until we have dealt with a subsequence of only two elements. This sorting method is called *straight selection*. Here is a C function, which sorts an array *a* of *n* floating-point numbers in this way:

```
/* SORT1.C: Straight selection, applied to an
            array of float numbers
*/
sort1(a, n) float a[]; int n;
{ int i, j, k;
  float min;
  for (i=0; i<n-1; i++)
  { k = i; min = a[k];
    for (j=i+1; j<n; j++)
      if (a[j] < min) {k = j; min = a[k];}
    /* Exchange a[k] ( = min) with a[i]: */
    a[k] = a[i]; a[i] = min;
  }
}
```

We could replace the *i*-loop with

```
for (i=0; i<n-1; i++)
{ k = i;
  for (j=i+1; j<n; j++)
    if (a[j] < a[k]) k = j;
  /* Exchange a[k] with a[i]:  */
  min = a[k]; a[k] = a[i]; a[i] = min;
}
```

However, if we modified *sort*1 in this sense the new version would be slightly slower, because in its inner loop we would perform the test $a[j] < a[k]$, instead of the simpler test $a[j] < min$. This test will often fail, so the higher speed of this test in the original version outweighs some extra work that is done only when the test suceeds (namely the work involved in assigning the value of $a[k]$ to the variable *min*). Far more important than considering these subtle modifications is the observation that the running time of the straight-selection algorithm is $O(n^2)$. (Recall that we discussed this 'big-oh' notation in Section 1.1.) There are two nested loops in *sort*1; if we doubled the value of *n* the range of the controlled variable *i*, in the outer loop, would approximately be doubled. (Actually, this range would increase by a factor $(2n-1)/(n-1)$ instead of 2, hence the word *approximately*, which from now on we will omit.) As for the inner loop, with controlled variable *j*, the *average* range would also be doubled, so as a result of increasing *n* by a factor 2, the total running time would increase by a factor 4, and, in general, increasing *n* by a factor *k* implies an increase in running time by a factor k^2. As we know, this is expressed very briefly by saying that the running time is $O(n^2)$, or equivalently, that the algorithm has *time complexity* n^2.

We shall also consider a version of the straight-selection sorting algorithm for strings. If we wish to compare two strings we want the addresses of their first characters. It is these addresses (also called *pointers*) that are technically called *strings*. Note that we use the term 'string' either for a sequence of characters or for the address of the first of these characters. This may seem confusing, but it is not in practice. If we write a literal string such as "ABC" in a program its value has type *pointer-to-char* and is in fact the address of the first character, ′A′, so regarding the string "ABC" as a pointer value is in accordance with the above technical terminology. On the other hand, it is obvious that the actual sequence of characters is meant if we talk about the *i*th character (or the length) of a string, or about comparing and copying strings. Recall that for strings *s* and *t* (i.e. the addresses of the first characters!), we write

```
strcmp(s, t) < 0
```

for 'string *s* precedes string *t* alphabetically', and

```
strcpy(s, t)
```

for 'copy (the characters of) string *t* to *s*'. Should we instead write $s < t$ and $s = t$, respectively, then this would manipulate addresses, not the character sequences starting at these addresses.

We conclude this recapitulation of strings by recalling the essential role of the terminating *null character*, '0', in string-handling routines such as *strcmp* and *strcpy*. This enables us to use a portion of a character array as a string, namely the portion that begins with a given address and ends with the first following null character.

In our first sorting function for strings we will deal with strings of maximum length 20. To accommodate the terminating null character, each string will occupy 21 bytes. The following function sorts an array of *n* such strings:

```
/* SORT2.C: Straight selection, applied to an array of
            fixed-length strings
*/
sort2(a, n) char a[][21]; int n;
{ char *p, min[21];
  int i, j;
  for (i=0; i<n-1; i++)
  { p = a[i];
    for (j=i+1; j<n; j++)
      if (strcmp(a[j], p) < 0) p = a[j];
    /* Exchange the character sequence starting at  p  */
    /* with that starting at  a[i]:                     */
    strcpy(min, p);
    strcpy(p, a[i]);
    strcpy(a[i], min);
  }
}
```

If the comparison *strcmp*(*a*[*j*], *p*) succeeds, we do not copy the characters themselves but, instead, we store the value of *a*[*j*], that is, the address of *a*[*j*][0], into the variable *p*. Copying the characters themselves to *min* at this stage would not lead to a simpler comparison as copying a floating-point value did in *sort*1.

Since the functions *sort*1 and *sort*2 (both based on the sorting method straight selection) have running time $O(n^2)$ they are suitable only for relatively small sequences. Besides straight selection, there are many other simple sorting methods which usually also have time complexity n^2. Collectively, we call them *straight methods*.

With straight selection the number of comparisons does not depend on the initial order of the elements to be sorted. This is different in another straight sorting method,

namely *shaker sort*. This method is even worse than straight selection if the elements
are initially in random order. However, it is extremely fast if only a few elements are
in a wrong position and all the others are in increasing order.

Consider, for example, the following sequence:

$$10 \quad 21 \quad \underline{92} \quad 35 \quad 50 \quad 69 \quad 80 \quad 83 \quad 90 \quad 95 \quad 100 \quad 120$$

The length of this sequence is $n = 12$. As usual in C, we number the positions of
the elements 0, 1, ..., $n-1$. Only the underlined element, 92, is in a wrong position.
If, starting at the left, we compare each two neighbour elements, and exchange them
if the left one is greater than the right one, then 92 is exchanged with 35, then with
50, and so on, until it is in its correct position, between 90 and 95. In this example
all elements are then in increasing order, but in general this need not be the case. If
we proceed from left to right, and if after exchanging the elements in the positions j
and $j+1$ no other exchanges are carried out during this scan, then all elements in the
positions $j+1$, $j+2$, ... $n-1$ are in their correct places, so only elements in the positions
0, 1, ..., j may still be wrong. We could now deal with these, again starting at the left.
We would then sort according to the method called *bubble sort*. However, we had better
work from right to left this time, since there might be only one wrong element which
is much too small for its position, so that it is to shift many positions to the left. We
therefore alternately proceed from left to right and from right to left, which explains the
name *shaker sort*. If, after proceeding from right to left, the final exchanged elements
are at the positions $j-1$ and j, then the elements 0, 1, ..., $j-1$ are in their correct
positions, so j is the leftmost position to be dealt with next. The following function is
based on this principle:

```
/* SORT3.C: Shaker sort, applied to an array
            of float numbers
*/
sort3(a, n) float *a; int n;
{ float *left=a, *right=a+n-1, *start=a, *p, *q, x;
  do
  { for (p=left; p < right; p++)
    { q = p + 1;
      if (*p > *q) {x = *q; *q = *p; *p = x; start = p;}
    }
    right = start;
    for (p=right; p > left; p--)
    { q = p - 1;
      if (*q > *p) {x = *q; *q = *p; *p = x; start = p;}
    }
    left = start;
  } while (left < right);
}
```

We have used pointer notation here, which turned out to be noticeably faster than
the corresponding array notation. With shaker sort there are usually more exchanges
to be carried out than with straight-selection sort. It is therefore worthwhile to use two
pointers p and q for the elements to be exchanged. With the more conventional array
notation and integer variables i, $i1$, l, r, j, instead of the pointers p, q, *left*, *right*, *start*,
the first of the above two for-loops would have read

```
for (i=1; i<r; i++)
{ i1 = i + 1;
  if (a[i] > a[i1])
  { x = a[i1]; a[i1] = a[i]; a[i] = x; j = i;
  }
}
```

which is somewhat slower. Besides, using pointers here is a good preparation for the next section, where we shall be dealing with a method that in general is much faster than straight methods such as the two we have been discussing. Remember, however, that our last method, shaker sort, is the best if all or almost all elements are already in increasing order.

2.2   QUICKSORT

We shall now discuss a sorting method which is very efficient for large sequences of objects. This method, called *quicksort* (C. A. R. Hoare, *Computer Journal*, April 1962), is based on partitioning the given sequence into two subsequences. For some rather arbitrarily chosen element x, all elements of the first resulting subsequence are not greater than x, and all elements of the second are not less than x. Then the same method is applied to both subsequences, and so on. Here is a recursive function, which applies quicksort to a sequence of floating-point numbers:

```
/* QSORT1.C: Quicksort, first version */
qsort1(left, right) float *left, *right;
{ float *p = left, *q = right, w,
        x = *(left + (right - left >> 1));
  /* >> shifts right to divide by 2 */
  do
  { while (*p < x) p++;
    while (*q > x) q--;
    if (p > q) break;
    w = *p; *p = *q; *q = w;
  } while (++p <= --q);
  if (left < q) qsort1(left, q);
  if (p < right) qsort1(p, right);
}
```

If, for example, we have defined

```
static float a[8] = {23, 398, 34. 100, 57, 67, 55, 320};
```

then we can use *qsort*1 as follows:

```
qsort1(a, a + 7);
```

In this example we have $x = 100$, since this is found in the address $left+(7 \gg 1)$, that is, in the address $left+3$. (Note that $right-left$ denotes a number of floating-point numbers, not a number of bytes!) The pointer variable p, starting at the left end, is then incremented until it points to an element greater than or equal to x, so in this example the first while-loop ends when p points to the number 398. Similarly, q starts at the right end, and moves to the left until it points to an element less than or equal to x, so here it will then point to 55. The two elements 398 and 55 are then exchanged, and in the comparison

```
++p <= --q
```

the pointers p and q take another step towards each other. The new situation is as follows:

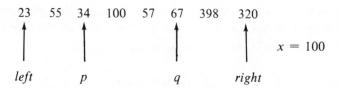

The first while-loop is executed again, so p is again incremented until it points to 100. Then p is no longer incremented, since it does not point to an element less than x any longer. In the second while-loop q is not decremented this time, since 67 is not greater than x. So the elements 100 and 67 are now exchanged, p is incremented and q is decremented, which gives:

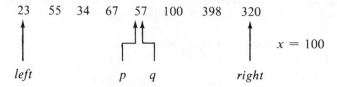

The pointers p and q now have equal values, so we still have $p \leq q$, and the first while-loop is executed again. Since 57 is less than x, the pointer p is incremented. It then points to 100, so this while-loop stops. In the second while-loop q is not decremented, since it points to 57, which is not greater than x. This time we have $p > q$, so the break-statement is executed, and the main (do-while) loop ends with values of *left, right, p, q* as shown below:

23   55   34   67   57 ‖ 100   398   320

left   *q*   *p*   *right*

$x = 100$

Numbers $\leq x$ Numbers $\geq x$

This completes the partitioning process. To the left of the double vertical line no element is greater than and to its right no element is less than x. It is interesting that this method will always work properly, even if x is unfortunately chosen. It would be ideal if x were the median, that is, if there were as many array elements less than x as there are elements greater than x. In less fortunate cases the resulting subsequences have unequal lengths, as in the above example, where these lengths are 5 and 3. After partitioning the given sequence it seems that we still have a long way to go before all elements are in increasing order. However, the only thing that remains to be done is to apply the same process to both the left and the right partitions. In *qsort*1 this is done recursively for both partitions, which is a very simple and elegant solution.

Except for the worst-case situation, which in practice is extremely unlikely to occur, the running time of quicksort is $O(n.\log n)$, so it will be approximately equal to $cn.\log n$, where c is some constant. Note that the base of the logarithm only influences the value of c, and, since we leave the latter unspecified, that base is irrelevant in our discussion. Remember that for large arguments logarithmic functions increase extremely slowly. For example, using base 10, we have

$$\log 1000 = 3$$
$$\log 10\,000 = 4$$

so if we switch from problem size $n_1 = 1000$ to problem size $n_2 = 10\,000$, the running time will increase by a factor

$$\frac{n_2 \cdot \log n_2}{n_1 \cdot \log n_1} = \frac{10\,000 \cdot 4}{1\,000 \cdot 3} \approx 13.3$$

whereas with a straight sorting method that factor would be

$$\frac{n_2^2}{n_1^2} = \frac{10\,000^2}{1000^2} = 100$$

This example illustrates the significance of the concept of time complexity, as introduced in Section 1.1. For any algorithm with running time $O(n \cdot \log n)$ and any other algorithm with running time $O(n^2)$ there is a value of n beyond which the former algorithm will be faster than the latter. In practice we may work with values of n that will not exceed some limit, and we should be aware that we have not really shown that quicksort is faster than straight sorting methods, for, let us say, $n = 1000$, although we will probably expect that to be the case. Both analytic and experimental investigations have confirmed such expectations, that is, they have shown that quicksort is really a very fast sorting algorithm, even for rather small values of n, such as, say, 100.

It is not difficult to avoid the second recursive call in *qsort*1, for after having performed the first, we can sort the right-hand partition iteratively. Function *qsort*2 shows how this is done.

```
qsort2(left, right) float *left, *right;
{ float *p=left, *q=right, w, x;
  do
  { x = *(left + (right - left >> 1));
    do
    { while (*p < x) p++;
      while (*q > x) q--;
      if (p > q) break;
      w = *p; *p = *q; *q = w;
    } while (++p <= --q);
    if (left < q) qsort2(left, q);
    left = p; q = right;
```

```
  } while (left < right);
}
```

The first of the two statements

```
left = p; q = right;
```

followed by a 'jump back to the beginning', means that the value of p is now used as the new value of the variable *left*. Then, as usual, *left* and *right* are again used as boundary pointers, which is similar to a recursive call *qsort2*(p, *right*). The variable *right* has not been changed, and q should again have the same initial value, hence the second of the above two assignment statements. As discussed in Section 1.6, recursion is associated with using a stack, so it is reasonable to ask if for certain large arrays the functions *qsort*1 and *qsort*2 might cause stack overflow. In practice this is most unlikely to happen, but such a vague remark is not completely satisfactory. If each recursive call should have to deal with a subsequence almost as long as the current sequence, then, indeed, the recursion depth could be considerable, which may even cause stack overflow. Although improbable, this is not impossible. It would be nice if each recursive call had to deal with a subsequence of, at most, half the size of the sequence under consideration. Fortunately, we can achieve this! In *qsort*2 we had a recursive call for the left partition, while we dealt with the right partition iteratively, regardless of the sizes of the partitions. Instead, we can always use a recursive call for the smaller partition, leaving the larger one to be dealt with iteratively. This is the way function *qsort*3 works:

```
/* QSORT3.C: Quicksort with limited recursion depth */
qsort3(left, right) float *left, *right;
{ float *p=left, *q=right, w, x;
  do
  { x = *(left + (right - left >> 1));
    do
    { while (*p < x) p++;
      while (*q > x) q--;
      if (p > q) break;
      w = *p; *p = *q; *q = w;
    } while (++p <= --q);
    if (q - left < right - p)
    { if (left < q) qsort3(left, q);
      left = p; q = right;
    } else
    { if (p < right) qsort3(p, right);
      right = q; p = left;
    }
  } while (left < right);
}
```

Since in each recursive call the sequence length is reduced by at least a factor 2, the recursion depth is not greater than the 2-logarithm of the original sequence length.

2.3 SORTING STRINGS OF VARIABLE LENGTH

If strings instead of numbers are to be sorted there is a problem, due to the variable length that strings usually have. We can, of course, reserve a fixed number of bytes for each string, as discussed in Section 2.1. Like the method *straight selection*, applied to fixed-length strings in SORT2.C, we can apply *quicksort* to such strings. However, this means that each string must not exceed a given length, which we probably wish to choose rather small. After all, each string, however small, will use that amount of space. This is particularly unpleasant and inefficient if the strings vary greatly in length, as, for example, in the index at the end of a book. For this application and others we will now consider a different method.

In contrast to the above two-dimensional array *list* we will use a one-dimensional array *str* of characters, in which we store all strings, including their final null characters. It will now normally not be possible to exchange two strings because of their unequal lengths. Therefore there will be another array, *ptr*, in which we store pointers to the individual strings. Initially, $ptr[0]$ points to the first string, that is, to character $str[0]$. If this first string is, for example, "*cos*", then we have

```
str[0] = 'c'
str[1] = 'o'
str[2] = 's'
str[3] = '\0'
```

so the second string begins in $str[4]$, and that is where the next pointer $ptr[1]$ initially points to. Now suppose that this second string is "*atan*". Then we logically place them in alphabetic order by exchanging the pointers $ptr[0]$ and $ptr[1]$ instead of the corresponding character sequences "*cos*" and "*atan*". After this exchange, $ptr[0]$ points to $str[4]$, and $ptr[1]$ points to $str[0]$, so if we used, for example,

```
printf("%s %s", ptr[0], ptr[1])
```

the output would be

```
atan cos
```

Program STRQSORT.C can actually be used as an intermediate step in producing the index of a book. Here we have in fact pairs of keywords and page numbers, but these can simply be combined. The program reads its input from the file UNSORTED.TXT, which, for example, may contain:

```
cos..3
atan..3
circle..4
pi..4
triangle..10
pythagoras..11
circle..17
tan..19
sin..19
cos..19
atan..20
point-of-intersection..20
plane..21
```

If we run program STRQSORT.C we obtain the file SORTED.TXT, with the following contents:

```
atan..20
atan..3
circle..17
circle..4
cos..19
cos..3
pi..4
plane..21
point-of-intersection..20
pythagoras..11
sin..19
tan..19
triangle..10
```

Notice that each keyword is combined with its page number into one string, which must not contain any blanks. Also, we write *pythagoras* with a small letter *p*, because the capital letters lie in a range different from the lower-case ones. It is now relatively simple to change this into the form that we actually need, namely:

```
atan, 3, 20
circle, 4, 17
cos, 3, 19
pi, 4
plane, 21
point of intersection, 20
Pythagoras, 11
sin, 19
tan, 19
triangle, 10
```

Especially for a real index of a book, of, say, a thousand keywords, it would take a lot of time if we had to sort them manually, so program STRQSORT.C may be quite useful:

```
/* STRQSORT.C:
     This program sorts variable-length strings,
     using quicksort.
*/

#include <stdio.h>
#define LEN 30000
#define NNAMES 2000
char a[LEN], *ptr[NNAMES];

main()
{ int n=0, i;
  char *q;
  FILE *fpin, *fpout;
  fpin = fopen("unsorted.txt", "r");
  if (fpin == NULL) {printf("???"); exit(1);}
  q = a;
  while(fscanf(fpin, "%s", q) > 0)
  { ptr[n++] = q;
    q += strlen(q) + 1;
```

```
      if (q - a + 50 > LEN)
      { printf("File too large\n"); exit(1);
      }
   }
   fclose(fpin);
   printf(
   "Total string length: %d\nThere are %d keywords\n",
    q - a + 1, n);
   strqsort(0, n-1);
   fpout = fopen("sorted.txt", "w");
   for (i=0; i<n; i++) fprintf(fpout, "%s\n", ptr[i]);
   fclose(fpout);
}

strqsort(left, right) int left, right;
{ int i, j; char *px, *pw;
   do
   { px = ptr[(left+right)/2]; i = left; j = right;
     do
     { while (strcmp(ptr[i], px) < 0) i++;
       while (strcmp(ptr[j], px) > 0) j--;
       if (i > j) break;
       pw = ptr[i]; ptr[i] = ptr[j]; ptr[j] = pw;
     } while (++i <= --j);
     if (j - left < right - i)
     { if (left < j) strqsort(left, j);
       left = i; j = right;
     } else
     { if (i < right) strqsort(i, right);
       right = j; i = left;
     }
   } while (left < right);
}
```

With the constants *LEN* and *NNAMES* defined in the program the maximum number of keyword occurrences is 2000, and the total length of the keywords, including the null characters, must not exceed 30 000 characters. If we had used the more conventional way of sorting, as discussed at the beginning of this section, with a maximum string length of 40 (including the null character), 2000 keywords would have required an array of

$$2000 \times 40 = 80\,000$$

characters. Furthermore, such a program would have been considerably slower, since it takes much more time to copy a string than to copy a pointer.

2.4 SORTING A FILE

So far, we have been discussing only *internal* sorting methods, with array elements as the objects to be sorted. In contrast to this, we can sort *externally*, that is, rearrange items in a file instead of in an array. Since on most computer systems files may be much larger than arrays, we need external sorting methods as soon as memory is insufficient for internal sorting. A good many years ago internal sorting methods could hardly ever be used for data-processing applications, because of memory limitations. Now that we are accustomed to large amounts of internal memory we should not reject internal sorting methods too soon. However, memory may still be insufficient to contain all data to be sorted, so we will also pay some attention to external sorting.

Note that the distinction between internal and external sorting methods is pragmatic rather than fundamental. Since in C we have *random access* to a disk file we can adapt the methods of the preceding sections to files. To illustrate this, we shall apply quicksort to a disk file, at the end of this section. On the other hand, sequential file access may be simulated with arrays. After all, it is not forbidden to use arrays purely sequentially. In practice, however, we should remember:

(1) With internal sorting methods we normally use only one array, which only contains the data to be sorted. External methods, on the other hand, need not be so economical with space, but may use several files for the same data at the same time if desirable for fast sorting.

(2) Sequential *array* access is not faster than random array access. This may be different for *files*, since with sequential file access large quantities of data can be buffered. So although random access is possible with a disk file it might be faster to use sequential access if we sort externally. With tapes, we are limited to sequential access, which means that in this case quicksort is out of the question.

Let us now be more concrete. We shall, for convenience, again sort a sequence of (floating-point) numbers. This time, they are not in an array but in a file. Since during the sorting process we have to read and to write them a great many times it is wise to use *unformatted* I/O. This means that the numbers are not converted from the external, decimal format to the internal, binary representation and vice versa. Instead, they have the same format, both internally and externally. We shall, however, begin with a normal ASCII file, which we read only once. Similarly, we end with writing the sorted file in ASCII format. Thus, we will actually perform conversions from the external to the internal format and vice versa, but, as they are rather time-consuming, we will separate them from the sorting process, as Fig. 2.1 shows:

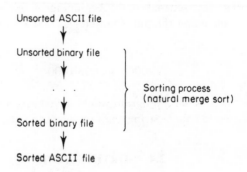

Fig. 2.1. Use of ASCII and binary files

Natural merge sort, as its name implies, is based on the principle of *merging*. We shall deal with this principle first, and at the same time demonstrate the use of unformatted I/O.

Suppose we have two ordered sequences of integers, in binary files, for example:

File *aaa*: 10 20 40 60 70 80
File *bbb*: 15 25 35 40 50 65 90

We want to form the following ordered sequence, consisting of all elements of the files *aaa* and *bbb*:

File *ccc*: 10 15 20 25 35 40 40 50 60 65 70 80 90

Here is function *merge* to accomplish this, along with a main program to demonstrate its working:

```
/* MERGE.C: Merging two files */
#include <stdio.h>

main()
{ FILE *fa, *fb, *f;
  int x;
  fa = fopen("aaa", "wb");   /* "wb" is system dependent */
  fb = fopen("bbb", "wb");
  printf(
  "Enter two monotonic nondecreasing sequences,\n");
    printf(
  "each followed by a zero as an end signal:\n\n");
  while (scanf("%d", &x), x)
    fwrite(&x, sizeof(int), 1, fa);
  while (scanf("%d", &x), x)
    fwrite(&x, sizeof(int), 1, fb);
  fclose(fa); fclose(fb);
  merge();             /* This is the function in question */
  f = fopen("ccc", "rb");
  printf("\nOutput:\n");
  while (fread(&x, sizeof(int), 1, f) > 0)
    printf("%4d", x);
  fclose(f);
}

merge()
{ FILE *fa, *fb, *f;
  int a, b, size=sizeof(int);
  fa = fopen("aaa", "rb");   /* "rb" is system dependent */
  fb = fopen("bbb", "rb");
  f = fopen("ccc", "wb");
  fread(&a, size, 1, fa);
  fread(&b, size, 1, fb);
  while (!feof(fa) && !feof(fb))
  { if (a < b)
    { fwrite(&a, size, 1, f);
      fread(&a, size, 1, fa);
    } else
    { fwrite(&b, size, 1, f);
      fread(&b, size, 1, fb);
    }
  }
  while (!feof(fa))
```

```
  { fwrite(&a, size, 1, f);
    fread(&a, size, 1, fa);
  }
  while (!feof(fb))
  { fwrite(&b, size, 1, f);
    fread(&b, size, 1, fb);
  }
  fclose(fa); fclose(fb); fclose(f);
}
```

In the function *merge* the first while-loop compares two numbers, *a* and *b*, read from the files *aaa* and *bbb*, respectively. Each time, the smaller of these two numbers is written to file *ccc*, and then the next number is read from the file from which the number just written had been read, that is, if there is still a next number on that file. If not, the first while-loop ends, and either the second or the third deals with the remaining numbers in one of the two files *aaa* and *bbb*. Note that at this stage either file *aaa* or file *bbb* is exhausted, so indeed, only one of the last two while-loops is effective.

Natural merge sort is based on ordered subsequences, called *runs*. Suppose that file *f* contains a number sequence as shown below:

$$f : \underline{29 \quad 32 \quad 34} \quad \underline{21} \quad \underline{19 \quad 50} \quad \underline{10 \quad 43} \quad \underline{33 \quad 49 \quad 100} \quad \underline{60}$$

The underlined runs are now distributed onto the two other files *fa* and *fb*:

$$fa : \underline{29 \quad 32 \quad 34} \quad \underline{19 \quad 50} \quad \underline{33 \quad 49 \quad 100}$$

$$fb : \underline{21} \quad \underline{10 \quad 43 \quad 60}$$

The first run of *f* has gone to *fa*, the second to *fb*, the third to *fa* again, and so on. Note that the fourth and the sixth run of file *f* form spontaneously one single run (10, 43, 60) on file *fb*. This is no problem whatsoever; we even appreciate it, since the fewer runs there are, the better.

It is now time to use merging. In contrast to program MERGE.C, we will merge runs rather than files. Repeatedly, two runs are read, one from *fa* and the other from *fb*, and they are merged into one new run, written to file *f* again:

$$f : \underline{21 \quad 29 \quad 32 \quad 34} \quad \underline{10 \quad 19 \quad 43 \quad 50 \quad 60} \quad \underline{33 \quad 49 \quad 100}$$

As soon as one of the two input files is exhausted any remaining runs on the other are simply copied to *f*, as is done here with the final run (33, 49, 100) of *fa*. File *f* now contains the same numbers as it did originally, but in fewer and longer runs. We then repeat these two actions of distributing and merging until there is only one run on file *f*. Sooner or later this will happen, and then we are ready with our sorting task.

Here is a complete program which reads real numbers from an ASCII file, and writes the sorted numbers to another ASCII file. As indicated in Fig. 2.1, binary files are used in the actual sorting process for reasons of efficiency:

```
/* NMSORT.C:
      This program sorts real numbers in a given
      ASCII file. The resulting sorted file is also
```

```
            an ASCII file. The program uses three (binary)
            scratch files. The user has to enter the names
            of these five files.
*/
#include <stdio.h>
int size = sizeof(float), number_of_runs;
FILE *f, *fa, *fb; /* Scratch files */
char  tmpfil[25], tmpfila[25], tmpfilb[25];
main()
{ char infil[25], outfil[25];
  FILE *fpin, *fpout;
  float x;
  long t0, t1; int count=0, dt;

  int i=0;
/* Ask user for file names:    */
  printf("Name of input file:      "); scanf("%s", infil);
  printf("Name of scratch file 1:"); scanf("%s", tmpfil);
  printf("Name of scratch file 2:"); scanf("%s", tmpfila);
  printf("Name of scratch file 3:"); scanf("%s", tmpfilb);
  printf("Name of output file:     "); scanf("%s", outfil);

/* Open both input file fpin and scratch file f: */
  fpin = fopen(infil, "r");
  if (fpin == NULL) {printf("Unknown name\n"); exit(1);}
  f = fopen(tmpfil, "wb");
                /* First argument:  Name of scratch file */
                /* Second argument: system dependent      */

/* Convert from ASCII to binary: */
  while (fscanf(fpin, "%f", &x) > 0)
  { fwrite(&x, size, 1, f); count++;
  }
  fclose(fpin); fclose(f);

/* The actual sorting process, applied to file f: */
  time(&t0);
  nmsort();
  time(&t1); dt = t1 - t0;
  printf(
  "nmsort    n = %d,   computing time: %d s\n", count, dt);


/* Open output file:   */
  fpout = fopen(outfil, "w");

/* Convert from binary to ASCII: */
  f = fopen(tmpfil, "rb");
  while (fread(&x, size, 1, f) > 0)
  { fprintf(fpout, "%8.2f", x); i++;
    if (i == 10) { fprintf(fpout, "\n"); i = 0; }
  }
  fclose(fpout);
  fclose(f);
  f = fopen(tmpfil, "wb");
            /* File f is now empty */
  fclose(f);
}

nmsort()
```

```
{ do
  { distribute();
    merge();
  } while (number_of_runs > 1);
  fa = fopen(tmpfila, "wb"); fclose(fa); /* Empty */
  fb = fopen(tmpfilb, "wb"); fclose(fb); /* Empty */
}

distribute()
{ float x;
  f = fopen(tmpfil, "rb");
  fa = fopen(tmpfila, "wb");
  fb = fopen(tmpfilb, "wb");
  fread(&x, size, 1, f);
  while (!feof(f))
  { copyarun(f, fa, &x);
    if (feof(f)) break;
    copyarun(f, fb, &x);
  }
  fclose(f); fclose(fa); fclose(fb);
}

copyarun(in, out, pnext) FILE *in, *out; float *pnext;
{ float old;
  do
  { fwrite(pnext, size, 1, out);
    old = *pnext;
    fread(pnext, size, 1, in);
  } while (!(feof(in) || *pnext < old));
  number_of_runs++;
}

merge()
{ float a, b, old;
  number_of_runs = 0;
  fa = fopen(tmpfila, "rb");
  fb = fopen(tmpfilb, "rb");
  f = fopen(tmpfil, "wb");
  fread(&a, size, 1, fa);
  fread(&b, size, 1, fb);
  while (!feof(fa) && !feof(fb))
  { if (a < b)
    { fwrite(&a, size, 1, f);
      old = a;
      fread(&a, size, 1, fa);
      if (feof(fa) || a < old) copyarun(fb, f, &b);
    } else
    { fwrite(&b, size, 1, f);
      old = b;
      fread(&b, size, 1, fb);
      if (feof(fb) || b < old) copyarun(fa, f, &a);
    }
  }
  while (!feof(fa)) copyarun(fa, f, &a);
  while (!feof(fb)) copyarun(fb, f, &b);
  fclose(f); fclose(fa); fclose(fb);
}
```

This program is somewhat complicated, which is mainly due to the fact that we can detect the end of a run only by reading the first element of the next run, if any. The function *copyarun* is therefore not a normal copying function. When it is called, the first element to be copied has already been read and is pointed to by its third argument. Similarly, just before returning to its caller, this function has read one element too far (unless the end of the file has been reached), and the third argument points to that element. Recall that in C the function *feof* tells us that a read attempt has failed, so we use it after a read attempt, not before (in the way *eof* is used in Pascal). We shall discuss the performance of this program in connection with a competitive program, which we will write first.

Traditionally, *sequential* access is used for external sorting. However, if we use disks we can instead use some *random-access* (or 'direct access') method, originally applied to arrays. Incidentally, not only the hardware but also the software may prohibit our using random file access, as (standard) Pascal does. In C, however, random access is a standard I/O facility.

After the call

```
fseek(fp, offset, code)
```

the next read or write operation for stream *fp* takes place at the position determined by *offset* and *code*. If *code* is zero the long int argument *offset* is counted from the beginning, that is, for the very first byte of a file we have *offset* $= 0L$. We also use *code* $= 2$, which means that we count from the position immediately after the file, so for the final byte of a file we have

```
offset = -1L, code = 2.
```

The position is expressed in a byte number. We can inquire the current position by the call

```
ftell(fp)
```

Its value has type *long int*, similar to the second argument of *fseek*. Note that this call gives the file length (in bytes) if it is preceded by the call *fseek*(*fp*, 0L, 2).

We are now in a position to consider another sorting program for real numbers in a file, which uses the method quicksort, discussed in Sections 2.2 and 2.3:

```
/* FQSORT.C:
      This program sorts real numbers in a given
      ASCII file. The resulting sorted file is also
      an ASCII file. The user has to enter the names
      of these two files. The sorting process
      itself deals with temporary binary files.
      Method: quicksort.
*/
#include <stdio.h>
int size = sizeof(float);
FILE *f;          /* Scratch file */
char  tmpfil[25];

main()
{ char infil[25], outfil[25];
  FILE *fpin, *fpout;
```

```
        float x;
        long t0, t1; int count=0, dt;

        int i=0;
 /* Ask user for file names:    */
        printf("Name of input file:     "); scanf("%s", infil);
        printf("Name of scratch file: "); scanf("%s", tmpfil);
        printf("Name of output file: "); scanf("%s", outfil);

 /* Open both input file fpin and scratch file f: */
        fpin = fopen(infil, "r");
        if (fpin == NULL) {printf("Unknown name\n"); exit(1);}
        f = fopen(tmpfil, "wb");
                        /* First argument:  Name of scratch file */
                        /* Second argument: system dependent      */

 /* Convert from ASCII to binary: */
        while (fscanf(fpin, "%f", &x) > 0)
        { fwrite(&x, size, 1, f); count++;
        }
        fclose(fpin); fclose(f);

 /* The actual sorting process, applied to file f: */
        time(&t0);
        filqsort();
        time(&t1); dt = t1 - t0;
        printf(
 "filqsort   n = %d,   computing time: %d s\n", count, dt);

 /* Open output file:    */
        fpout = fopen(outfil, "w");

 /* Convert from binary to ASCII: */
        f = fopen(tmpfil, "rb");
        while (fread(&x, size, 1, f) > 0)
        { fprintf(fpout, "%8.2f", x); i++;
          if (i == 10) {fprintf(fpout, "\n"); i = 0;}
        }
        fclose(fpout);
        fclose(f);
        f = fopen(tmpfil, "wb");
                   /* File f is now empty */
        fclose(f);
 }


filqsort()
{ long left, right;
  f = fopen(tmpfil, "rb+");
  left = 0L;
  fseek(f, (long) -size, 2); right = ftell(f)/size;
  fqsort(left, right);
  fclose(f);
}

fqsort(left, right) long left, right;
{ long i=left, j=right, middle; float x, xi, xj;
  do
  { middle = left + ((right - left) >> 1);
    fseek(f, middle * size, 0);
```

```
    fread(&x, size, 1, f);
    do
    { while(fseek(f, i * size, 0),
            fread(&xi, size, 1, f), xi < x) i++;
      while(fseek(f, j * size, 0),
            fread(&xj, size, 1, f), xj > x) j--;
      if (i > j) break;
      fseek(f, i * size, 0); fwrite(&xj, size, 1, f);
      fseek(f, j * size, 0); fwrite(&xi, size, 1, f);
    } while (++i <= --j);
    if (j - left < right - i)
    { if (left < j) fqsort(left, j);
      left = i; j = right;
    } else
    { if (i < right) fqsort(i, right);
      right = j; i = left;
    }
  } while (left < right);
}
```

Note the similarity between the function *fqsort* and *qsort3*, discussed in Section 2.2. Again, only the smaller partition is dealt with recursively, so that the recursion depth will not exceed the two-logarithm of the number of objects to be sorted.

We will now compare the two programs NMSORT.C and FQSORT.C. The running time for either program is $O(n.\log n)$, so both can be used for large files. In an experiment on the IBM PC, FQSORT.C turned out to be much faster than NMSORT.C, that is, when applied to files on a diskette. Instead of the latter, the experiment was also carried out with 'virtual disk', also called 'ramdisk', which means that input and output operations are simulated in main memory. (This principle is frequently used with programs running on a machine with more memory than for which they have been designed.) With virtual disk, NMSORT.C did much better than FQSORT.C. Sorting 500 real numbers in this way took about 20 s, which is not much if we take into account that floating-point operations take a long time (see also the remark at the end of Section 1.6.) Curiously enough, FQSORT.C sorted relatively slowly on a virtual disk. (Of course, this slowness is not due to the method quicksort itself but rather to our way of using it. Originally, quicksort was meant for internal memory (see Sections 2.2 and 2.3.) We then wrote the special version FQSORT.C, which runs fast with real files on disk, but, with virtual disk, we are using this version to sort in internal memory again, which is hardly a sensible thing to do!)

Anyway, we see that much depends on the circumstances, that is, on the hardware and software that is available. The above two programs are easy to use, so if you are interested in their performances on a particular machine, the best thing to do is to experiment with them yourself! Since the names of all files are to be entered by the user it is possible to include information about the disk drive to be used. For example, on a certain PC we may enter *A:AAA*, *B:BBB*, *C:CCC*, where *A:* denotes a diskette, *B:* a hard disk, and *C:* a virtual disk. As to NMSORT.C, we must remember, first, that this program uses much more file space than the other program, FQSORT.C, and, second, that the three temporary files should preferably be located on distinct physical devices. The following points are worth remembering:

(1) NMSORT.C uses much more file space than FQSORT.C.

(2) The three scratch files used by NMSORT.C should preferably be located on distinct devices.
(3) We cannot use FQSORT.C if tapes instead of disk storage are to be employed.
(4) If the file happens to be in ascending order already, NMSORT.C is faster than FQSORT.C.
(5) Natural merge sort is a stable method, while quicksort is not (see below).
(6) The number of key comparisons with NMSORT.C is more than twice the corresponding number with FQSORT.C. (Though determined experimentally, this fact is device-independent.) In addition to key comparisons, FQSORT.C also performs comparisons of long integers, but the latter may be much faster than the former, as is the case in our sample programs, where the keys are floating-point numbers.

Point 5 deserves some explanation. Usually we do not sort just numbers but rather records, as mentioned at the beginning of this chapter. For example, let us assume that we have records with a number and a name, and that the number is the key, so that we are comparing the numbers. If two records have identical keys we may require the old order of these two records to be maintained. This implies that the sequence

   345 *Patterson*
   289 *Taylor*
   345 *Johnson*

should give the following result after sorting:

   289 *Taylor*
   345 *Patterson*
   345 *Johnson*

With a stable sorting method this will indeed happen. If the method is not stable the following result may appear:

   289 *Taylor*
   345 *Johnson*
   345 *Patterson*

In most applications the sorting method need not be stable, either because we have unique keys or (more rarely) because the order of elements with identical keys is irrelevant. In particular, if the objects to be sorted have no other fields than their keys then obviously their order is irrelevant. This is the case if we sort either a sequence of numbers, as in most of our sample programs, or a sequence of strings, as in Section 2.3.

2.5   BINARY SEARCH

This section deals with searching ordered sequences. Similar to our introduction to sorting algorithms in Section 2.1, we shall be dealing with sequences of numbers, keeping in mind that in practice we normally have records with keys and data. The records will have unique keys, so in our case all numbers in the given sequence are different from each other. Besides, the sequence is increasing, so that with elements $k[i](i = 0, 1, \ldots, n-1)$ we have:

$$k[0] < k[1] < \ldots < k[n-1].$$

Let us declare

```
int k[M], x;
```

where M is greater than or equal to n. The variable x denotes a given integer, for which array k is to be searched. We can benefit from the fact that the sequence is in increasing order, and search it very efficiently. The method to be discussed is widely known as *binary search*.

We begin with an element in the middle of the sequence, and, if this is not the one we are looking for, we proceed by searching either the left or the right half of the original sequence, depending on whether x is less or greater than the element in the middle, and so on. This rough description of the method is inaccurate and incomplete, since x may be unequal to all elements $k[i]$, and when writing a function for binary search we have to provide a means to enable the user of the function to know whether or not x has been found. One solution would be to make the function return either -1 if x is not found or i if x is found and equal to $k[i]$. We will go a step further and, in case x is not found, provide the user with information about where it logically belongs in the sequence. Our function *binsearch* will therefore return the integer value i, determined as follows:

$$i = \begin{cases} 0 \text{ if } x \le k[0] \\ n \text{ if } x > k[n-1] \\ j \text{ if } k[j-1] < x \le k[j] \text{ for some } j(1 \le j \le n-1) \end{cases}$$

In Sections 4.2.4 and 4.2.5 we will apply binary search to B-trees, and then we will really need such a value i, both where x is present and not present in a given sequence. The first line of *binsearch* will read as follows:

```
int binsearch(x, k, n) int x, k[], n;
```

Before we proceed with binary search we observe that we can also obtain the desired value i by using linear search, for which the following function would suffice:

```
int linsearch(x, k, n) int x, k[], n;
{ int i=0;
  while (i < n && x > k[i]) i++;
  return i;
}
```

Note that, for all possible values of x, function *linsearch* returns the correct value. However, linear search is relatively slow, since its running time is $O(n)$. As we are given an ordered array, using linear search here is as foolish as searching a dictionary for a word without using the fact that the words are listed in alphabetic order. We therefore want to replace the latter function with *binsearch* which gives the same result as *linsearch*, but runs in $O(\log n)$ time. If the range to be searched is exactly twice as small each time, then we need k steps, where

$$2^k = n$$

so

$$k = {}^2\log n$$

which explains the time complexity mentioned.

Writing a function for binary search is a well-known and instructive programming exercise. We have to be cautious to avoid both wrong results and an endless loop. If we test for the two trivial cases $x \le k[0]$ and $x > k[n-1]$ in advance, the remaining case to be considered is:

$$k[0] < x \le k[n-1]$$

We have to reduce this condition to

$$k[j-1] < x \le k[j]$$

and we note that both conditions are special cases of

$$k[left] < x \le k[right] \tag{1}$$

so we begin with $left = 0$, $right = n-1$, and all we have to do is to halve the range $left, \ldots, right$ in such a way that (1) also holds for the reduced range, and to repeat this until we have

$$right - left = 1 \tag{2}$$

At this moment, both (1) and (2) are true, which means that $right$ is the desired value i. Here is the function $binsearch$, which works in this way:

```
/* BINSEARCH.C: Function for binary search.
      Array k[0], k[1], ..., k[n-1] is searched for x.
      Returned value:  0 if x <= k[0], or
                       n if x > k[n-1], or
                       i, where  k[i-1] < x <= k[i].
*/
int binsearch(x, k, n) int x, k[], n;
{ int middle, left, right;
   if (x <= k[0]) return 0;
   if (x > k[n-1]) return n;
   left = 0; right = n-1;
   while (right - left > 1)
   { middle = right + left  >> 1;
      if (x <= k[middle]) right = middle;
                    else left = middle;
   }
   return right;
}
```

We assign the value of *middle* to the variable *right* if

$$x \leq k[middle]$$

so that afterwards we have

$$x \leq k[right]$$

Similarly, if

$$k[middle] < x$$

we assign the value of *middle* to *left*, so that

$$k[left] < x$$

holds after this assignment. Since there are no other assignments to the variables *left* and *right* in the loop, condition (1) will always be satisfied. We also have to verify that the loop terminates. This is rather simple, since each time, the inner part of the loop is entered only for a subrange

$$left, \ldots, right$$

of at least three elements, which means that the computed value of *middle* satisfies

$$left < middle < right.$$

This implies that either *left* will increase or *right* will decrease, so it is guaranteed that the length of the subrange under consideration really decreases each time.

When discussing condition (2) for loop termination we implicitly assumed that the sequence consists of at least two elements. However, function *binsearch* also allows the sequence length 1. In that case, the loop is not entered at all, since then $k[n-1]$ is in fact $k[0]$, so we have either $x \leq k[0]$ or $x > k[n-1]$. The returned value is 0 in the former case and 1 (that is, *n*) in the latter, as it should be. The case $n = 1$ may seem farfetched, but it is not. It will actually occur in Section 4.2.4, and, in general, when dealing with a sequence of length *n* we ought to know which values for *n* are allowed. For our binary-search algorithm *n* may be any positive integer, including 1. Binary search is notorious for its pitfalls when programmed sloppily, and it is one of the rare cases in programming in which a more or less formal correctness proof is both worthwhile and feasible.

It may not be superfluous to point out how *binsearch* should be used. If *i* is an int variable and, coincidentally, the actual arguments have the same names as the formal parameters of binsearch, we can write:

```
i = binsearch(x, a, n);
if (i < n && x == a[i])
{ /* Found.
      The given integer x is equal to a[i].
  */
  ...
} else
{ /* Not found.
      Either a[i] is the first element
```

```
        that is greater than x (and i < n),
        or  x > a[n-1] (and i = n).
    */
      ...
  }
```

The test $i < n$ after the call is essential, since otherwise the memory location following the final element $a[n-1]$ would be inspected if x happened to be greater than that final element. In the first place, this would be fundamentally incorrect because we may have no access to that memory location. Note that the operator $\&\&$ guarantees the second operand not to be evaluated if the first is 0, so in our function the case that i should be equal to n causes no such problems. Second, that memory location might contain a value equal to x, so if our computer system allows us to inspect it (which is the more probable case), the test $x == a[i]$ may succeed, and our program would behave as if x had been found.

2.6 HASHING

We will now discuss a well-known technique, called *hashing*, to store and retrieve objects very efficiently. We shall call these objects *records* and assume each of them to contain a unique key which, as usual, serves as a means to search the set of all stored records. It would be nice if we could derive the position of records from their keys. If the keys were natural numbers lying in a range that is small enough, we could indeed store each record in the position given by its key, so that we would know its place when we needed it later. Unfortunately, that is not the case in most practical situations. If the keys are natural numbers their range is usually much larger than the amount of space available. If the keys are strings we can transform them into natural numbers, but the requirement that unequal strings should give unequal numbers would lead to very large numbers, so again, their range would be too large. However, the idea of transforming keys into a reasonable range of natural numbers is useful, not only if the keys are strings but also if they are numbers.

We will assume storage space to be available for, at most, n records, numbered

$$0, 1, \ldots, n-1$$

and we will apply a so-called *hashing function* to the keys to obtain a nonnegative integer i which is less than n. Although a one-to-one mapping remains desirable, we shall not require this. Thus we do not require our hashing function to transform any two distinct keys $k1$ and $k2$ into two distinct integers $i1$ and $i2$. In other words, the situation

$$h(k1) = h(k2) = i$$

called a *collision*, may happen. A very simple (but not the best) way to cope with collisions is known as *linear probing*, which works as follows.

When we are storing objects we distinguish between occupied and empty locations. If we want to store a record with key k, and the location computed as $i = h(k)$ happens to be already occupied, we simply try the next one, that is, location

$$i+1 \quad \text{if } i < n, \quad \text{or}$$
$$0 \quad \text{if } i = n$$

and so on. When, later, we want to find that record, we simply use the same procedure, that is, we compute $i = h(k)$, and see if the key of the record stored in location i is the given key k. If not, we try the next location, and so on, until, if we keep finding keys other than the given one, we have either tried n locations or found an empty location.

Before we discuss some improvements, this simple method should be absolutely clear, so let us use an example and work it out in detail. We shall assume that we have character strings of maximum length 20 as keys, and associated integers to be stored as useful data. The character strings are the keys k and the integers are the data fields d. There will be, at most, 1000 records.

First a large number of pairs (k, d) are read, say, from the file named $DATA$ and stored in the array a, and then we are given some key value k and have to find the record with that key because we need the corresponding data field d. If you are somewhat familiar with assembly language you may think of the way an assembler translates 'symbols' into addresses. Then our key k denotes such a symbol, that is, a symbolic notation for an address, and our data field d is the numerical value of that address. In the first scan the assembler stores symbols and addresses, and in the second it generates object code with concrete addresses, found in the symbol table and corresponding to the symbols it encounters. As an assembler usually consults the symbol table a great many times it is a good illustration of the fact that speed may be an important factor, even if the table is only of moderate size. The following main program is a less realistic example, since each time that we enter a string on the keyboard the table is consulted only once.

```
/* HASH1.C: Demonstration of hashing
*/
#include <stdio.h>
#define LEN 1000
struct { char k[21]; int d; } a[LEN];
        /* Field k is initialized with null strings! */
main()
{ FILE *fp;
  char key[100];
  int dat;
  fp = fopen("DATA", "r");
  if (fp == NULL) { printf("File DATA ???"); exit(1); }
  while (fscanf(fp, "%s %d", key, &dat) > 0)
  { key[20] = '\0';              /* Truncate if length > 20 */
    if (store(key, dat) == 0)
      { printf(
        "Table full or duplicate key, (%s, %d) not stored\n",
        key, dat);
      }
  }
  fclose(fp);
  while
  (printf("\nEnter a string, or ! to stop: "),
    scanf("%s", key),
    key[20] = '\0',       /* Truncate if length > 20   */
    strcmp(key, "!")      /* strcmp returns 0 if equal */
```

```
      ) if (lookup(key, &dat))
           printf("Data field:%6d\n", dat);
         else printf("Key not stored in hash table\n");
   }

   /* Linear probing:   */

   int store(key, dat) char *key; int dat;
   { int i, count=0;
     i = hash(key);
     while (strlen(a[i].k))      /* Location i is occupied?  */
     { if (strcmp(a[i].k, key) == 0      /* Duplicate key      */
       ¦¦ ++count == LEN) return 0;      /* or table full?     */
       if (++i == LEN) i = 0;
     }
     strcpy(a[i].k, key); a[i].d = dat;
                                      /* Use empty location */
     return 1;
   }

   int lookup(key, pdat) char *key; int *pdat;
   { int i, count=0;
     i = hash(key);
     while (strcmp(a[i].k, key))      /* Strings unequal?     */
     { if (strlen(a[i].k) == 0        /* Empty location       */
       ¦¦ ++count == LEN) return 0;   /* or table exhausted?  */
       if (++i == LEN) i = 0;
     }
     *pdat = a[i].d;                    /* Found!             */
     return 1;
   }

   int hash(key) char *key;
   { int slen = strlen(key);
     return
       (101 * key[0] + 103 * key[slen-1] + 107 * slen) % LEN;
   }
```

The function *hash* was chosen rather arbitrarily. It is based only on the first and the final characters and on the length of the key. Thus, for example, we have

$$hash("ABC") = (101 * 65 + 103 * 67 + 107 * 3)\%1000 = 787$$

but, unfortunately, also

$$hash("ARC") = 787$$

This does not mean that this hash function is a bad one, because collisions similar to this one will also occur with other hash functions. It is not a particularly good one either, since we can easily replace it by others that are equally good. The multiplication factors were introduced to give all locations a reasonable chance to be chosen. For example, if we had written

```
   return key[0] + key[slen-1] + slen;
```

then the higher part of the hash table would only have been used after a great many collisions. On the other hand, we could have used a more sophisticated hash function, based on all characters of the string, but that would have been slower. The choice of the numbers 101, 103, 107 in our hash function was quite arbitrary.

After this brief discussion of hash functions we have to pay some attention to the method of collision handling. First, we should know that storing all records in a fixed-size table, as we are doing, is called *closed* hashing; instead, we can use *open* hashing, that is, use such a table only to contain pointers to the records themselves, stored elsewhere in memory, as we will see in Exercise 4.5 at the end of Chapter 4. Here we will confine the subject to closed hashing, and discuss collision handling in this context.

Linear probing, that is, simply trying the next location after each collision, is known to lead to clusters. There are several more advanced methods, of which we will consider only one, namely *double hashing*. According to this method, we use another function to compute some increment to be applied to the subscript i, instead of using the increment 1 as we did with linear probing. This increment is also derived from the key, and we again count cyclically, so that 0 follows $LEN - 1$. We shall replace the above functions *store* and *lookup*, and add the function *incrhash* as the hash function to compute increment values. It is most desirable that the table length LEN should now be some prime number, say 1009, instead of 1000. (Note that 1009 is the least prime number greater than 1000.) If we used 1000, as before, and the increment should be, for example, 50, then after 20 steps we would be back at the location where we started, so not all locations would be visited. We avoid such situations by using a prime number for the table length. Thus the #*define*-line at the top of program HASH1.C is to be replaced with the one shown in HASH2.C:

```
/* HASH2.C: Double hashing
*/
#include <stdio.h>
#define LEN 1009

/* Insert the definition of array 'a' and the
   functions 'main' and 'hash'; see HASH1.C.
*/

int store(key, dat) char *key; int dat;
{ int i, inc, count=0;
  i = hash(key);
  if (strlen(a[i].k))
  { inc = incrhash(key);
    do
    { if (strcmp(a[i].k, key) == 0      /* Duplicate key   */
      !! ++count == LEN) return 0;      /* or table full   */
      i += inc; i %= LEN;
    } while (strlen(a[i].k));  /* Location i occupied?  */
  }
  strcpy(a[i].k, key); a[i].d = dat;  /* Empty location */
  return 1;
}

int lookup(key, pdat) char *key; int *pdat;
{ int i, inc, count=0;
  i = hash(key);
  if (strcmp(a[i].k, key))                /* Strings unequal? */
  { inc = incrhash(key);
```

```
   do
   { if (strlen(a[i].k) == 0        /* Empty location or*/
     ¦¦ ++count == LEN) return 0;    /* table exhausted? */
     i += inc; i %= LEN;
   } while (strcmp(a[i].k, key));    /* Strings unequal? */
 }
 *pdat = a[i].d;                     /* Found!           */
 return 1;
}

int incrhash(key) char *key;
{ return ((53 * key[0] + 57 * key[1]) & 511) + 1;
  /* The returned value lies in the range 1, ..., 512 */
}
```

We could have written the functions *store* and *lookup* in a somewhat simpler form by computing the value of *inc* unconditionally at the beginning. After this, we could have used a while-statement, similar to the previous versions of these functions. However, the 'primary index value' *i*, returned by the function *hash*, may quite frequently be the subscript that actually will be used. Then no collision handling is needed, and it would be a waste of time to call the function *incrhash* in this important special case. We therefore compute *inc* only if there is really a collision. Again, the given function *incrhash* is only an example. It will work satisfactorily, but the peculiar way of computing its returned value, like most examples, is based on no scientific theory whatsoever.

It is obvious that searching a hash table will be slow if the table is almost full. Therefore it is recommended that the table length *LEN* should be much greater than the number of records actually stored. Usually we do not know in advance how many records are to be stored, so whenever we store things in a table, it is quite normal for only a small portion of its space to be actually in use. In the most primitive way of storing and searching, we would fill a table consecutively as far as we need, starting at the top, and use linear search (see Section 1.2) to look things up. Compared with this, closed hashing is very sophisticated in that it makes use of the whole table straightaway. If we are economical enough to use only a small fraction of all locations available we are rewarded with fast access, so with hashing we immediately benefit from what we have paid.

EXERCISES

2.1 We have been discussing four sorting methods, namely straight selection, shaker sort, quicksort and natural merge sort. Which of these methods are stable? Use records with at least one data field besides the key to give a demonstration.

2.2 Rewrite *qsort*3 in Section 2.2, replacing pointers with array notation. This makes it more suitable for a subsequent translation into another high-level language. (If *qsort*1 were to be translated into assembly language, the given version would immediately be suitable, since pointer values are addresses, which in assembly language are quite normal objects to deal with.)

2.3 Use natural merge sort for internal sorting. Use three arrays instead of three files. Compare the speed of the resulting function with *qsort*3 in Section 2.2.

2.4 Use the method shaker sort for external sorting. Although this will be slow in general, it may be useful in applications where almost all elements in the given file are already in increasing order.

2.5 Our versions of quicksort chose the element in the middle of the subsequence under consideration to compare it with all other elements. Ideally, the chosen element should be the median of that subsequence. To improve the choice, use three elements in the middle of the subsequence, and choose the median of these three elements to compare it with all other elements of the subsequence. (If we are given three elements, two or three of which may be equal, and we omit both one that is greatest and one that is least, then the remaining element is the median.)

2.6 Apply the method binary search to a file of which all elements are in increasing order.

2.7 Apply the hashing method to a file, and compare linear probing with double hashing in an experiment. (Linear probing might be faster in this case, since a sequence of adjacent locations to be searched may be located in a buffer in main memory, so that, after dealing with some location, examining the next may not involve real disk access.)

CHAPTER 3

Some Combinatorial Algorithms

3.1 A VARIABLE NUMBER OF NESTED LOOPS

Suppose that we have an integer array r, say, of length 3, and that we want some action to be performed for all possible values $r[0]$, $r[1]$, $r[2]$, where each $r[i]$ ranges from a given lower bound *lower*$[i]$ to a given upper bound *upper*$[i]$. For example, let us use global variables for these arrays, defined as:

```
int r[3],
    lower[3] = {5, 2, 8},
    upper[3] = {7, 2, 9};
```

Then we want array r to obtain the following values, in this order:

$r[0]$	$r[1]$	$r[2]$
5	2	8
5	2	9
6	2	8
6	2	9
7	2	8
7	2	9

Obviously, we achieve this using three nested loops:

```
for (r[0] = lower[0]; r[0] <= upper[0]; r[0]++)
for (r[1] = lower[1]; r[1] <= upper[1]; r[1]++)
for (r[2] = lower[2]; r[2] <= upper[2]; r[2]++) action();
```

To avoid any vagueness, we may imagine the task of the function *action* to consist of printing the values of array r, which would produce the above table of three columns. So far, everything is extremely simple. We now wish to generalize these three nested loops to n nested loops, where n is variable. Again, we will use the three arrays r, *lower*, *upper*, but we will now distinguish between their physical length *LEN* and their logical length n which is not greater than *LEN*. Only the first n elements of both *lower* and *upper* will now be used, and it is our task to achieve the effect that we can write symbolically as:

```
for (r[0] = lower[0]; r[0] <= upper[0]; r[0]++)
for (r[1] = lower[1]; r[1] <= upper[1]; r[1]++)
          . . .
for (r[n-1] = lower[n-1]; r[n-1] <= upper[n-1]; r[n-1]++)
  action();
```

For simplicity, let us define

```
action()
{ int i;
  for (i=0; i<n; i++) printf("%6d", r[i]);
  printf("\n");
}
```

as suggested previously. Thus we want our program to print a table similar to the one shown above for the simple case with $n = 3$. (Obviously, this table is empty if, for some i, the value *lower*[i] is greater than *upper*[i].)

We are now faced with the problem that we cannot write a variable number of nested for-loops. However, with recursion there is a simple and elegant solution to this problem. We shall use a function *loopfun*, with one integer argument, k. Its effect will be:

```
for (r[k] = lower[k]; r[k] <= upper[k]; r[k]++)
for (r[k+1] = lower[k+1]; r[k+1] <= upper[k+1]; r[k+1]++)
          . . .
for (r[n-1] = lower[n-1]; r[n-1] <= upper[n-1]; r[n-1]++)
  action();
```

Here we have $n-k$ nested loops. With $k = 0$, we have our original n nested loops. If we take care that the call *loopfun*(n) should result in the call *action*(), then we can describe the effect of *loopfun*(k) for $k < n$ as follows:

```
for (r[k] = lower[k]; r[k] <= upper[k]; r[k]++)
  loopfun(k+1);
```

If this is fully understood, the following program should also be clear:

```
/* NESTED.C: A variable number of nested loops
*/
#define LEN 10
int n, r[LEN], lower[LEN], upper[LEN];

main()
{ int i;
  printf("Enter n (not greater than %d): ", LEN);
  scanf("%d", &n);
  printf("Enter n pairs (lower, upper):\n");
  for (i=0; i<n; i++)
    scanf("%d %d", lower + i, upper + i);
  printf("\nOutput:\n\n ");
  for (i=0; i<n; i++) printf("  r[%d]", i);
  printf("\n");
  loopfun(0);
}
```

```
loopfun(k) int k;
{ if (k == n) action(); else
    for (r[k] = lower[k]; r[k] <= upper[k]; r[k]++)
       loopfun(k+1);
}

action()
{ int i;
    for (i=0; i<n; i++) printf("%6d", r[i]);
    printf("\n");
}
```

Here is a demonstration of this program:

```
Enter n (not greater than 10): 3
Enter n pairs (lower, upper):
5   7
2   2
8   9

Output:

   r[0]   r[1]   r[2]
      5      2      8
      5      2      9
      6      2      8
      6      2      9
      7      2      8
      7      2      9
```

Although statically there is only one occurrence of a recursive call in function *loopfun*, this call will normally be executed more than once, so dynamically there are several recursive calls. Each call of *loopfun* may therefore be associated with a tree, as we discussed in Section 1.5. In the above example, the call *loopfun*(0) in the main program corresponds to the tree shown in Fig. 3.1, where we have used the abbreviations $f(k)$ for *loopfun*(k) and r_k for $r[k]$.

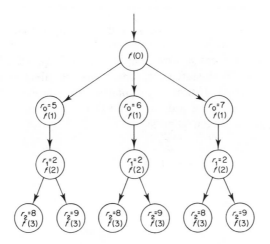

Fig. 3.1. Tree to illustrate recursion

The root of this tree is $f(0)$ and the leaves are the six calls $f(3)$. Each leaf results in the call *action*(), which prints all values r_i encountered on the path from the root to that leaf. In many recursive programming problems it will be helpful to imagine a tree similar to this one.

It is instructive to compare our function *loopfun* with a nonrecursive function for the same task. In *loopfun* the argument k was necessary because we used the function both in the main program and recursively, and all calls had to be distinguished from one another. With a nonrecursive version there is only one function call, say *loopfun*1(), and no argument is needed.

We begin with copying the values of $lower[0], \ldots, lower[n-1]$ into $r[0], \ldots, r[n-1]$. At the same time we check if each of these values is less than or equal to the corresponding element of array *upper*, since otherwise no further actions are to be performed and we can return to the main program. After copying *lower* to r, we enter a while-loop in which we immediately perform the call *action*(). In the same while-loop we then update array r. Since the final element, $r[n-1]$, changes most frequently, it is this element that is incremented. Only when it is equal to $upper[n-1]$ do we have both to reset it to the value of $lower[n-1]$ and go back to $r[n-2]$. If this is less than $upper[n-2]$ we increment it, otherwise we reset it to the value $lower[n-2]$ and go back to $r[n-3]$, and so on:

```
loopfun1()
{ int i, n1=n-1;
  for (i=0; i<n; i++)
    if ((r[i] = lower[i]) > upper[i]) return;
  while (1)
  { action();
    i = n1;
    while (1)
    { if (r[i] < upper[i]) {r[i]++; break;}
      r[i] = lower[i];
      if (--i < 0) return;
    }
  }
}
```

Function *loopfun*1 is harder to understand and longer than the elegant recursive version *loopfun*, but it will be somewhat faster. In *loopfun* a recursive call takes place each time $r[n-1]$ is incremented, which happens quite frequently. In the same situation, *loopfun*1 executes the break-statement, which has the effect of jumping back to the call of the function *action*. However, in applications where the function *action* takes comparatively much time, as in program NESTED.C, the difference in speed between *loopfun*1 and *loopfun* will be negligible.

3.2 PERMUTATIONS

With n (distinct) objects we can form

$$n! = 1 \times 2 \times \ldots \times n$$

distinct (ordered) sequences. We verify this as follows. We can choose n objects as the first, that is, the leftmost element of the sequence. Then for the second element of the sequence we have to choose among the $n-1$ remaining objects. Since such a choice of $n-1$ elements can be made after each of the n previous choices for the first element we have

$$n\times(n-1)$$

possible choices for the first two elements of the sequence. Now there are only $n-2$ objects left, among which we choose the third element, so for the first three elements we have

$$n\times(n-1)\times(n-2)$$

possible choices, and so on. Continuing in this way until there is only one object left, we find that altogether the number of choices (that is, the number of possible sequences) is

$$n\times(n-1)\times(n-2)\times \ \ldots \ \times2\times1$$

which is written as $n!$. We call each sequence a *permutation*, so there are $n!$ permutations of n distinct objects.

Without loss of generality we shall use the numbers

$$1, \ 2, \ \ldots, \ n$$

for these objects, and we now want to write a program which reads n and generates all permutations of those n numbers. Each of these permutations can be regarded as a (long) integer in the number system with base m, where m can be any number greater than n. Quite simply, if n is less than 10 we can associate each sequence with an integer written as n decimal digits. For example, with $n = 6$, the permutation

$$3 \quad 6 \quad 1 \quad 5 \quad 4 \quad 2$$

corresponds to the long integer 361542. With this association of permutations and integers we can order the permutations according to the 'less than' relation for integers. For example, if $n = 3$ our program is to generate the permutations

$$\begin{array}{ccc}
1 & 2 & 3 \\
1 & 3 & 2 \\
2 & 1 & 3 \\
2 & 3 & 1 \\
3 & 1 & 2 \\
3 & 2 & 1 \\
\end{array}$$

in that order. As in the previous section, we shall distinguish between a function (*permut*) that generates all sequences and a function (*action*) that is called each time some global array r contains a new sequence.

Let us use a function *action* which simply prints the permutation just generated and stored in $r[1], r[2], \ldots, r[n]$. Function *action* is called in *permut*, which in turn is called both recursively and in a main program. In this main program we store the initial values

1, 2, ..., n in array r, before we call *permut*. Using the array elements

$$r[1], \ r[2], \ ..., \ r[n]$$

for this purpose, we initially have

$$r[i] = i(i = 1, \ 2, \ ..., \ n)$$

After considering all this, we have to begin with thinking how to write *permut*. Let us assume that we know how to generate all permutations of $n-1$ objects, so that we can use this to generate all permutations of n objects. For example, if $n = 4$, array r is initially as follows:

$$1 \quad 2 \quad 3 \quad 4$$

We can divide the 4! permutations to be generated into four classes of 3! permutations each. Each class has a unique first element in all its permutations. Thus we have:

$$
\begin{array}{ll}
1 \ . \quad . \quad . & \\
\quad ... & \text{Class 1} \\
1 \ . \quad . \quad . & \\
& \\
2 \ . \quad . \quad . & \\
\quad ... & \text{Class 2} \\
2 \ . \quad . \quad . & \\
& \\
3 \ . \quad . \quad . & \\
\quad ... & \text{Class 3} \\
3 \ . \quad . \quad . & \\
& \\
4 \ . \quad . \quad . & \\
\quad ... & \text{Class 4} \\
4 \ . \quad . \quad . & \\
\end{array}
$$

By assumption, we can generate all permutations of $n-1 = 3$ elements, and since for each class there are only three variable elements, all permutations of each class can be generated, which in principle solves our problem.

However, there is a flaw in the above reasoning. Our assumption about the initial situation is correct if we only consider a call of *permut* in the main program, but if we include recursive calls we have to be aware that generating all permutations of n numbers does not imply that these should be the numbers

$$1, \ 2, \ ..., \ n$$

For example, in class 1 we have to generate permutations of three elements, but these are the numbers 2, 3, 4 instead of 1, 2, 3. We therefore need a slightly more general approach. We may require, however, that the numbers to be permuted are given in ascending order. So we should have assumed the initial contents of array r to be

$$a \quad b \quad c \quad d$$

where

$$a < b < c < d$$

Then all permutations in the first class begin with a, those in the second with b, and so on. This order is important, since we want the permutations to appear in the natural order, that is, in increasing order of the corresponding long integers. Since a is less than b, all permutations beginning with a are to appear before those beginning with b, and so on. In class 1, the 'variable' elements b, c, d are initially in increasing order, so we can safely apply a recursive call of our function *permut* to these elements. In class 2, we have to rearrange the elements in such a way that b comes in position 1, and the other elements in positions 2, 3, 4 in increasing order. This means that for class 2 the elements are to be in the order

$$b \quad a \quad c \quad d$$

before we can apply a recursive call to the last three of these elements. Similarly, in class 3 we begin with

$$c \quad a \quad b \quad d$$

and in class 4 with

$$d \quad a \quad b \quad c$$

We see that for class m we have to remove the mth element of the initial sequence

$$a \quad b \quad c \quad d$$

We fill the gap by shifting any preceding elements one position to the right. The resulting gap in the leftmost position is then filled with the removed element. Together, these operations form a rotation to the right, applied to the first m elements. We then perform the recursive call, and finally, restore the old situation by the inverse rearrangement in order to begin with an increasing sequence in the next class.

Program PERM.C shows how these ideas are implemented. In function *permut* we do not change the elements of array r in the positions 1, 2, ..., $k-1$. Within the for-loop, where i runs from k to n, the element in position i is to move to position k, so here the rotation applies to

$$m = i - k + 1$$

elements, starting at position k.

```
/* PERM.C: Generation of permutations in natural order
*/
#define LEN 11
int n, r[LEN];

main()
{ int i;
  printf("Enter n ( < %d): ", LEN); scanf("%d", &n);
  if (n >= LEN) exit(1);
  for (i=1; i<=n; i++) r[i] = i;
  printf("\nOutput:\n\n");
```

```
    permut(1);
}

permut(k) int k;
/* Generate all permutations of the n - k + 1 numbers
   r[k], r[k+1], ..., r[n]
*/
{ int i, j, aux;
  if (k == n) { action(); return; }
  for (i=k; i<=n; i++)
  { /* For each i, a class of permutations is generated.
       Move r[i] to position k, and shift the (old)
       elements in positions k, k+1, ..., i-1 one position
       to the right, in other words, rotate the elements
       in positions k, k+1, ..., i one position to the
       right:
    */
    aux = r[i];
    for (j=i; j>k; j--) r[j] = r[j-1];
    r[k] = aux;
    /* Recursive call: */
    permut(k+1);
    /* Restore old situation: */
    for (j=k; j<i; j++) r[j] = r[j+1];
    r[i] = aux;
  }
}

.action()
{ int i;
  for (i=1; i<=n; i++) printf("%3d", r[i]);
  printf("\n");
}
```

As in the previous section, a tree may be helpful to understand how this program works. For $n = 3$ this tree is shown in Fig. 3.2.

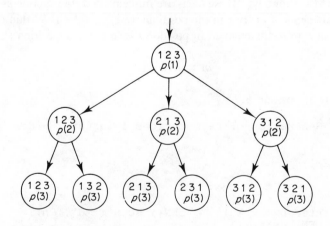

Fig. 3.2. Tree illustrating the generation of permutations

Each call *permut*(k) is abbreviated $p(k)$, and the contents of array r are shown at the moment this call takes place. The leaves of this tree shows the six permutations that are generated.

3.3 COMBINATIONS

If we are given both a set of n objects, say, the numbers

$$1, 2, \ldots, n$$

and an integer k ($0 \le k \le n$), we may be interested in all possible subsets of k objects. There are

$$\binom{n}{k} = \frac{n(n-1)(n-2) \ldots (n-k+1)}{k!} = \frac{n!}{k!(n-k)!}$$

such subsets, each of which is called a *combination*. For example, if $n = 5$ and $k = 3$, we have the following ten combinations:

```
1  2  3
1  2  4
1  2  5
1  3  4
1  3  5
1  4  5
2  3  4
2  3  5
2  4  5
3  4  5
```

Since each combination is a subset, the order of the elements in it is irrelevant, as the order of the elements in any set is irrelevant. For example, the triple

$$3 \quad 2 \quad 1$$

is not included in these ten lines since it would represent the same combination as

$$1 \quad 2 \quad 3$$

Let us write each combination as an ascending number sequence. We now want to write a program to generate all combinations of k elements out of n objects, where n and k are given. Besides representing each combination by an ascending sequence we also want these representations to appear in the 'natural' order, in the same way as the permutations were ordered in the previous section. Note that the ten combinations listed above are in this order. This time, we begin with a tree for the above example with $n = 5$ and $k = 3$, as Fig. 3.3 shows.

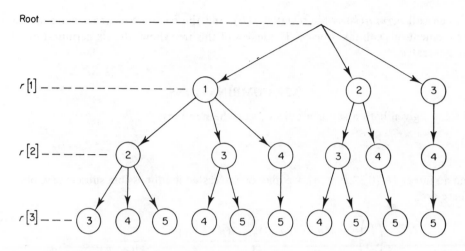

Fig. 3.3 *Tree illustrating the generation of combinations*

Each node of this tree contains only a single number, which is to be placed in $r[1]$, $r[2]$, or $r[3]$, as mentioned in the leftmost column. For each leaf, the function *action* will be used, and the contents of r, which form the desired combination, are then given by the path from the root to that leaf. For the first element, $r[1]$, we can choose 1, 2, or 3; not 4 or 5, for then no greater numbers would be available to follow $r[1]$. In general, $r[1]$ ranges from 1 to $n-k+1$. Depending on $r[1]$, we can make one or more choices for $r[2]$. More precisely, $r[2]$ ranges from $r[1]+1$ to $n-k+2$. In the same way, $r[3]$ ranges from $r[2]+1$ to $n-k+3$, and so on. So conceptually we need the following nested for-statement:

```
for (r[1] = 1; r[1] <= n - k + 1; r[1]++)
for (r[2] = r[1] + 1; r[2] <= n - k + 2; r[2]++)

                     . . .

for (r[k] = r[k-1] + 1; r[k] <= n; r[k]++)
   action();
```

This problem is similar to our subject of Section 3.1. Again we can implement this variable number of loops by means of a recursive function. The above nested loops can be given a more homogeneous appearance if we define $r[0] = 0$, since then the first line can be replaced with

```
for (r[1] = r[0] + 1; r[1] <= n - k + 1; r[1]++)
```

which makes it more similar to the second. The complete program for the rather complex task is surprisingly small:

```
/* COMB.C: Generate combinations
*/
#define LEN 100
int n, k, r[LEN];
```

```
main()
{ printf("Enter n ( < %d): ", LEN); scanf("%d", &n);
  if (n >= LEN) { printf("Too large"); exit(1); }
  printf("Enter k ( < %d): ", n+1); scanf("%d", &k);
  if (k > n) { printf("Too large"); exit(1); }
  printf("\nOutput:\n\n");
  combin(1);
}

combin(m) int m;
{ int i;
  if (m > k) action(); else
  for (i=r[m-1]+1; i <= n-k+m; i++)
  { r[m]=i; combin(m+1);
  }
}

action()
{ int i;
  for (i=1; i<=k; i++) printf("%3d", r[i]);
  printf("\n");
}
```

3.4   THE KNAPSACK PROBLEM

The combination problem in the last section was essentially about finding subsets of a given set. This is also the case in the classic *knapsack problem*, where we have to choose among several items, to be carried on our back. Each item has both a weight and a utility value, and the choice must be made such that the total weight of the selected items does not exceed some limit (the maximum load that can be carried), and, at the same time, the total utility of the chosen items should be maximized.

We will simplify this problem in two respects. First, we will require the total weight to be exactly equal to the given limit, and, second, we will assume the utility values of the items to be proportional to their weights. This means that we only have to find a subset consisting of items whose weights sum to exactly the total weight to be carried, if there exists such a subset. It will be clear that we can think of many similar problems: for example, how to choose a subset of the coins and banknotes that are in our purse to pay some amount of money.

In general, we are given a sum s and n positive integers

$$d_0, \; d_1, \; \ldots, \; d_{n-1}$$

and we are to find a subset of these integers (each occurring at most once) whose sum is s. To solve this problem, we shall develop a function *exactsum*, called in the main program as follows:

```
if (exactsum(s, 0))
  printf("\nThe problem has been solved\n"); else
  printf("\nNo solution\n");
```

In general, the call *exactsum*(t, i) is to examine if the target t can be formed as the sum of some integers chosen among the sequence

$$d_i, d_{i+1}, \ldots, d_{n-1}$$

If this is possible, the chosen integers are to be printed and the value to be returned is
1; if not, the value 0 should be returned. Function *exactsum* is recursive; as usual in
recursion, we have an 'escape clause' to prevent the function from calling itself forever.
If $t = 0$ the problem is solved by using an empty subset, and the problem cannot be
solved if $t < 0$ or $i = n$. If t is positive and i is less than n, *exactsum* (with arguments
t and i) finds out if the target $t-d_i$ can be formed as the sum of some integers chosen
among the sequence

$$d_{i+1}, d_{i+2}, \ldots, d_{n-1}$$

For this, we use the recursive call

```
exactsum(t - d[i], i + 1)
```

If its value is 1 we know that there is a solution, and we print the value of d_i, which is
included in the solution. If it returns 0, we perform the call

```
exactsum(t, i + 1),
```

to examine if there is a solution that does not include d_i. If this is not the case either,
there is no solution. Program KNAPSACK.C shows both the definition of function
exactsum and the way this function can be used.

```
/* KNAPSACK.C:
      This program solves the (simplified)
      knapsack problem: given a sum s and a set
      of positive integers, it finds a subset whose
      elements sum to exactly s if there is such a
      subset.
*/

#define NULL 0
char *malloc();
int *d, n;

main()
{ int s, i;
  printf("Enter the desired sum: ");
  scanf("%d", &s);
  printf("Enter n, followed by the n given ");
  printf("integers themselves:\n");
  scanf("%d", &n);
  d = (int *)malloc(n * sizeof(int));
  if (d == NULL)
  { printf("Not enough memory\n");
    exit(1);
  }
  for (i=0; i<n; i++) scanf("%d", d+i);
  printf("\nOutput:\n");
  if (exactsum(s, 0))
```

```
        printf("\nThe problem has been solved\n"); else
        printf("\nNo solution\n");
}

int exactsum(t, i) int t, i;
{ if (t == 0) return 1; else
   if (t < 0 || i == n) return 0; else
   if (exactsum(t - d[i], i+1))
   { printf("%d ", d[i]); return 1;
   } else
   return exactsum(t, i+1);
}
```

Here is a demonstration of this program:

```
Enter the desired sum: 18
Enter n, followed by the n given integers themselves:
7
2  2  2  5  5  9  11

Output:
9 5 2 2
The problem has been solved
```

We see that program **KNAPSACK.C** simply gives the first solution it finds. Instead, we may want to select the best, or *optimal*, solution in some particular sense. In our example, we may require the sum s to consist of as few terms as possible. We see that besides the computed solution

$$18 = 9+5+2+2$$

there is also the solution

$$18 = 11+5+2$$

which, according to the above requirement, would be required instead, because this sum consists of only three terms instead of four. Program **KNAPSACK.C** would actually have found the latter solution if we had entered the numbers d_i in the reverse order, that is, as the sequence

$$11 \quad 9 \quad 5 \quad 5 \quad 2 \quad 2 \quad 2$$

We could, of course, sort the numbers d_i in the program itself, and use them in decreasing order, no matter in what order they are entered. However, a decreasing sequence does not guarantee finding the 'shortest' solution either, as the following demonstration shows:

```
Enter the desired sum: 18
Enter n, followed by the n given integers themselves:
7
7  7  6  6  6  2  2

Output:
2 2 7 7
The problem has been solved
```

Unfortunately, the shorter solution $18 = 6+6+6$ is not found. Although in most cases it is a good strategy to use the largest number available, there are exceptions. An algorithm based on the strategy of selecting what 'looks best' is called *greedy*. (For some problems, there are greedy algorithms that always lead to an optimal solution, so 'greedy' is not necessarily a bad qualification as far as algorithms are concerned.) In the next section we will find an optimal solution for a problem for which we cannot use a greedy algorithm.

3.5 DYNAMIC PROGRAMMING

We will now deal with a problem similar to the previous one. Again, an integer s is given, along with n positive integers

$$d_0, d_1, \ldots, d_{n-1}$$

In contrast to the knapsack problem, solved in Section 3.4, each integer d_i may now occur more than once as a term in the solution. A perhaps more interesting new point is that we will now insist on using as few terms as possible in forming sum s. For example, if we have

$$s = 18$$
$$n = 3$$
$$d_0 = 2, \ d_1 = 6, \ d_2 = 7$$

then we want the sum s to be formed as

$$18 = 6+6+6$$

not as, for example,

$$18 = 7+7+2+2$$

or as

$$18 = 6+2+2+2+2+2+2$$

An application of this is making change in a shop, assuming that we have plenty of coins and banknotes. If, for example, we have coins with values of 1c, 5c, 10c, 25c, and we have to pay 42c, we immediatedly compute

$$42 = 25+10+5+1+1$$

if we want to use as few coins as possible. With the coin values mentioned we always obtain the optimal solution by using a *greedy* algorithm. As mentioned in Section 3.4, this means that, each time, we simply use the largest coin that does not exceed the remaining amount to be paid. However, we will use a more general algorithm, which gives an optimal solution even in cases where a greedy algorithm would not. We really need such an algorithm if there are no coins of 5c available. With

$$s = 42$$
$$n = 3$$
$$d_0 = 1, \ d_1 = 10, \ d_2 = 25$$

a greedy algorithm would yield

$$42 = 25+10+1+1+1+1+1+1+1$$

instead of the optimal solution

$$42 = 10+10+10+10+1+1$$

In cases like this (and in many others) we can use a tabular technique, called *dynamic programming*. Explaining this important technique in full would be beyond the scope of this book, so we will discuss it only in connection with our problem.

We define function $F(x)$ as the minimum number of terms (or coins) needed to form the sum x. It follows that F is defined only for those values x for which there is a solution. So if the least value d_i is greater than 1, then, for example, $F(1)$ is undefined. Dynamic programming, applied to our application, is based on the equation

$$F(x) = \min_{0 \le i < n} F(x-d_i)+1$$

for certain positive integers x (see below) and on

$$F(0) = 0$$

If, with the given range of i, some values $F(x-d_i)$ exist, we select the minimum of them and add 1 to this minimum to obtain the value $F(x)$. If no such values $F(x-d_i)$ exist, then $F(x)$ does not exist either. Although the above formula suggests recursion, we had better take the 'bottom-up' approach this time (see also Section 1.5, where we analysed a simple recursive function in a similar way). Thus, we will not begin with the given sum s but rather try to compute $F(1)$, $F(2)$, ... , $F(s)$, in that order. The resulting program would be very simple if only the value $F(s)$ were needed, since then we would only have to use an array of integers to store the computed values $F(x)$. As we are also interested in the selected values d_i we shall instead use an array of p of pointers. If $F(x)$ is undefined, then $p(x)$ is equal to the special pointer value usually written as *NULL*. Otherwise, $p(x)$ will point to a sequence of integers; the first of these is the value $F(x)$, and it is followed by $F(x)$ selected values d_i, which sum to exactly x. Again we benefit from the possibility of allocating a block of memory, using the standard function *malloc*, as program DYNPRO.C shows.

```
/* DYNPRO.C: An application of dynamic programming.
      With a given integer s and a set of positive
      integers, we try to write s as a minimal sum
      using these integers zero or more times.
*/

#define NULL 0
typedef int *pint;
int n, *d, *getints();
pint *p;
char *malloc();
```

```
main()
{ int s, i, j, m, *row, *solution();
  printf("Enter the desired sum: ");
  scanf("%d", &s);
  printf("Enter n, followed by the n given ");
  printf("integers themselves:\n");
  scanf("%d", &n);
  d = getints(n);
  p = (pint *)malloc((s+1)*sizeof(pint));
  if (p == NULL)
  { printf("Not enough memory\n");
    exit(1);
  }
  for (i=0; i<n; i++) scanf("%d", d+i);
  row = solution(s);
  if (row == NULL) printf("\nNo solution\n"); else
  { printf("\nSolution:\n\n    %d = ", s);
    m = row[0];
    for (j=1; j<=m; j++)
      printf("%d %s", row[j], j<m ? "+ " : "\n");
  }
}

int *getints(n) int n;
{ int *q;
  q = (int *)malloc(n * sizeof(int));
  if (q == NULL)
  { printf("Not enough memory\n");
    exit(1);
  }
  return q;
}

#define BIG 30000

int *solution(s) int s;
{ int x, u, i, j, min, imin, *destin, *source, aux;
  p[0] = getints(1); p[0][0] = 0; /* = F(0) */
  for (x=1; x<=s; x++)
  { min = BIG;
    for (i=0; i<n; i++)
    { u = x - d[i];
      if (u >= 0 && p[u] != NULL && p[u][0] < min)
      { min = p[u][0]; imin = i;
      }
    }
    if (min < BIG)
    { p[x] = destin = getints(min + 2);
      aux = x-d[imin]; source = p[aux];
      destin[0] = min + 1;
      for (j=1; j<=min; j++) destin[j] = source[j];
      destin[min+1] = d[imin];
    } else p[x] = NULL;
  }
  return p[s];
}
```

Here are three demonstrations of this program:

```
Enter the desired sum: 42
Enter n, followed by the n given integers themselves:
3
1   10   25

Solution:

    42 = 10 + 10 + 10 + 10 + 1 + 1


Enter the desired sum: 11
Enter n, followed by the n given integers themselves:
3
5   7   9

No solution


Enter the desired sum: 18
Enter n, followed by the n given integers themselves:
3
2   6   7

Solution:

    18 = 6 + 6 + 6
```

It may be instructive to see what actually has been computed in a relatively simple case as the last example. The values of $F(x)$ and the corresponding selected integers are as shown in Table 3.1.

Table 3.1   Internal results in the example with $s = 18$, $n = 3$, $d_0 = 2$, $d_1 = 6$, $d_2 = 7$

x	$F(x)$	Selected integers
0	0	
1	—	
2	1	2
3	—	
4	2	2+2
5	—	
6	1	6
7	1	7
8	2	6+2
9	2	7+2
10	3	6+2+2
11	3	7+2+2
12	2	6+6
13	2	7+6
14	2	7+7
15	3	7+6+2
16	3	7+7+2
17	4	7+6+2+2
18	3	6+6+6

To determine the final value, $f(18)$, the minimum of the three values

$$F(18-2) = F(16) = 3$$
$$F(18-6) = F(12) = 2$$
$$F(18-7) = F(11) = 3$$

is chosen and increased by 1, so we have

$$F(18) = F(18-6)+1 = 3$$

EXERCISES

3.1 Write a program to generate 'words' The program should read the word length n and, for each of the n positions, it should also read the letters that are allowed in that position. For example, with $n = 3$, the following letters may be given:

Position 1: B, L, N, R
Position 2: A, E, O, U
Position 3: L, M, N, S, T

This should lead to $4 \times 4 \times 5 = 80$ words:

$$BAL$$
$$BAM$$
$$\ldots$$
$$RUS$$
$$RUT$$

(It may disappoint you that only few of such generated 'words' have a meaning. It shows that if we need an unused letter combination for a new word there are plenty, even if we want the word to be very short!)

3.2 In Section 3.2 we were generating permutations in a certain order. To achieve this, each recursive call was preceded by a rotation to the right. If the order in which the permutations appear is irrelevant it is faster to exchange two elements instead. Again, the inverse operation is to be performed after the recursive call. Write a program that uses this faster method.

3.3 Write a program which reads a positive integer n, followed by n distinct capital letters. The program is to generate all words that are permutations of the given n letters, except for words with more than two successive vowels and words with more than two successive consonants. The five letters A, E, I, O, U are vowels, the 21 others are to be regarded as consonants.

3.4 Write a program which reads the positive integers n and $k(k \leq n)$, followed by n names. Generate all combinations of k names out of the given n names. This program may be useful if for some game we want a list of all possible teams of k persons, to be formed out of a population of n persons.

CHAPTER 4

Linear Lists

4.1 INTRODUCTION

In this chapter we shall use blocks of memory locations which are linked together. Each of these blocks contains at least one component that may refer to another block. If each block (except the final one) contains exactly one pointer to a next block, so that they form a chain, then the entire collection of linked blocks, together with a pointer to the initial block, is called a *linear list* or, equivalently, a *linked list*. Of course, if there is no danger of confusion with other list types (discussed later) we may as well simply call it a *list*. The blocks of memory locations of a list are usually called the *elements* or *nodes* of the list. They are *structures* (in some other languages called *records*), and for a given list they all have the same type and size. Every node of a linear list, except the final one, contains a pointer to its (immediate) *successor*, and every node except the first one is pointed to by its (immediate) *predecessor*.

Figure 4.1 shows an example of a linear list, each node of which contains an integer and a pointer field. We have an additional pointer variable, *start*, pointing to the first node. The first and the final nodes are called *head* and *tail*, respectively. The pointer field of the tail contains the value *NULL*; all other pointer fields point to the next node in the list. If the list is empty, there is neither a head nor a tail and the variable *start* has the value *NULL*. If the list consists of only one node, this node is both head and tail at the same time.

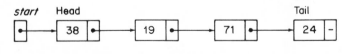

Fig. 4.1. Linear list

Program LIST.C reads integers from the keyboard and builds a linear list to store them. Any special character (such as a #) may be used to end the number sequence. Then the numbers in the list are printed. If we enter the numbers 24, 71, 19, 38, in that order, the list of Fig. 4.1 will be the resulting (internal) data structure and the sequence 38, 19, 71, 24 will be the output of the program.

79

```
/* LIST.C: Read numbers from the keyboard, and build a
          linear list to store them.
*/
#define NULL 0

main()
{ int x;
  struct node {int num; struct node *next;} *start, *p;
  char *malloc();
  start = NULL;
  printf(
  "Enter a sequence of integers, followed by #:\n");
  while (scanf("%d", &x) > 0)
  { p = start;
    start = (struct node *)malloc(sizeof(struct node));
    if (start == NULL)
    { printf("Not enough memory"); exit(1);
    }
    start->num = x;
    start->next = p;
  }
  printf(
"\nIn reverse order, the following numbers were read:\n");
  for (p = start; p != NULL; p = p->next)
    printf("%5d\n", p->num);
}
```

If you are not familiar with the C notation for pointers or with the standard function *malloc* you should consult a textbook on C, such as, for example, *C for Programmers* (Ammeraal, 1986). Linear lists usually do not have only one information field containing an integer, as in our example, but they may contain all sorts of information. Extending the above type *struct node* to a more realistic structure type is obvious and simple. From a programmer's point of view, however, it is more interesting to extend our subject in another direction, as the next section will show.

4.2   MANIPULATING LINEAR LISTS

In almost all applications of linear lists the lists are searched. Not surprisingly, the search method involved is linear search, so we can benefit from a *sentinel*, in a way similar to our array search in Section 1.2. In a linear list, a sentinel is an extra node at the end, as shown in Fig. 4.2.

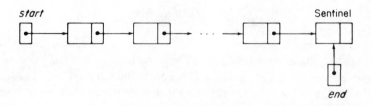

Fig. 4.2. Linear list with a sentinel

If we define

```
struct node {int num; struct node *next;};
typedef struct node NODE;
NODE *start, *p, *end, *getnode();
#define NULL 0

NODE *getnode()
{ char *malloc(); NODE *p;
  p = (NODE *)malloc(sizeof(NODE));
  if (p == NULL) {printf("Not enough memory"); exit(1);}
  return p;
}
```

we can set up an empty list, that is, a list with a sentinel as its only node, as follows:

```
/* Set up an empty list: */
start = end = getnode();
```

The contents of the sentinel are irrelevant. We can use the pointer variable *end* to distinguish the sentinel from all other nodes, so there is no need for the value *NULL* to be stored in the sentinel.

The following program fragment inserts a given integer *x* at the head of the list.

```
/* Insert the given integer x at the head of the list: */
p = start;
start = getnode();
start->next = p;
start->num = x;
```

Instead, we can insert *x* at the tail of the list. We then create a new sentinel and store *x* in the node that previously was the sentinel:

```
/* Insert the given integer x at the tail of the list: */
p = end;
end = getnode();
p->next = end;
p->num = x;
```

Assuming some integer *x* to be given, we will now search the list for it. The list may not contain *x*; in particular, it may be empty:

```
/* Search the list for the given integer x:  */
end->num = x;   /* Sentinel */
p = start;
while (p->num != x) p = p->next;
if (p == end) {/* Not found */ ... }
else  {/* Found in the node pointed to by p */ ... }
```

If the integers stored in the list are in increasing order, then we can stop as soon as we encounter a node with an integer not less than *x*:

```
/* Search an ordered list for the given integer x:   */
end->num = x;   /* Sentinel */
p = start;
while (p->num < x) p = p->next;
if (p->num == x   &&   p != end)
{ /* Found in the node pointed to by p */ ...
} else
{ /* Not found */ ...
}
```

Suppose that pointer variable *p* points to some node of the list and that a new node, say, with a given integer *x* in its *num* field is to be inserted just before the node pointed to by *p*. Figure 4.3 shows such a situation. A new node is to be inserted such that 25 will occur between 20 and 30.

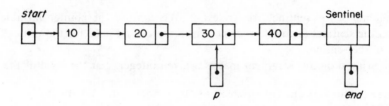

Fig. 4.3. A list in which a new node (with contents 25) is to be inserted

This seems a difficult problem, since *p* does not enable us to find the preceding node, that is, the node whose *next* field contains the same value as *p*. To solve this problem, we use a trick, the first part of which is shown in Fig. 4.4.

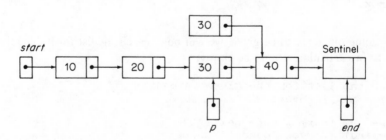

Fig. 4.4. Creating a duplicate of the node pointed to by p

We create a new node and fill it with the contents of the node pointed to by *p*. The latter node is then used to store the given integer *x*, and we make its pointer field point to the newly created node, as shown in Fig. 4.5.

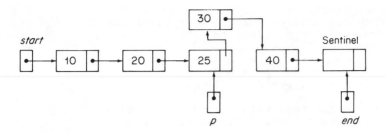

Fig. 4.5. List after insertion

Curiously enough, the program text that corresponds to Figs 4.3–4.5 is very short. We assume that the pointer variable *q* has been declared in the same way as *p*, and write:

```
/* Insert a new node with a given value x in its
   information field, just before the node pointed
   to by p, see Fig. 4.3.
*/
q = getnode();                  /* Create a new node.    */
if (p == end) end = q;          /* See explanation below */
   else *q = *p; /* Copy the entire node, see Fig. 4.4. */
p->next = q;      /* See Fig. 4.5.                        */
p->num = x;       /* Store new information in old node.   */
```

In Figs 4.3–4.5 pointer *p* pointed to a real node, not to the sentinel. Since we want a method to insert a new node that should precede the node pointed to by *p* it is reasonable to admit *p* to point to the sentinel, for otherwise we would not be able to insert a node just before the sentinel. Thus we also have to consider the case that the pointer values of *p* and *end* are equal. In this case we need not copy the contents of the sentinel, since those contents are irrelevant. On the other hand, we should realize that the newly generated node will be the new sentinel, so this is the node that the pointer *end* is to point to. This explains the above if-statement.

If we begin with an empty list and we combine the last two program fragments we obtain a useful algorithm to build an ordered list. Let us simply read integers from the keyboard; the following program fragment builds an ordered linear list to store them. If an integer is read and it is already in the list, we will display a message and not store it twice:

```
/* Build an ordered linear list with integers read from
   the keyboard (in any order):
*/

struct node {int num; struct node *next;}
typedef struct node NODE;
NODE *start, *p, *end, *getnode(), *q;
int x;

/* Set up an empty list: */
start = end = getnode();
```

```
while (scanf ("%d", &x) > 0)
{ /* Search the ordered list for the given integer x:    */
  end->num = x;   /* Sentinel */
  p = start;
  while (p->num < x) p = p->next;
  if (p->num == x  &&  p != end)
  { printf ("Already present\n"); continue;
  }
  /* Insert a new node with x in its information field, */
  /* just before the node pointed to by p:              */

  q = getnode();   /* Create a new node.                 */
  if (p == end) end = q; else *q = *p;
                   /* Copy entire node, see Fig. 4.4.    */
  p->next = q;     /* See Fig. 4.5.                      */
  p->num = x;      /* Store new information in old node. */
}
```

Finally, we want to *delete* *p, that is, the node pointed to by p, as shown in Fig. 4.6.

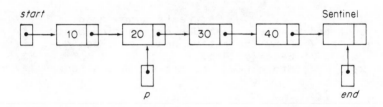

Fig. 4.6. The node pointed to by p is to be deleted

Again we use the trick of copying an entire node. We first make an auxiliary pointer q point to the successor of *p, and copy the contents of *q to *p. (Recall that in C the notation *p is used for the node pointed to by p.) This gives the situation of Fig. 4.7.

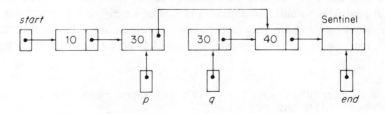

*Fig. 4.7. Situation after copying *q to *p*

Now the only thing that remains to be done is deleting node *q. (Recall that the standard function *free* does the opposite of *malloc*, that is, it returns memory space to the operating system.) Here is the program text that we need:

```
/* Delete the node pointed to by p, or, at least,
   perform an action with that effect:              */
q = p->next;
if (q == end) end = p; else    /* See explanation below */
   *p = *q;                     /* See Fig. 4.7          */
free(q);
```

Again, we have taken a special measure in connection with the end of the list. If the node to be deleted immediately precedes the sentinel then it is the (old) sentinel that is pointed to by q and that will be returned to the operating system by *free*. The node pointed to by p will then be the new sentinel, so in this case we have to assign the value of p to the pointer variable *end*. We now need not copy the contents of the old sentinel, so in this special case we perform *end* $= p$ instead of $*p = *q$.

4.3 LINEAR LISTS AND VARIABLE-LENGTH STRINGS

We will now deal with a linear list which contains some more information than only integers. Every node of the list will contain two data fields *name* and *num* and a pointer field *next*. Data field *name* contains a pointer to a sequence of nonnumeric characters representing a name, and data field *num* contains a long integer (for example, the telephone number of the person with the given name). The nodes of the list will be in alphabetic order of the names. For example, the list may contain, in this order, the following data:

```
Atherton,P.R.    600312
Atkinson,J.      551288
Ellis,F.         371103
Miller,B.        300611
Wood,E.G.        600228
```

As this example illustrates, blank space is not allowed within a name, not even after a comma. The name length will not be limited. Although the list elements will be in increasing order, the data may be entered in any order. Besides adding new items we will also provide for the possibility of deleting existing items. For this purpose we shall use the slash (/) to be used instead of a number in the input. Also, it will be possible to change the stored number (in case of any mistakes in previous input data): if there is already a list element with the given name, the new number will overwrite the old one. Thus if the list is as shown above and we supply the following data

```
Miller,B.          /
Ellis,F.         371104
Atherton,P.R.      /
Armstrong,M.     301205
```

the new list will contain the following data:

```
Armstrong,M.     301205
Atkinson,J.      551288
Ellis,F.         371104
Wood,E.G.        600228
```

To obtain a person's number, we enter his or her name (as usual, followed by one or more spaces) and then a question mark. For example, if we enter

```
Ellis,F.    ?
```

we obtain the following answer:

```
Ellis,F.                        371104
```

Finally, we introduce the following three commands:

.L Load data from a permanent file into a linear list.
.P Print the contents of the entire list.
.S Save the contents of the list in a permanent file.
.Q Quit.

(Lower-case letters *l*, *p*, *s*, *q* may be used instead of the corresponding capitals.) After .S and .L the system asks us to enter a file name, as program INFSYS1.C shows.

```
/* INFSYS1.C: An information system based
                on a linear list.
*/
#include <stdio.h>
struct node {char *name; long num; struct node *next;};
typedef struct node NODE;
NODE *start, *end, *getnode();

main()
{ char str[100], ch;
  long ii;
  int indic, found;
  NODE *p;
  /* Install empty list: */
  start = end = getnode();
  /* Load, save, print or update the list:  */
  while (1)
  { printf(">>");
    scanf("%s", str);
    if (str[0] == '.')
    switch (toupper(str[1]))
    { case 'L': loadlist(); break;
      case 'P': printlist(); break;
      case 'S': savelist(); break;
      case 'Q': exit(0);
      default:  printf(
                "\nWrong command; use L, P, S, or Q\n");
    } else
    { /* Search list for string str:  */
      end->name = str;  /* Sentinel */
      p = start;
      while ((indic = strcmp(p->name, str)) < 0)
        p = p->next;
      found = p != end  &&  indic == 0;
      /* If '?', display; */
      /* if '/', delete:  */
```

```
          if (scanf("%ld", &ii) == 0)
          { ch = getchar();
            if ((ch == '?' !! ch == '/') && !found)
            printf("Unknown name\n"); else
            if (ch == '?')
               printf("\n%-40s %8ld\n", str, p->num); else
            if (ch == '/') delete(p); else
            { printf("A name must be followed by a number,");
              printf(" a question mark, or a slash.\n");
            }
          } else  /* Update or insert:  */
          if (found) p->num = ii; else insert(p, str, ii);
      }
   }
}

NODE *getnode()
{ NODE *p;
  char *malloc();
  p = (NODE *)malloc(sizeof(NODE));
  if (p == NULL) printf("Not enough memory\n");
  return p;
}

printlist()
{ NODE *p;
  printf("\n\nContents:\n\n");
  p = start;
  while (p != end)
  { printf("%-40s %8ld\n", p->name, p->num);
    p = p->next;
  }
}

loadlist()
{ NODE *p;
  char filnam[50], str[100], *malloc();
  long ii;
  FILE *fp;
  if (start != end)
  { printf("List is not empty\n"); return;
  }
  printf("File name: "); scanf("%s", filnam);
  fp = fopen(filnam, "r");
  if (fp == NULL) {printf("Unknown file\n"); return;}
  while (fscanf(fp, "%s %ld", str, &ii) == 2)
  { p = end;
    end = getnode();
    p->next = end;
    p->name = malloc(strlen(str) + 1);
    strcpy(p->name, str);
    p->num = ii;
  }
  fclose(fp);
}

savelist()
{ NODE *p;
  char filnam[50];
  FILE *fp;
```

```
    printf("File name: "); scanf("%s", filnam);
    fp = fopen(filnam, "w");
    p = start;
    while (p != end)
    { fprintf(fp, "%s %ld\n", p->name, p->num);
      p = p->next;
    }
    fclose(fp);
}

insert(p, str, ii) NODE *p; char *str; long ii;
{ NODE *q; char *malloc();
  q = getnode();
  if (p == end) end = q; else *q = *p;
  p->next = q;
  p->name = malloc(strlen(str) + 1);
  strcpy(p->name, str);
  p->num = ii;
}

delete(p) NODE *p;
{ NODE *q;
  free(p->name);
  q = p->next;
  if (q == end) end = p; else *p = *q;
  free(q);
}
```

Note that in this example we use *malloc* to reserve memory space not only for nodes but also for strings. In each node the field called *name* is a pointer to the first character of a name which is stored elsewhere. For example, in the function *loadlist* we use *getnode* (which in turn calls *malloc*) to reserve memory space for a node. All nodes have exactly the same size, since the only objects of variable size, that is, the character sequences representing the names themselves, are stored elsewhere, namely in memory locations obtained by the call

```
malloc(strlen(str) + 1)
```

If *str* is the name "*Smith*", then *strlen(str)* is equal to 5, but we need $5 + 1 = 6$ positions to accommodate the terminating null character as well. We also use the standard function *free* for two purposes, as the function *delete* in program INFSYS1.C shows. A nice aspect of separating the actual strings from the node where they logically belong is that we need not limit the length of the name to some fixed maximum. Recall that we also discussed variable-length strings in Section 2.3, where we applied the sorting method Quicksort to such strings. In Section 2.6 we used fixed-length strings in our hashing example, but we could have used variable-length strings there in the same way as we are doing here.

Our 'information system' INFSYS1.C works reasonably as long as the *heap* is large enough. (For our purposes, we can define a *heap* as a large area of memory of which portions become available when we call the standard function *malloc*.) If we search a linear list for some item the time this takes depends on the position of that item in the list: if the item is at the end of the list we have to traverse the entire list to reach that item. Remember that we are doing linear search, with running time $O(n)$. This may be a real drawback if we have to search the list very frequently. However, using program INFSYS1.C for a list of, say, a thousand elements we will find the program quickly enough, because searching the list is a very fast operation compared with our entering input lines.

As we have seen, we can update linear lists very efficiently. In our discussion about hashing (in Section 2.6) we could only *insert* items, for if we had *deleted* items there we would have had problems with the distinction between free and occupied locations. Here we have no such problems. If it is fast enough, a linear list is very suitable in cases where insertions and deletions may occur in any order. Of course, this holds only if enough memory is available; we should not forget that, besides the real information to be stored, all pointer fields together also use a considerable amount of memory.

4.4 STACKS AND QUEUES

In Section 4.1 we inserted new nodes at the head of the list. If we insert nodes only in this way and also delete nodes only at the head then we say that we are using the list as a *stack*, that is, we follow the principle *Last In First Out* (LIFO). Implementing a stack by means of a linear list is not always the best solution; in many cases it has no real advantages over the more usual method, that is, with an array. In the latter case we use an integer variable as a stack pointer, which is incremented when an element is pushed onto the stack and decremented when it is popped from the stack, as the following program fragment shows:

```
#define STSIZE 1000
int stack[STSIZE], stptr=0;
/* stack[stptr] is the first free stack location */

push(x) int x;
{ if (stptr == STSIZE) error("Stack overflow"); else
  stack[stptr++] = x;
}

int pop();
{ if (stptr == 0) error("Pop attempt with empty stack");
  else return stack[--stptr];
}
```

Note that our stack pointer *stptr* points to the free location next to the last occupied location. Instead, we can make the stack pointer point to the last occupied location. Both solutions are correct, but we must always carefully realize which choice we have made and be consistent. For C programmers our choice is perhaps the more natural, since we often use n elements

$$a[0], \ a[1], \ \ldots, \ a[n-1]$$

Here, too, $a[n]$ is the first array element beyond those which are actually in use, so we may regard n as 'pointing to' the first free location.

For many applications an array is a good means to implement a stack. Note, however, that a maximum stack size must be specified in advance (although we can solve this problem by using the standard functions *malloc* and *realloc*, as we shall see shortly). We have no such problems with a linear list, as shown in the following program fragment:

```
#define NULL 0
char *malloc();
struct node {int num; struct node *link;}
  *start=NULL, *p;

push(x) int x;
{ p = (struct node *)malloc(sizeof(struct node));
  if (p == NULL) error("Stack overflow"); else
  { p->link = start;
    p->num = x;
    start = p;
  }
}

int pop()
{ int x;
  if (start == NULL) error("Pop from empty stack");
  else
  { x = start->num;
    p = start;
    start = start->link;
    free(p); return x;
  }
}
```

Note that in both solutions we perform tests to prevent misusing an *empty* stack. These tests take time, so we should remove them in applications where we know them to be superfluous. This is often the case, since all we have to do is take care that we do not try to fetch more items from the stack than we have stored on it.

Tests for stack *overflow*, also included in the above program fragments, are usually not superfluous. It is wise to perform them whenever there is the slightest chance that the stack should grow larger than the amount of available memory permits. In the latter solution (using a linear list) a considerable fraction of the memory locations that we use contain pointers, so with a stack of a given actual size the former solution uses fewer memory locations than the latter. On the other hand, with an array we will normally reserve more memory for the stack than we actually need, which is not efficient either. If we use a conventional array declaration the array size will often be some compromise, partly based on the available amount of memory; if we choose the array too large, we run into troubles on a small computer system, and choosing a rather small array means that the program may be more restrictive than the computer on which it runs. However, the C language offers a better solution. As we have done several times, we can benefit from the possibility of allocating a block of memory, pointed to by a pointer variable, and then use this pointer variable as an array. With memory space allocated by *malloc* rather than by an array declaration we can cope with 'stack overflow' by enlarging the reserved amount of memory space, using *realloc*. We may then obtain an entirely new block of memory to which the old stack contents are automatically copied. As this will take some time we had better not use *realloc* for each new item to be placed on the stack but rather increase the stack size by a block of, say, 50 items (or by, say, 10% of the current size). (See also Exercise 4.6, at the end of this chapter.)

A linked list is more elegant in this regard: on a large machine the function *malloc* will simply supply more memory than on a small one if we call this function a great many times. Apart from testing the pointer value returned by *malloc*, as usual, we need no special provisions in our program. Also, when items are popped from the stack their memory locations are immediately returned by *free* to the operating system in the case of a linear list, while with an array they will normally remain reserved. Thus, there may be good reasons for implementing stacks as linear lists. In Sections 8.3 and 8.4 we shall actually use such stacks, and refer to them as *linked stacks*.

Instead of the LIFO principle, on which a stack is based, we may want to use the rule *First In First Out* (FIFO), which corresponds to a *queue*. In this case a linear list is certainly much easier to use than an array. In Fig. 4.8 we have a queue in the form of a linear list, with two special pointer variables *new* and *old*. New nodes are inserted at the tail, pointed to by *new*, and old nodes are deleted from the head, pointed to by *old*.

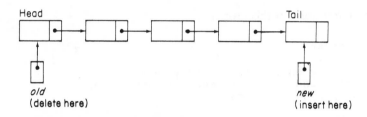

Fig. 4.8. A queue

Program QUEUE.C uses a queue. Repeatedly, it reads an integer, preceded by an exclamation mark from the keyboard, and stores it in a newly created node; this node is then inserted at the tail of the list. Instead of an exclamation mark, we may enter a question mark, which is a signal to delete a node from the list and to print the integer it contains. A dollar sign will stop program execution.

```
/* QUEUE.C   Demonstration of a queue.   */
#include <stdio.h>

main()
{ int x;
  struct node {int num; struct node *link;}
    *old, *new=NULL, *p;
  char ch, *malloc();
  printf("Each time, enter:\n\n");
  printf("  !  followed by an integer to be stored\n");
  printf(
    "  ?   (to print the oldest integer in the queue)\n");
  printf("  $   (to stop program execution)\n\n");
  while (1)
  { do  ch = getchar(); while (ch != '!' && ch != '?'
                            && ch != '$');
    if (ch == '!')
    { if (scanf("%d", &x) > 0)
      { p = (struct node *)malloc(sizeof(struct node));
        if (p == NULL)
        { printf("Memory full; use ? first, or use $\n");
```

```
      } else
      { if (new == NULL) old = p; else new->link = p;
        p->num = x;
        new = p;
      }
    } else printf("Integer expected\n");
  } else
  if (ch == '?')
  { if (new == NULL)
      printf("Use  !... first, or use $\n");
    else
    { printf("%30d\n", old->num);
      p = old;
      if (old == new) new = NULL; else old = old->link;
      free(p);
    }
  } else break; /* ch == '$' */
  }
}
```

Here is a demonstration of this program:

```
Each time, enter:

   !  followed by an integer to be stored
   ?  (to print the oldest integer in the queue)
   $  (to stop program execution)

! 1492
! 1945
?
                              1492
! 1813
?
                              1945
?
                              1813
?
Use  !... first, or use $
$
```

The numbers in the left column are input data and those in the right column form the output. Since in both columns we find the same numbers in the same order this demonstration clearly shows the FIFO principle. In this example the length of the queue was successively 0, 1, 2, 1, 2, 1, 0.

4.5 CIRCULAR, DOUBLY LINKED LISTS

A list is called *circular* if its tail contains a pointer to its head, as shown in Fig. 4.9.

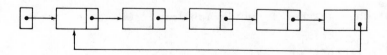

Fig. 4.9. A circular list

We obtain a more interesting extension of the simple linear list if we supply each node with two pointers, such that one, as usual, points to its successor and the other to its predecessor. The resulting data structure is called a *doubly linked list*, an example of which is shown in Fig. 4.10.

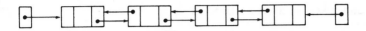

Fig. 4.10. A doubly linked list

Finally, we can combine both concepts to obtain a circular, doubly linked list, as Fig. 4.11 illustrates.

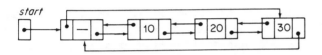

Fig. 4.11. A circular, doubly linked list

The leftmost node, that is, the node pointed to by *start*, is a *dummy header node*. It is useful as a sentinel, and it enables us to deal with an empty list more easily than without it. For example, let us assume that each information field consists of only an integer, as shown in Fig. 4.11. Then we set up an empty list as follows:

```
struct node {int num; struct node *left, *right;} *start;
char *malloc();
...
start = (struct node *)malloc(sizeof(struct node));
if (start == NULL) {printf("Not enough memory"); exit(1);}
start->right = start->left = start;
```

This gives the situation of Fig. 4.12.

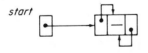

Fig. 4.12. An empty circular, doubly linked list

Starting with this empty list we can insert new nodes (containing integers read from the keyboard) as follows:

```
while (scanf("%d", &i))
{ p = (struct node *)malloc(sizeof(struct node));
  if (p == NULL)
  { printf("Not enough memory"); exit(1);
  }
  p->num = x;
```

```
    q = start->left;
    start->left = p;
    p->right = start;
    q->right = p;
    p->left = q;
}
```

where *i*, *p*, and *q* are variables declared as

```
int i;
struct node *p, *q;
```

If we apply the above while-loop to the input data

    10   20   30$

then we obtain the list of Fig. 4.11. (The dollar sign acts as an end signal; it is the next character to be read after the above while-loop.) With a given pointer to some node we can insert a new node either to the right or to the left of the given node, without copying an entire node as we did with the simple linear list. For example, if *p* is the given pointer and *i* is a given integer to be placed in a new node to the left of the node pointed to by *p*, we write:

```
q = (struct node *)malloc(sizeof(struct node));
if (q == NULL) {printf("Not enough memory"); exit(1);}
q->left = p->left;
q->num = i;
q->right = p;
p->left->right = q;
p->left = q;
```

Here *q* is an auxiliary pointer, pointing to the newly created node (see Fig. 4.13).

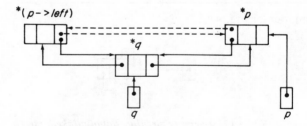

Fig. 4.13. Inserting a node. (- - - = old; _____ = new)

We can delete the node pointed to by a given pointer *p* in an elegant and efficient way:

```
p->left->right = p->right;
p->right->left = p->left;
free(p);
```

Verifying this in a diagram is left as an exercise for the reader. Note that in real applications it may be wise to include a test in this program fragment. If the given pointer p depends on input data that may be incorrect we ought to verify that p is unequal to *start* (see Figs 4.11 and 4.12). Should p and *start* have equal values, then p points to the dummy header node, which should always be present, even in an empty list.

Interesting as our last two program fragments are, a more important new aspect is that we can traverse (and search) a circular doubly linked list in two directions. In either case we can use the dummy header node as a sentinel. There are many applications where a collection of data is to be traversed both forward and backward. As an important example, we consider a text editor (or a word processor). We assume that during an edit session, except for the beginning and the end, we are all the time updating a data structure in internal memory, even though we call that data structure a *workfile*. It may be a good idea to implement this data structure as a circular, doubly linked list, with a node for each line of text. In this way, inserting and deleting lines are very efficient operations, and so are forward and backward scans. We had better not include the text lines themselves in the nodes, since we want all nodes to have the same size and, at the same time, we want short lines to occupy less memory than long ones. We therefore use dynamic memory allocation not only for the nodes but also for character strings, each containing a line of text, and in each node we include a pointer field to contain the begin address of the corresponding line. (Recall that this most useful aspect of the C language was also discussed in Section 4.2.) We shall not work out this application in full detail but discuss only the main operations on the data structures involved.

Consider, for example, the following contents of the workfile at a certain moment:

```
Believe Me, If All Those Endearing Young Charms (Irish)
All Through the Night (Welsh)
Auld Lang Syne (Scottish)
Greensleeves (English)
Home on the Range (American)
```

Adopting the convention that & & & at the beginning of an input line denotes end-of-input, we can enter the above five lines (followed by & & &) on the keyboard and place them in a circular doubly linked list, as follows:

```
#include <stdio.h>
char str[150], *plin, *malloc();

struct node {char *line; struct node *left, *right;}
    *start, *current, *insert(), *delete(), *p;

...

while (gets(str), strcmp(str, "&&&"))
{ plin = malloc(strlen(str) + 1);
    if (plin == NULL) error("Not enough memory");
    strcpy(plin, str);
    current = insert(current, plin);
}
```

We shall discuss the function *insert* shortly, but let us first consider what we want to achieve with it. With the five given input lines, the variable *plin* successively points to each of these five strings, stored somewhere in memory; in other words, the begin addresses of these strings are the successive values of *plin*, and, each time, such a begin address is passed to function *insert*. The desired data structure is shown in Fig. 4.14.

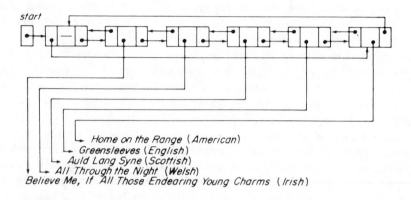

Fig. 4.14. Data structure used by text editor

The pointer variable *current* is to point to the current line, that is, the line under consideration. There may be an edit command *TOP*, to be executed if the first line is to be the current line. As a result of this command, we perform the following statement:

```
current = start->right;
```

Thanks to the circular nature of the list, an edit command *BOTTOM*, to go to the bottom line of the workfile, leads to an equally simple statement:

```
current = start->left;
```

Once the above data structure exists, we can list the entire workfile, using the following program fragment:

```
current = start->right;
while (current != start)
{ printf("%s\n", current->line);
  current = current->right;
}
```

Obviously, an editor must have the possibility of storing the workfile on disk. We can achieve this with almost the same program fragment as the last one, using *fprintf* (*fp*, ...) instead of *printf* (...). It might be noted that a very simple (though possibly not useful) change in the last program fragment would cause the file to be listed in the reverse order, that is, the bottom line first and the top line last. Replacing *right* with *left* twice is all that would be needed.

If the variable *current* has a value different from *start* then there is a current line and we can implement a command to go to the next line, so that the latter becomes the current line. This command should be ignored if the current line should be the bottom line, because then there is no next line:

```
p = current->right; /* Go to next line, if any */
if (p != start) current = p;
```

Similarly, a command to go back to the previous line, if there is one, is implemented as follows:

```
p = current->left; /* Go to previous line, if any */
if (p != start) current = p;
```

Note that the variable *current* is altered only if there is a next or a previous line, respectively.

The above operations assume that the circular doubly linked list exists. However, we have not yet discussed the function *insert* to build the list. There is one thing, though, that must be done in advance, namely creating an empty list, that is, a list with only a dummy header node:

```
start = (struct node *)malloc(sizeof(struct node));
start->left = start->right = current = start;
```

Thus, the variable *current* initially points to the dummy header node **start*. The following function *insert* can handle this situation as well. In general, it inserts a new node immediately after the node pointed to by its first argument. The second argument is the begin address of the actual sequence of characters, which have already been placed somewhere in memory. The function returns a pointer to the inserted node. The main program that calls *insert* can use this return value to make the inserted node to be the new current node. In this way we can easily insert more than one line in the right order.

```
struct node *insert(pcur, pstr)
  struct node *pcur; char *pstr;
/* Create a new node, store the address pstr in it,
    and insert it after  *pcur                       */
{ struct node *pnew;
  pnew = (struct node *)malloc(sizeof(struct node));
  if (pnew == NULL) error("Not enough memory");
  pnew->left = pcur;
  pnew->line = pstr;
  pnew->right = pcur->right;
  pcur->right->left = pnew;
  pcur->right = pnew;
  return pnew;
}
```

Note that we have used the standard function *malloc* twice, namely both for the actual line of text and for the node that refers to it.

Analogously, deleting the current line of the workfile involves two calls of the standard function *free*. We use the statement

```
current = delete(current);
```

The function *delete* returns the node representing the new current line, that is, the line that follows the deleted line:

```
struct node *delete(pcur) struct node *pcur;
{ struct node *pnext;
  if (pcur == start) return start;
  pnext = pcur->right;
  free(pcur->line);
  pcur->left->right = pnext;
  pnext->left = pcur->left;
  free(pcur);
  return pnext;
}
```

The if-statement takes care that we maintain a correct empty list, with a dummy header node, in case the function should be applied to an empty workfile.

EXERCISES

In the following exercises the contents of the data structures under consideration are to be printed wherever this is necessary to show that the program in question works properly.

4.1 Write a program which reads a sequence of integers and builds a linear list to store these integers. The order of the stored integers, from head to tail, is to be the same as the order in which the numbers are read.

4.2 Extend the program of Exercise 4.1, and delete all even integers (2, 4, ...) from the list. Use the standard function *free* to release the nodes that contain the even integers.

4.3 Write a program which reads text from a file. Let us define *words* as strings separated by one or more white-space characters. Each word read from the file is to be stored in some memory locations obtained by the standard function *malloc*, but if a word is read several times it is to be stored only once. Build a linear list whose nodes contain two fields, namely a pointer to the stored word and a pointer to the next node. The order of the word pointers in the list must be the same as that of the corresponding words in the file.

4.4 Write a program to read two positive integers n and k. Build a circular list (as shown in Fig. 4.9) in which the numbers 1, 2, ..., n, in that order, are stored. Starting at the node with number 1, delete each kth node from the list, going round until all nodes have been deleted. For example, if $n = 8$ and $k = 3$, we delete the nodes with the integers

3, 6, 1, 5, 2, 8, 4, 7

in that order. (This process, illustrated by initially having n persons arranged in a circle and by repeatedly eliminating the kth of those who are still present, is known as the *Josephus* problem.)

4.5 Instead of using only one linear list to store data we can have a great many of them, each starting in an element $p[i]$ of an array of pointer elements. Use this principle to implement *open hashing*, mentioned in Section 2.6. As with closed hashing, the keys are used to compute a 'primary' index i. All records with keys resulting in the same value i are stored in the list starting at $p[i]$. Compare open hashing with closed hashing, discussed in Section 2.6. With either hashing method investigate the possibily of deleting items.

4.6 In Section 4.4 we observed that to implement a stack as an array we have to specify a fixed maximum size in advance, unless we allocate memory by using the standard functions *malloc* and *realloc*. Write a program to implement such a more flexible stack.

4.7 Use a fixed-size array to implement a queue. The first array element should be considered the successor of the final one, so that we regard the array as a circle. A certain portion of the circle represents the queue; it continally grows at one end and shrinks at the other.

4.8 Write a simple text editor based on a doubly linked circular list and on program fragments listed in Section 4.5.

CHAPTER 5

Binary Trees

5.1 BASIC OPERATIONS ON BINARY SEARCH TREES

As we saw in Chapter 4, searching a linear list is done by means of linear search, which is slow compared with binary search, discussed in Section 2.5. We now want to apply the latter search method to dynamic data structures. A *binary tree*, as shown in Fig. 5.1, enables us to do this. It consists of a pointer variable, the so-called *root*, and (zero or more) nodes. The tree is said to be *empty* if there are no such nodes; in that case the root has the value *NULL*. Let us use the term *root node* for the node pointed to by the root (in a non-empty tree). Each node has one or more information fields and precisely two fields with pointers, each of which acts as a root: it either points to another node or has the value *NULL*. If a node contains any pointers to other nodes these latter nodes are said to be the *children* of the former, and we distinguish between a *left* and a *right* child. A node that has children is said to be the *parent* of these children. Unlike a traditional family situation, every child has only one parent, in other words, any two distinct pointers point to distinct nodes. Each pointer is in fact the root of a subtree, so each node has a left and a right subtree. This holds even if a pointer field has the value *NULL*, since a subtree may be empty. A *leaf* is defined as a node that has no children, which means that a leaf has two pointer fields whose values are *NULL*. With each node we can associate a *level*. The root node of a non-empty binary tree is said to be at level 1, and if a node at level i has any children then these are at level $i+1$. In addition to this, we say that the root of a tree is at level 0. Thus, the level of a node is in fact the number of branches to be traversed if we follow the shortest path from the root of the tree to that node. The highest level that occurs in a binary tree is called the *height* of that tree. For example, the binary tree shown in Fig. 5.1 has height 6. (The reader should be aware that there are books that give other definitions. What we are calling a 'root node' is sometimes termed a 'root'; some authors define that node to be at level 0, and, if it is the only node of the tree, they sometimes define the height of that tree to be 0. Our definitions, with a root being a special pointer variable and with an empty tree having height 0, are very useful from a programmer's point of view.)

Let us now develop a useful program which uses a binary tree to store words, read from a textfile and consisting of letters. We want to store the words in such a way that we can quickly search the tree for a given word. We shall also print a list of all words stored in the tree, in alphabetic order. If a word is read more than once we will store it only once in the tree, but it will be accompanied by a word count, which says how often the word has been read. Besides the two pointers to its children, if any, each node will contain both a pointer to a word, stored somewhere else, and the (integer) word count just mentioned. We will use each word as a *key*, which implies that it will be used when we search the tree. In general, each node of a binary tree may contain several data items, one of which, the key, is used in search operations. In each node the key is both greater than the key in the left child and less than the key in the right child, that is, as far as the node in question has a left and a right child. As this enables us to use the binary-search method we call this type of a binary tree a *binary search tree*. In our example every key is a string, and we shall use the words *greater* and *less* in the sense of string comparison, referring to the usual alphabetic order.

Consider, for example, the following text fragment:

> *'To be or not to be,*
> *that is the question'.*
> *William Shakespeare.*

Since we do not want to distinguish between capital and lower-case letters, we shall convert any lower-case letters into the corresponding capitals. Blanks and newline characters will act as word separators, and any other non-alphabetic characters will be ignored, so for our purpose the above fragment is equivalent to

> ### TO BE OR NOT TO BE THAT IS THE
> ### QUESTION WILLIAM SHAKESPEARE

With either fragment as input, our program will build the tree shown in Fig. 5.1.

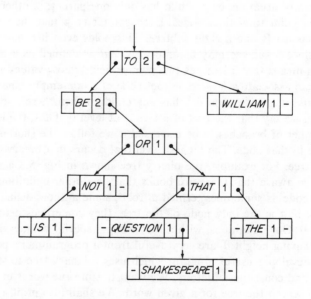

Fig. 5.1. Binary search tree

We may call a binary tree a *recursive* data structure, because it can be expressed in terms of smaller binary trees. Since each non-empty binary tree has more than one (namely precisely two) subtrees, we are dealing with 'genuine' recursion (see also Section 1.6). It will therefore not surprise us that in this context recursive functions are extremely useful. For example, if we have to print all information stored in a binary tree then we can express this task in terms of printing all information stored in its subtrees (which are also binary trees); all we have to do is:

If the tree is empty, nothing is to be printed.
If the tree is not empty, we successively perform the following three tasks:
(1) Print all information stored in the left subtree.
(2) Print the information fields in the node pointed to by the given root.
(3) Print all information stored in the right subtree.

As follows from the definition of a binary search tree, this procedure leads to an output sequence in increasing order. Searching a binary search tree is also easily expressed recursively; using a key as the value to be searched for, we proceed as follows:

If the tree is empty, the key is not found.
If the tree is not empty, then:
(1) If the given key is less than the key in the node referred to by the given root, search the left subtree.
(2) If it is greater than that key, search the right subtree
(3) If neither less nor greater, it is equal, so the object is found and the root of the subtree under consideration is the desired pointer.

To add new data (including a key) to a binary search tree we begin with searching the tree. If we find the given key we increment the count field, that is, if the application requires this, as in our example. If the key is not found, we create a new node for that object. The address of the new node (returned by *malloc*) is then placed in the pointer field (with the old value *NULL*) that we have reached during searching, as program BINTREE.C shows.

```
/*  BINTREE.C:
        This program builds and searches a binary search
        tree and prints its contents.
        The program produces a frequency distribution of
        words read from a text file.
        We can also search the tree for a given word, to
        inquire how often that word occurs.
*/
#include <stdio.h>
#include <ctype.h>
struct node
    { char *pword; int count; struct node *left, *right; };
typedef struct node NODE;
char buffer[100];

main()
{ NODE *root, *ptr, *buildtree(), *search();
  root = NULL;
```

```
    root = buildtree(root);
    printf("\nFrequency distribution:\n\n");
    printtree(root);
    while (
      printf("\n\nEnter a word, or type &&& to stop: "),
      fillbuffer(stdin),
      strcmp(buffer, "&&&")) /* &&& is the end signal */
    { ptr = search(root);
      if (ptr == NULL) printf("Does not occur.\n"); else
      printf("Number of occurrences: %d\n", ptr->count);
    }

}

NODE *buildtree(root) NODE *root;
{ char filnam[40];
  FILE *fp;
  NODE *addnode();
  int indic;
  printf("Input file: "); scanf("%s", filnam);
  fp = fopen(filnam, "r");
  if (fp == NULL)
  { printf("File not available"); exit(1);
  }
  while (indic = fillbuffer(fp)) /* that is, indic != 0 */
    if (indic > 0) root = addnode(root);
  fclose(fp);
  return root;
}

int fillbuffer(fp) FILE *fp;
{ char *dest, *source, ch;
  if (fscanf(fp, "%s", buffer) <= 0) return 0;
  if (strcmp(buffer, "&&&") == 0) return 1;
  dest = source = buffer;
  while (ch = *source++) /* that is, while ch != '\0' */
  { ch = toupper(ch);
    if (isalpha(ch)) *dest++ = ch;
  }
  *dest = '\0';
  return dest > buffer ? 1 : -1;  /* -1: empty string */
}

NODE *addnode(p) NODE *p;
{ char *my_alloc();
  int indic;
  if (p == NULL)
  { p = (NODE *)my_alloc(sizeof(NODE));
    p->pword = my_alloc(strlen(buffer) + 1);
    strcpy(p->pword, buffer);
    p->count = 1;   p->left = p->right = NULL;
  } else
  { indic = strcmp(buffer, p->pword);
    if (indic < 0) p->left = addnode(p->left); else
    if (indic > 0) p->right = addnode(p->right); else
      p->count ++;
  }
  return p;
}
```

```
char *my_alloc(n) int n;
{ char *p, *malloc();
  p = malloc(n);
  if (p == NULL)
  { printf("Not enough memory\n"); exit(1);
  }
  return p;
}

printtree(p) NODE *p;
{ if (p != NULL)
  { printtree(p->left);
    printf("%5d %s\n", p->count, p->pword);
    printtree(p->right);
  }
}

NODE *search(p) NODE *p;
{ int indic;
  if (p == NULL) return NULL;
  indic = strcmp(buffer, p->pword);
  return indic < 0 ? search(p->left) :
         indic >0 ? search(p->right) : p;
}
```

Assuming the above text fragment to be available in the file *SHAKESPEARE*, we can use program BINTREE.C as follows:

```
Input file: SHAKESPEARE

Frequency distribution:

    2 BE
    1 IS
    1 NOT
    1 OR
    1 QUESTION
    1 SHAKESPEARE
    1 THAT
    1 THE
    2 TO
    1 WILLIAM


Enter a word, or type &&& to stop: to
Number of occurrences: 2


Enter a word, or type &&& to stop: something
Does not occur.


Enter a word, or type &&& to stop: &&&
```

Program BINTREE.C does not contain a function for node deletion, which is more difficult than most other operations on trees; we will discuss this subject in Section 5.3.

5.2   PERFECTLY BALANCED BINARY TREES

It will be clear that we want a binary tree to be reasonably 'balanced'. Even without a definition of this adjective, we feel that the tree shown in Fig. 5.2 is hardly worth calling a binary tree, let alone a balanced binary tree. Of course, searching a degenerated tree of this type is not faster than searching a linear list.

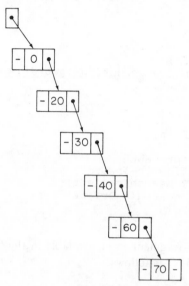

Fig. 5.2. A degenerated binary tree

However, this is really a binary tree, and with the numbers (instead of strings, just for a change) shown in the nodes, it is even a binary search tree. A degenerated tree such as this one will be built by program BINTREE.C or any similar program if the objects given in the input file are in increasing order. As we have developed good sorting algorithms in Chapter 2, files with objects in increasing order are not exceptional, so a warning not to use sorted files is not misplaced here. This example makes it clear that we need some definition about how well or how ill a binary tree is balanced. We shall distinguish two such definitions.

We call a binary tree *perfectly balanced* if each node has a left and a right subtree in which the numbers of nodes differ by at most one. The binary tree in Fig. 5.3 is perfectly balanced but the binary tree in Fig. 5.4 is not.

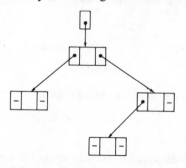

Fig. 5.3. A perfectly balanced binary tree

   The tree shown in Fig. 5.4 is an example of a *height-balanced binary tree*, which is a binary tree with the characteristic that for every node the *heights* of its left and right subtrees differ by at most one. (A height-balanced binary tree is also called an *AVL tree*, after its inventors Adelson-Velskii and Landis.) Every perfectly-balanced binary tree is a height-balanced binary tree, but the converse is not true, as Fig. 5.4 shows.

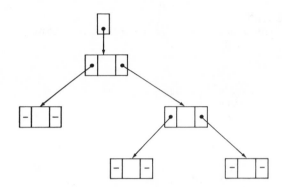

Fig. 5.4. A height-balanced binary tree that is not perfectly balanced

   We usually require the two types of balanced trees to be binary search trees. We then have to face the problem that without special measures the trees will lose their balance property if we insert or delete nodes arbitrarily. There are efficient algorithms for height-balanced binary trees to maintain their balance property, but there are none for perfectly balanced binary trees. Transforming a given binary tree into a perfectly balanced tree is rather time-consuming. However, with a simple and elegant algorithm we can build a perfectly balanced binary tree straightaway, provided that:

(1) The objects to be read are given in increasing order(!)
(2) We know in advance how many objects are to be read.

(In Exercise 5.2, at the end of this chapter, we will also use this algorithm to replace a given binary search tree with one that is perfectly balanced.)
   We assume that all data (including keys) to be stored in the tree be given in a file. To fulfil (1) we can sort this file, and this can be done efficiently, using, for example, the method quicksort. Requirement (2) is not difficult either, since we can read the file just to count the number of keys, then rewind it, and, finally, build the tree with the special algorithm mentioned. A special sorting method such as quicksort is not needed if we use the output produced by a function such as *printtree*, since this output is already sorted. We can in fact regard program BINTREE.C as a sorting program; this method of sorting is called *treesort*.
   Let us now assume that we are given a sorted file, along with the number of items in the file. Suppose, for example, that the file NUM.DAT contains the following sequence of integers:

   10
   11   12   13   14   15   16   17   18   19   20

With this input file, we want our program to store the ten integers 11, 12, ..., 20 in a
perfectly balanced binary search tree. Program PERFBAL.C accomplishes this; since
it does nothing else, it is not exactly a practical program but it illustrates the method
under discussion more clearly than would a complex program.

```
/* PERFBAL.C: This program builds a perfectly-balanced
      binary search tree.
*/
#include <stdio.h>
struct node { int num; struct node *left, *right; };
FILE *fp;

main()
{ int n;
  struct node *root, *pbtree();
  fp = fopen("NUM.DAT", "r");
  fscanf(fp, "%d", &n);
  root = pbtree(n);
  fclose(fp);
}

struct node *pbtree(n) int n;
{ int nleft, nright; char *malloc();
  struct node *p;
  if (n == 0) return NULL;
  nleft = (n - 1) >> 1;
  nright = n - nleft - 1;
  p = (struct node *)malloc(sizeof(struct node));
  p->left = pbtree(nleft);
  fscanf(fp, "%d", & p->num);
  p->right = pbtree(nright);
  return p;
}
```

The recursive function *pbtree* builds a perfectly balanced tree containing n nodes,
where n is its argument, and it returns the root of this tree. If, in a recursive call, n is
zero the function returns the value *NULL*, or, as we may say, it builds an empty tree. In
the main program we call *pbtree* with $n = 10$. We now compute the number of nodes
that are to be placed both in the left and in the right subtrees. Since there will be one
node (the root node) not belonging to either subtree there are $10 - 1 = 9$ nodes left for
the two subtrees. We divide this number by 2 and use the truncated quotient, for which
we use the right-shift operator in

```
nleft = (n - 1) >> 1;
```

Thus, we find *nleft* = 4, *nright* = 5. We then create the root node, pointed to by
the auxiliary pointer p, but we do not read the integer to be placed in it yet. Instead,
we first call *pbtree* recursively with *nleft* as its argument, which means that the four
numbers 11, 12, 13, 14 are read and placed in the left subtree, which is created at the
same time. Only now do we read the integer (15) to be placed in the root node. Finally,
we call *pbtree* once more to read the remaining five numbers and to create the right
subtree for them. Since *nleft* and *nright* differ by one in this case, the numbers of nodes
in the left and the right subtrees will also differ by one, which is required for the tree

to be perfectly balanced. In each recursive call we are again building a tree with two
subtrees of about the same size, and so on. If the argument of *pbtree* is odd, the two
subtrees will have exactly the same number of nodes, which is even better. Thanks to
our reading the number for the root node immediately after the construction of the left
subtree, the tree will be a binary search tree, provided that the input data is given in
increasing order. Figure 5.5 shows the resulting tree.

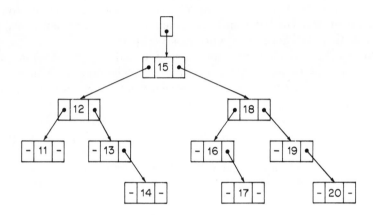

Fig. 5.5. Perfectly balanced binary search tree, built by program PERFBAL.C

Let us now use a perfectly balanced binary tree in a useful program. The tree will
represent a set of items, each consisting of a person's name and a non-negative number
associated with that person (for example, a telephone number or a registration number).
We shall use type *long int* to admit reasonably long numbers, such as 12345678. The
names are used as keys, so they must be unique; in other words, we do not admit two
persons whose names are spelled exactly the same. Our program will be capable of:

(1) Loading all items from a file and storing them in a perfectly balanced binary search
    tree;
(2) Reading names from the keyboard to search the tree for the corresponding numbers;
(3) Adding new items;
(4) Deleting items;
(5) Changing the number of an item;
(6) Saving all items, writing them to a file at the end of the session;
(7) Displaying an alphabetically ordered list of all items.

Recall that in Section 4.3 we discussed a similar program based on a linear list.
Should that program be too slow for some application, then the program discussed here
may be tried instead. However, we will be using a little more memory space, since each
node of a binary tree has two pointer fields, while each node of a linear list has only
one. The names of the files mentioned in points (1) and (6) will be entered by the user.
Normally, we will use the same file for both purposes. The items in this file are ordered,
that is, the names are in alphabetic order. However, the file may be empty, which will
be the case the very first time we use the program. At this initial stage we add items to

an empty set in the same way as we would add items to a non-empty set, using point (3). We then apply point (6) to obtain an ordered file. Thus, instead of first using a conventional text editor to create a file and then sorting this file by another program we use the very program we are discussing. Later, we can apply point (1) to build a perfectly balanced binary search tree which will then not be empty. To be honest, we must note that the tree may not remain perfectly balanced while we are adding and deleting items. However, as soon as we apply points (6) and (1) again we start with a fresh, perfectly balanced tree. In practice, the number of updates is usually small compared with the total number of items, so it is most unlikely that the tree should degenerate considerably. The latter may occur only if a great many new items, given in (almost) alphabetic order, are entered during one session.

Before we can write a complete program we have to deal with the *user interface*, that is, we must define how to use it. Since a user may not be familiar with binary trees we shall use the more elementary term *workfile* instead. Like a workfile used by an editor, our workfile is not a permanent file on disk, so its contents are lost at the end of the session, unless they are explicitly saved. We shall use the same commands as those discussed in Section 4.3, and only summarize them here. They begin with a period:

> .L Load the contents of a permanent file into an empty workfile.
> .P Print the contents of the workfile.
> .S Save the workfile onto a permanent file.
> .Q Quit

The lower-case letters *l*, *p*, *s*, *q* may be used instead of the corresponding capitals. We can add an item by typing the name, without any internal spaces, then one or more spaces, followed by a number; for example:

```
Johnson,P.H.     452319
```

If the name *Johnson,P.H.* already occurs in the workfile then the new number overwrites the old one. By typing

```
Johnson,P.H.     /
```

we remove the item with that name. The question mark in

```
Johnson,P.H.     ?
```

means that we want to know Johnson's number.

This is all the user has to know. As for the implementation of all this, we can borrow useful material both from program INFSYS1.C (listed in Section 4.3) and from our last program, PERFBAL.C. The most difficult new aspect is the above point (4). If an item is to be deleted we shall not immediately remove the corresponding node in the tree but instead mark it as unused by setting its number field to −1. The program will behave as if the node really is removed. However, when we save all information onto a disk file any 'garbage nodes', with a number −1, are ignored, so when we run the program later and load the file, we have a 'clean', perfectly balanced binary search tree again.

So the inefficiency of logically deleted nodes that are still occupying memory space is only temporary, in the same way as the tree may temporarily be unbalanced. (We shall discuss a more sophisticated way of deleting nodes in Section 5.3.)

Recall that in program PERFBAL.C we required the input file to contain the number of input items that are following. Although we could read an input file twice, counting the items in the first scan and using them in the second, there is a more efficient solution. We shall count the items as they are entered, and, after the command .S, write this item count to the file before the items themselves. As a result of command .L we begin with reading this item count, so that we can use our algorithm for a perfectly balanced tree immediately. During the process the process of updating the tree we change the variable *itemcount* accordingly. Since this variable is of type *int* the size of the tree is limited not only to the available amount of memory but also to the maximum integer value. Should this be a problem, then using type *long int* for that variable is the obvious solution. It is instructive to compare program INFSYS1.C., of Section 4.3, with our new program, INFSYS2.C. The former uses memory space more efficiently than the latter, but the latter wins in speed.

```
/* INFSYS2.C: An information system based on a
                perfectly-balanced binary search tree.
*/
#include <stdio.h>
struct node
. { char *name; long num; struct node *left, *right; };
typedef struct node NODE;
NODE *root=NULL;
FILE *fp;
long itemcount=0;
char strbuf[100];
int intbuf;

main()
{ char ch;
  NODE *p, *search(), *add_or_change();
  while (1)
  { printf(">>");
    scanf("%s", strbuf);
    if (strbuf[0] == '.')
    switch (toupper(strbuf[1]))
    { case 'L': loadtree(); break;
      case 'P': printf("\n\nContents:\n\n");
                printtree(root); break;
      case 'Q': exit(0);
      case 'S': savetree(); break;
      default:  printf(
                "\nWrong command; use L, P, Q, or S\n");
    } else
    { if (scanf("%ld", &intbuf) == 0)
      { ch = getchar();
        if (ch == '?' || ch == '/')
        { p = search(root);
          if (p == NULL) printf("Unknown name\n"); else
          if (ch == '?') printf("%8ld\n", p->num);
          else                    /* ch == '/' */
          { p->num = -1L;    /* delete    */
            itemcount--;
```

```
          }
        } else
        { printf("A name must be followed by a number, ");
          printf("a question mark, or a slash\n");
          while (ch != '\n') ch = getchar();
        }
      } else root = add_or_change(root);
    }
  }
}

loadtree()
{ char filnam[50];
  NODE *pbtree();
  if (itemcount)
  { printf("Workfile is not empty\n"); return;
  }
  printf("File name: "); scanf("%s", filnam);
  fp = fopen(filnam, "r");
  if (fp == NULL) { printf("Unknown file\n"); return; }
  if (fscanf(fp, "%d", &itemcount) == 0)
  { printf(
    "File %s does not begin with an item count\n", filnam);
    return;
  }
  root = pbtree(itemcount);
  fclose(fp);
}

NODE *pbtree(n) int n;
{ int nleft, nright;
  NODE *p;
  char *my_alloc();
  if (n == 0) return NULL;
  nleft = n >> 1;
  nright = n - nleft - 1;
  p = (NODE *)my_alloc(sizeof(NODE));
  p->left = pbtree(nleft);
  if (fscanf(fp, "%s %ld", strbuf, & p->num) < 2)
  { printf("Error in input file\n"); return NULL;
  }
  p->name = my_alloc(strlen(strbuf) + 1);
  strcpy(p->name, strbuf);
  p->right = pbtree(nright);
  return p;
}

NODE *add_or_change(p) NODE *p;
{ char *my_alloc();
  int indic;
  if (p == NULL) /* Insert */
  { p = (NODE *)my_alloc(sizeof(NODE));
    p->name = my_alloc(strlen(strbuf) + 1);
    strcpy(p->name, strbuf);
    p->num = intbuf;
    p->left = p->right = NULL;
    itemcount++;
  } else
  { indic = strcmp(strbuf, p->name);
```

```
     if (indic < 0) p->left = add_or_change(p->left); else
     if (indic > 0) p->right = add_or_change(p->right);
     else
     { if (p->num == -1L) itemcount++;
       p->num = intbuf; /* Insert (if -1L), or change */
     }
   }
   return p;
}

char *my_alloc(n) int n;
{ char *p, *malloc();
  p = malloc(n);
  if (p == NULL) {printf("Not enough memory\n"); exit(1);}
  return p;
}

printtree(p) NODE *p;
{ if (p != NULL)
  { printtree(p->left);
    if (p->num != -1L)
      printf("%-40s %8ld\n", p->name, p->num);
    printtree(p->right);
  }
}

NODE *search(p) NODE *p;
{ int indic;
  if (p == NULL) return NULL;
  indic = strcmp(strbuf, p->name);
  return indic < 0 ? search(p->left)  :
         indic > 0 ? search(p->right) :
         p->num == -1L ? NULL : p;
}

  savetree()
  { char filnam[50];
    printf("File name: "); scanf("%s", filnam);
    fp = fopen(filnam, "w");
    fprintf(fp, "%d\n", itemcount);
    writetree(root);
    fclose(fp);
  }

  writetree(p) NODE *p;
  { if (p != NULL)
    { writetree(p->left);
      if (p->num != -1L)
        fprintf(fp, "%s %ld\n", p->name, p->num);
      writetree(p->right);
    }
  }
```

5.3   ADDRESSES OF POINTERS AND NODE DELETION

We now want to be able to remove nodes from a binary search tree. The way we dealt
with deletion in Section 5.2 may not be satisfactory if a great many deletions and
insertions take place in a single session, during which the workfile is not saved. Program

INFSYS2.C is already rather complex, so we had better deal with the subject of node deletion separately in this section. Let us once again develop a complete program, but this time each node will have only one information field containing an integer. Throughout this section we shall use a type *NODE*, as defined in:

```
struct node { int info; struct node *left, *right; };
typedef struct node NODE;
NODE *root, *p, **pp;
```

Although complete, the program will not be useful for real applications; its only purpose is to clarify the subject we are discussing. The problem of removing a node from a tree is related to an aspect of pointer variables that we have not discussed yet. We normally want to designate a node by a pointer to that node, and up to now we have been using auxiliary pointer variables to which we copied the pointer values in question. However, a copy of a pointer to some node does not enable us to remove that node from the tree, even if that node is a leaf. For example, if we have a tree of only one node, the root node, and assuming that the statement

```
p = root;
```

has been executed, we cannot satisfactorily delete that node using only *p*. The point is that although

```
free(p);
```

frees the memory space for the node, this is not sufficient, since we also have to assign the value *NULL* to the variable *root*, and the address of *root* is not given by *p*. In this special case we could write

```
root = NULL;
```

but this would obviously not be correct in more complex situations. Yet we can do the job using only one auxiliary variable. In our example of a tree with only one node this variable is a pointer to the pointer variable *root*, or, in simpler terms, the value of this variable is the address of the pointer variable *root*. In the above variable declarations its name is *pp*. After the statement

```
pp = &root;
```

variable *pp* contains all information we need. We can now delete the node in question as follows:

```
free(*pp); *pp = NULL;
```

The latter statement actually assigns *NULL* to *root*. Note that two asterisks occur in the declaration of *pp*, which implies that:

    **pp   has type *NODE*

*pp   has type *pointer-to-NODE*

pp   has type *pointer-to-pointer-to-NODE*

The idea of using pointers to pointers is useful not only to delete nodes but also for other operations on binary search trees. In some programs in the previous section we used a function *search* to obtain information stored in the tree, but we did not benefit from this function when we had to insert new nodes, for which, after all, we had to search the tree as well. We will now develop improved functions both for searching and for inserting, based on our new concept of pointers to pointers. (This is not really a digression from our subject, since searching will also be needed in the framework of tree deletion. Besides, searching and inserting are easier subjects than deletion, so we had better deal with them first.)

Besides duplicating the program code for searching in some previous programs we have also used recursion where we could easily have used iteration instead. Recall that in Section 1.6 we called a function *genuinely* recursive if it calls itself more than once. This is the case, for example, with function *printtree* in program BINTREE.C, discussed in Section 5.1. (Incidentally, we shall use a special function *printtree* here, which in the output reflects the tree structure!) In contrast to *printtree*, function *search*, in the same program, calls itself, at most, once. It is true that textually there are two recursive calls, but only one of these is actually executed. The following function *search* has been improved in two respects:

(1) It returns a pointer to a pointer field belonging to the tree.

(2) It is nonrecursive.

```
NODE **search(pp, x) NODE **pp; int x;
{ NODE **qq;
   qq = pp;
   while (*qq != NULL  &&  x != (*qq)->info)
     qq = (x < (*qq)->info ? &(*qq)->left : &(*qq)->right);
   return qq;
}
```

If our tree is to be searched for a given integer, say, 123, we can write

```
pp = search(&root, 123);
if (*pp == NULL) { ... /* 123 has not been found */ }
else
{ ... /*  (*pp)->info == 123, and pp is the address of
          either the variable  root, or some pointer field
          in a node of the tree.
       */
}
```

It is instructive to verify this for three special cases:

(1) An empty tree. The function *search* returns the address of the variable *root*. We find *NULL* not in the returned value itself but as the contents of that address.

(2) A tree with only one node (the *rootnode*) containing the given integer (123). The

function again returns the address of *root*, but now this address contains a pointer to the root node.

(3) A tree with only one node containing an integer, say 246, different from the integer (123) searched for. The while-loop in the function *search* is executed once, and since 123 is less than 246, the function returns the value $\&(*qq) \rightarrow \mathit{left}$, which is the address of the left pointer field of the node. This address contains the value *NULL*.

The following function, *insert*, adds a node with a given integer x to the tree in the correct position, that is, if x does not occur in the tree yet. Note that it uses the above function *search* and that it is not recursive.

```
insert(pp, x) NODE **pp; int x;
{ NODE **qq, **search();
  char *malloc();
  qq = search(pp, x);
  if (*qq == NULL)
  { *qq = (NODE *)malloc(sizeof(NODE));
    if (*qq == NULL)
    { printf("Not enough memory\n"); exit(1);
    } else
    { (*qq)->info = x;
      (*qq)->left = (*qq)->right = NULL;
    }
  }
}
```

We now turn to our main subject, deletion, but before dealing with the deletion of a single node we shall delete entire subtrees, which, surprisingly enough, is simpler! If we are given an integer, say 123, stored in some node in the tree we can delete the subtree whose root node is the node just mentioned by writing:

```
deltree(search(&root, 123));
```

where the function *deltree* is as given below:

```
deltree(pp) NODE **pp;
{ if (*pp != NULL)
  { deltree(&(*pp)->left); deltree(&(*pp)->right);
    free(*pp);
    *pp = NULL;
  }
}
```

Note that the type of the value returned by *search* is just what *deltree* expects as its argument: not a pointer to a node, but the address of such a pointer.

After all these preliminaries we shall discuss a function to delete a single node. It is used in the same way as our last function, but instead of deleting an entire subtree it will delete only the node pointed to by a pointer the address of which is given as an argument. So with this new function, *delnode*, we can delete the node containing 123 (if there is such a node) by the call

```
delnode(search(&root, 123));
```

and, in general, the call

```
delnode(pp);
```

will delete the node pointed to by *pp. Using the unary operator * once more, we can also say that the latter call deletes the node **pp.

Now that we have paid so much attention to matters of notation we must not forget to find a method of maintaining a binary search tree after we have removed the node in question. Let us first consider the simple case that this node has only one child, as shown in Fig. 5.6, where we want to delete the root node.

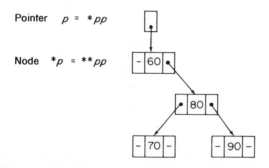

Fig 5.6. Node to be deleted has only one child

This case and the case with only a left child can be dealt with as follows:

```
p = *pp;
if (p->right == NULL) {*pp = p->left; free(p);} else
if (p->left == NULL) {*pp = p->right; free(p);} else ...
```

(Here ... stands for the more difficult case that the node *p has two children.) In Fig. 5.6 this program fragment has the effect that pointer p will point to the node with integer 80. There is still a simpler case, namely with a node that has neither a left nor a right child, which means that the node is a leaf. The above program fragment works properly in this case as well, as we can easily verify.

If the node in question has two children we will not really delete the node itself. Instead, we delete one of its descendants, after having copied the data fields of the latter node into the former. As we want the tree to remain a binary search tree we must be very particular about which descendant to choose. We shall select the key that would appear as the left neighbour of the key in question, if all keys stored in the tree were written down as an increasing sequence. Starting in the given node (with two children), we first go to its left child and then further downward to the right as far as possible. Thus, of all integers stored in the tree, we find the largest that is less than the one in the given node. This is precisely what we need to maintain a binary search tree. In Fig. 5.7 the tree contains the integers

$$30 \quad 40 \quad 50 \quad 55 \quad 60 \quad \underline{90} \quad 95$$

The node with 90 is to be deleted. Out of all the above integers less than 90, we choose the greatest, 60. By first taking the left child we decide to restrict our choice to the left subsequence, so, in any case, we will use a value less than 90. Having said that, we have to take care that we repeatedly go to the right-hand child, as long as possible. As a result, we arrive at the desired node with integer 60.

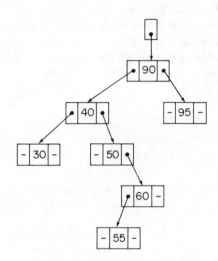

Fig. 5.7. Path from 90 to 60 is taken to find the greatest integer less than 90, stored in the tree

Here is the function *delnode*. It is nonrecursive but yet surprisingly short.

```
delnode(pp) NODE **pp;
{ NODE *p, **qq, *q;
  if (*pp != NULL)
  { p = *pp;
    if (p->right == NULL) {*pp = p->left; free(p);} else
    if (p->left == NULL) {*pp = p->right; free(p);} else
    { qq = & p->left;
      while ((*qq)->right != NULL) qq = & (*qq)->right;
      q = *qq;
      *qq = q->left;
      p->info = q->info;
      free(q);
    }
  }
}
```

For the development of an instructive demonstration program we now want a function to print a binary tree as a binary tree, using indentation. Here is a special version of our well-known function *printtree*, which accomplishes this. The tree printed has its root on the left instead of at the top. For each node we print its right subtree before its left one, to obtain the same tree representations as we get by rotating the usual tree pictures counter-clockwise through 90 degrees.

```
printtree(p) NODE *p;
{ int i;
  static indent=0;
  if (p != NULL)
  { indent += 6;
    printtree(p->right);
    for (i=6; i<indent; i++) printf(" ");
    printf("%6d\n", p->info);
    printtree(p->left);
    indent -= 6;
  }
}
```

The way it prints a tree is shown at the end of this section. The following demonstration program, PTREE.C, shows how pointers pointing to pointer fields are used for deleting either an entire subtree or just a node. The program reads a sequence of integers from a file to build a binary tree, and then asks the user whether a subtree or a node is to be deleted and to type in the integer that says which subtree or node is meant. The program is to be appended by the functions listed above in this section.

```
/* PTREE.C: Demonstration program for tree deletion,
            using pointers to pointers
*/
#include <stdio.h>
#include <ctype.h>

struct node { int info; struct node *left, *right; };
typedef struct node NODE;

main()
{ NODE *root, **search();
  char filnam[50], ch;
  FILE *fp;
  int x;
  printf("Name of input file: "); scanf("%s", filnam);
  fp = fopen(filnam, "r");
  if (fp == NULL) { printf("???\n"); exit(1); }
  root = NULL;
  while (fscanf(fp, "%d", &x) > 0) insert(&root, x);
  fclose(fp);
  printf("\n"); printtree(root); printf("\n");
  while (1)
  { printf(
    "Enter N (node deletion), T (subtree deletion),\n");
    printf("or Q (quit):\n");
    do
    { ch = getchar(); ch = toupper(ch);
    } while (ch != 'N' && ch != 'T' && ch != 'Q');
    switch (ch)
    { case 'N':
        printf("Integer in node to be deleted: ");
        scanf("%d", &x); delnode(search(&root, x)); break;
      case 'T':
        printf("Integer in root node of subtree: ");
        scanf("%d", &x); deltree(search(&root, x)); break;
      case 'Q':
        exit(0);
```

```
      }
      printf("\n"); printtree(root); printf("\n");
   }
}

/* The functions  search, insert, delnode, deltree,
   and printtree, listed in this section, are to be
   inserted here.
*/
```

Here is a demonstration of this program, based on the input file NUM.DAT, containing the integer sequence:

$$90 \quad 95 \quad 40 \quad 30 \quad 50 \quad 60 \quad 55$$

The sets of indented numbers below are printed by *printtree*. They represent three binary search trees, which should be turned through 90 degrees clockwise to obtain the usual orientation. The first two of these trees correspond to our above discussion, illustrated by Fig 5.7. The third is the result of deleting a subtree.

```
Name of input file: NUM.DAT

            95
    90
                        60
                                55
                50
        40
                30

Enter N (node deletion), T (subtree deletion),
or Q (quit):
N
Integer in node to be deleted: 90

            95
    60
                                55
                50
        40
                30

Enter N (node deletion), T (subtree deletion),
or Q (quit):
T
Integer in root node of subtree: 40

            95
    60

Enter N (node deletion), T (subtree deletion),
or Q (quit):
Q
```

EXERCISES

All functions to be developed in the following exercises are to be complemented by program fragments to demonstrate them. In most cases, program text listed in this chapter can be used for this purpose.

5.1 Write a function which deletes a binary tree and builds a similar one. In the given tree the information field of each node consists of a pointer to a block of memory, which has been allocated by the standard function *malloc* and contains a (null-terminated) character string. The tree to be built should have the same structure as the original one, but now each node is to contain only an integer as its information field, which denotes the length of the string pointed to in the corresponding node of the original tree. As for the original tree, the memory space used by the tree nodes and that for the character strings should be released by means of the standard function *free*.

In the following exercises each node in the binary tree in question has an information field which contains only an integer.

5.2 Write a function to transform a given binary search tree into one that is perfectly balanced. The demonstration program should (also) print the heights of the old and the new tree.
Hint: First count the number of nodes in the given tree, and then build a perfectly balanced binary search tree in a way similar to what we did in Section 5.2 but based on the given tree instead of on an input file. Each time we insert a node in the new tree we also delete a node in the old one, to keep the total amount of used memory space to a minimum. In the final situation the old tree no longer exists so that we have only a perfectly balanced tree.

5.3 Write a function to determine if a given binary tree is perfectly balanced.

5.4 Write a function to determine the height of a binary tree (see Section 5.1).

5.5 Write a function to determine if a given binary tree is height-balanced.

5.6 Write a function to determine if a given binary tree is a binary search tree.

5.7 Write a function to print all integers stored in a binary tree, along with the levels of all nodes.

5.8 Write a function to print all integers stored in the leaves of a given binary tree (ignoring the integers stored in all other nodes).

5.9 Write a function which for a given binary search tree swaps the left and right children of every node and, at the same time, replaced each integer i in the tree with $-i$. Thus, the resulting tree is again a binary search tree.

CHAPTER 6

B-trees

6.1   BUILDING AND SEARCHING A B-TREE

So far, we have been using only binary trees that existed in main memory. We also want to store trees in *secondary storage*, that is, on disk, and load information from it into main memory only when we need it. There are two reasons for this. First, information in main memory exists only temporarily, whereas on disk it is permanent, and second, the amount of available main memory will probably be less than the amount of secondary storage. However, disk access is slower than memory access. In order to reduce the number of I/O operations we will no longer use binary trees, which, as we know, have as many nodes as there are keys. Instead, we want to use larger blocks of information, grouping together several items, each including a key, into one node. We shall therefore use multiway trees of a certain type, called *B-trees*. For some fixed number M, each node of a B-tree contains at most $2M$ and at least M items, the latter condition having one exception, namely the root node, which contains at least one item. The constant M is called the *order* of the B-tree.

We shall avoid dealing with two new subjects, B-trees and secondary storage, at the same time, so our first B-tree will still be in main memory. Let us, for example, use the following definitions:

```
#define M 2
#define MM 4
struct node {int cnt, key[MM]; struct node *ptr[MM+1];};
typedef struct node NODE;
```

Here we have $M = 2$, so the constant MM, which stands for $2M$, is 4. In real applications we use larger values for example, $M = 100$, $MM = 200$. We always use unique keys, so no two items will have the same key. In our example every item will contain no data other than its key, so we will use the terms *item* and *key* interchangeably. In practical applications we usually have more complex items containing other relevant data besides the keys. As with binary search trees, we use the keys to search the tree in an efficient way. In the above definition of type *struct node* each array element *key*[i] can contain a key (or, in the general case, an item that includes a key). The field *cnt* is a counter, which in B-trees, in contrast to binary trees, is essential. It says how many of the $2M$ information fields are actually used. In our discussion we shall use the simple notations n, k_i and p_i instead of $t\!\rightarrow cnt$, $t\!\rightarrow key[i]$ and $t\!\rightarrow ptr[i]$, respectively, where t is a pointer to the node under consideration. Thus we have:

$$1 \leq n \leq 2M \qquad \text{for the root node}$$
$$M \leq n \leq 2M \qquad \text{for all other nodes}$$

Each node has at most $2M+1$ children, so there are $2M+1$ pointer fields in each node. However, exactly $n+1$ of these are actually in use. Thus, the number of items stored in a node is one less than the number of stored pointers. Figure 6.1 shows an example of a B-tree, corresponding to the above definitions.

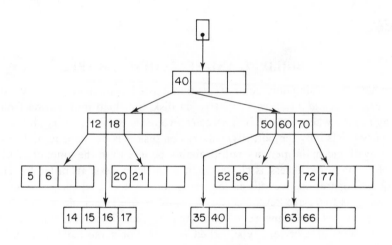

Fig. 6.1. A B-tree of order 2

Notice the position of the pointers emanating from each node. For example, the pointer from node [12, 18] to node [14, 15, 16, 17] leaves the former node between 12 and 18, which corresponds to the fact that the numbers 14, 15, 16, 17 in the latter node lie between these two values. Logically, we consider the pointers p_i and the keys k_i in each node to be arranged as follows:

$$p_0,\ k_0,\ p_1,\ k_1,\ \ldots,\ p_{n-1},\ k_{n-1},\ p_n$$

where

$$k_0 < k_1 < \ldots < k_{n-1}$$

The values n, though stored in the nodes, are not shown in Fig. 6.1, but for each node n is equal to the number of integers listed, that is, 1 for the root node and 2, 3, or 4 for the other nodes. For each node its pointer values p_i are as follows:

If the node is a leaf, the value of each pointer p_i in the node is *NULL*.
If the node is not a leaf, each of the $n+1$ pointers p_i points to another node, a child of the given node. Also, if i is greater than 0, all keys in the child pointed to by p_i

are greater than k_{i-1}. Similarly, if i is less than n, all keys in the child in question are less than k_i.

The B-tree of Fig. 6.1 is well balanced, which is no coincidence, but it is characteristic for B-trees:

All leaves of a B-tree are at the same level.

(As defined in Section 5.1 for binary trees, the level of a node is the length of the path from the root to that node.) Recall that this characteristic did not apply to perfectly balanced binary trees, so B-trees seem to be 'better than perfect'. However, in binary trees we have exactly one information item in each node, which in general makes it impossible to meet a similar requirement about equal path lengths. The nice shape of B-trees is not without its price, since memory space is also reserved for unused information and pointer fields. Yet B-trees are elegant and efficient in many applications, especially since there are good algorithms available to manipulate them. Not all of these are particularly simple, however. We shall first discuss the insertion of new items.

Let us begin with an empty B-tree, in which the first four numbers, say 60, 20, 80, 10, are to be inserted. This gives the tree shown in Fig. 6.2(a). There is now only one node *root*, which contains the following data:

$$n = 4$$
$$p_0 = p_1 = p_2 = p_3 = p_4 = NULL$$
$$k_0 = 10$$
$$k_1 = 20$$
$$k_2 = 60$$
$$k_3 = 80$$

Since n is now equal to MM there is no room for the next number to be inserted, say 15. Ignoring the limitation to four items for one moment, we write down the augmented sequence

$$10, \quad 15, \quad 20, \quad 60, \quad 80$$

(which would appear if there were enough room) to select the item in the middle, 20. We then remove this item, to store it in another node later, and we move the subsequence on the right of it, [60, 80], to a newly created node. If the node under consideration had a parent which could accommodate the removed item 20 we would store it in that parent. We will consider that situation shortly. In the present case there is no parent at all, so we have to create another node to store 20. This will be a new root node, which means that the height of the tree increases. This new root node contains one number (20), so we have to use two pointer fields. Fortunately, we have two other nodes to point to, namely both the original one, in which we set the count field to 2, and the one created to store 60 and 80. This leads to Fig. 6.2(b). If we now have to insert a new number, say 30, it might be tempting to store it in the root node, since this node has plenty of room. However, this would not be correct because then the root node would have as many information items as it has children. The general rule is that we always try to insert a new item in a leaf node. So 30 is placed in the right child, which makes it necessary to shift 60 and 80 one position to the right. Let us add another item, say 70, which will be placed in the same node because it is also greater than 20. This gives the result shown in Fig. 6.2(c). We have now reached the maximum number of information items for that node, so adding another item, say 22, will cause some item to move upward. To find out which, we again forget about the limitation for one moment, and write down the augmented sequence

$$22, 30, 60, 70, 80$$

As we did for the root node, we choose the item (60) in the middle and split the remaining sequence into

$$22, 30 \qquad \text{and} \qquad 70, 80$$

The node 60 is now inserted in the parent node, if possible. In our case this is indeed possible, so we obtain the tree shown in Fig. 6.2(d). As a result of splitting a leaf node there is some new room in the leaves for subsequent items. If we keep inserting new items we will again reach the situation that a leaf is selected in which already $2M(=4)$ items have been stored. Then again we have to split that leaf and to move some item to its parent, and so on. In this way, we sooner or later have five leaves, which is the maximum number of children for any parent. For example, if we proceed with the tree of Fig. 6.2(d), and we insert the numbers

$$12, 18, 19, 4, 5, 6, 2, 3$$

in that order, we obtain the tree shown in Fig. 6.2(e). Let us now insert the number 1 in the latter tree. Since 3 is the item in the middle of the sequence 1, 2, 3, 4, 5, obtained by augmenting the bottom-left node, this item 3 is to move upward, and the remaining items are divided between the subsequences [1, 2] and [4, 5]. However, the parent node is already full, so this node, too, is to be split. We first write the sequence of five items

$$3, 6, 15, 20, 60$$

and select the element 15, in the middle. Since the parent node in question happens to be the root node, we have to create a new root node to store 15, and at this moment the height of the tree increases again. Figure 6.2(f) shows the resulting tree.

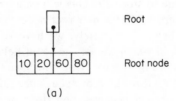

(a)

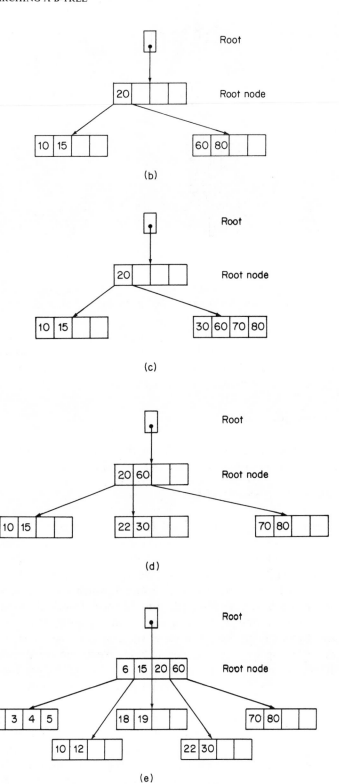

(b)

(c)

(d)

(e)

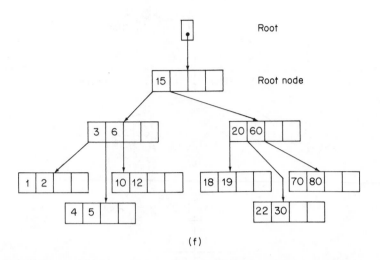

Fig. 6.2. Growth of a B-tree of order 2. Successive input and resulting trees: (a) 60, 20, 80, 10; (b) 15; (c) 30, 70; (d) 22; (e) 12, 18, 19, 4, 5, 6, 2, 3; (f) 1

Now that we understand how a B-tree grows we want a program to demonstrate this growth. It will be clear from the above discussion that a function to insert an item in a B-tree will be rather complex. We will actually use two functions, namely the function *insert*, to be called in the main program as follows:

```
root = insert(x, root);
```

(where *x* is the item to be inserted), and another function, *ins*, used in the following statement, which occurs in the function *insert* just mentioned:

```
code = ins(x, t, &xnew, &tnew);
```

The variables *xnew* and *tnew* are local to the function *insert*; we will discuss them shortly. The (recursive) function *ins* returns the value 1 if it has completely fulfilled its task. If *x* happens to have been inserted previously, the present request is ignored and *ins* returns the value 2. In these two cases we do not use *xnew* and *tnew*. In the third, and most interesting, case, *ins* returns the value 0, which means that we are not ready yet. Although *x* may have been inserted, some additional work has to be done. Function *ins* has now placed an integer value in *xnew* and a pointer value in *tnew*, which we made possible by supplying the addresses of these local variables as arguments.

We are now dealing with the case of node overflow, and we therefore still have to insert the item *xnew*. So *ins* has inserted *x*, but it had to remove the value placed in *xnew* to accomplish this. Another remaining task is storing a pointer to a newly created node. In fact the old node **t* was split; it now contains only *M* instead of *2M* items, the other *M* items having been stored in a new node. The address of this new node is returned through the fourth argument, &*tnew*; in other words, the local pointer variable *tnew* now points to this new node. Thus, if the above call of *ins*, occurring in the function *insert*, returns the value 0, then we have to create a new root node, in which we store the values of *xnew* and *tnew*, and at this moment the height of the tree increases.

Let us now turn to the function *ins*, viewed from the inside. Its first line reads:

```
int ins(x, t, y, u) int x, *y; NODE *t, **u;
```

As follows from our above discussion, its task is to insert item x in the (sub-)tree whose root is t. If this succeeds completely, the parameters y and u are irrelevant and the function is to return the value 1. If, on the other hand, there is overflow, the value to be returned is 0, and in this case we have to place the extra item in the address y, and, similarly, we are to return a pointer value though the fourth parameter, u. At first sight, we may be confused by the two asterisks in $**u$, but it might be helpful to notice that, as far as their types are concerned, u is related to t in the same way as y is related to x. Since we have to return results through y and u we specify them with an extra asterisk. Parameter u is a pointer to a pointer, or, less confusing, its value is an address of a pointer variable (see also Section 5.3).

One case in which 0 is to be returned is obvious, namely when t has the value *NULL*. In this case we cannot do very much, since we have no pointer to an existing node at our disposal. We report that x could not be accommodated and that t did not point to a node yet, by executing:

```
*y = x;
*u = NULL;
return 0;
```

If t is not *NULL*, it points to a node. We then locate the position where x belongs by comparing it with the items stored in this node. In this way we find the pointer value p_i, stored in the node, and we perform the recursive call:

```
ins(x, p[i], &xnew, &tnew)
```

This may return the value 1, which means that x has successfully been inserted in the subtree with root p_i. In that case we are ready, and we can immediately return 1. If this recursive call returns 2, we know that x was found in the subtree, and again we return immediately with the same value 2. In the third case, with 0 as the returned value, we have to pay attention to *xnew* and *tnew*. We try to place them in the current node *t, which may or may not be possible. If it is, we can return the value 1, after all, since the insertion task is then completed. If it is not, we split the node, as shown in our example, which yields both an item extracted from the middle of an augmented sequence and a pointer to a newly created node. We place these in the addresses y and u (the third and the fourth parameters) and we return the value 0, so that, one level higher, the correct information will be available.

Program BTREE.C shows further details of B-tree insertion. The program first inserts a given sequence of integers in a B-tree, which initially is empty. In its present form, the program builds a B-tree of order 2, but if a higher order is desired, we only have to alter M and MM in two #*define*-lines. Once the B-tree has been built, we can enter another integer to search the tree for it. The program prints the complete search path, starting at the root and ending in the node where the integer is stored, or, if we are searching in vain, ending in the leaf where it would have been stored if it had been included in the given input data. This search process is performed in the function *search*. We use binary search, as discussed in Section 2.5, which will increase speed if we choose large values for *M* and *MM*. At the end of the program there are some functions for tree deletion. This is a new subject, to be discussed in the next section. It has already been included in this program to avoid a duplication of program text or a rather fragmentary presentation.

```c
/* BTREE.C  Demonstration program for a B-tree.
            After building the tree by entering integers
            on the keyboard, we can repeatedly search the
            tree for a given integer. Each time, a
            search path from root to leaf is displayed.
            The B-tree can be updated interactively.
*/
#include <stdio.h>
#include <ctype.h>
#define M 2
#define MM 4
struct node {int cnt, key[MM]; struct node *ptr[MM+1];};
typedef struct node NODE;
NODE *root;

main()
{ int x;
  char ch;
  NODE *insert(), *delete();
  root = NULL;
  printf(
  "Enter some integers, followed by the character /\n");
  while (scanf("%d", &x) > 0) root = insert(x, root);
  getchar();
  while (1)
  { printf(
    "\nDelete (D), Insert (I), Search (S) or Quit (Q): ");
    do
    { ch = getchar(); ch = toupper(ch);
    } while (ch != 'D' && ch != 'I' &&
             ch != 'S' && ch != 'Q');
    if (ch == 'Q') exit(0);
    printf("Enter an integer: "); scanf("%d", &x);
    switch (ch)
    { case 'D': root = delete(x, root); break;
      case 'I': root = insert(x, root); break;
      case 'S': search(x, root); break;
    }
  }
}

search(x, t) int x; NODE *t;
{ int i, j, *k, n;
  printf("Trace:\n");
  while (t != NULL)
  { k = t->key; n = t->cnt;
    for (j=0; j < n; j++) printf(" %d", k[j]);
    printf("\n");
    i = binsearch(x, k, n);
    if (i < n && x == k[i]) { found(t, i); return; }
    t = t->ptr[i];
  }
  notfound(x);
```

```
}

int binsearch(x, a, n) int x, *a, n;
/* Search array a[0], a[1], ..., a[n-1] for x.         */
/* Returned value:   0 if x <= a[0],   n if x > a[n-1],  */
/*                   or r, where   a[r-1] < x <= a[r]    */
{ int i, left, right;
  if (x <= a[0]) return 0;
  if (x > a[n-1]) return n;
  left = 0; right = n-1;
  while (right - left > 1)
  { i = right + left  >> 1;
    if (x <= a[i]) right = i; else left = i;
  }
  return right;
}

found(t, i) NODE *t; int i;
{ printf("Found in position %d ", i);
  printf("of node with contents: ");
  for (i=0; i < t->cnt; i++) printf(" %d", t->key[i]);
  printf("\n");
}

notfound(x) int x;
{ printf("Item %d not found\n", x);
}

NODE *insert(x, t) int x; NODE *t;
/* Driver function for node insertion, called only in the
   main program. Most of the work is delegated to 'ins'.
*/
{ NODE *tnew, *u, *getnode();
  int xnew, code;
  code = ins(x, t, &xnew, &tnew);
  if (code == 2) printf("Duplicate key %d ignored\n", x);
  if (code) return t;
  u = getnode();
  u->cnt = 1; u->key[0] = xnew;
  u->ptr[0] = t; u->ptr[1] = tnew;
  return u;
}


int ins(x, t, y, u) int x, *y; NODE *t, **u;
/* Insert x in B-tree with root t. If not completely
   successful, the integer *y and the pointer *u
   remain to be inserted.
   Returned value:
        0 if insertion not completely successful,
        1 if insertion successful,
        2 if x is already present in B-tree.
*/
{ NODE *tnew, *getnode(), *p_final, **p = t->ptr;
  int i, j, xnew, k_final, *n=&(t->cnt), *k = t->key,
      code;

  /* Examine whether t is a pointer field in a leaf:
  */
  if (t == NULL) { *u = NULL; *y = x; return 0; }
```

```
    /* Select pointer p[i] and try to insert x in
       the subtree of which p[i] is the root:
    */
    i = binsearch(x, k, *n);
    if (i < *n && x == k[i]) return 2; /* Duplicate key */
    code = ins(x, p[i], &xnew, &tnew);
    if (code) return code;

    /* Insertion in subtree did not completely succeed;
       try to insert xnew and tnew in the current node:
    */
    if (*n < MM)
    { i = binsearch(xnew, k, *n);
      for (j= *n; j>i; j--)
      { k[j] = k[j-1]; p[j+1] = p[j];
      }
      k[i] = xnew; p[i+1] = tnew; ++*n; return 1;
    }

    /* The current node was already full, so split it. Pass
       item k[M], in the middle of the augmented sequence,
       back through parameter y, so that it can move
       upward in the tree. Also, pass a pointer to the newly
       created node back through u. Return 0, to report
       that insertion was not completed:
    */
    if (i == MM) { k_final = xnew; p_final = tnew; } else
    { k_final = k[MM-1]; p_final = p[MM];
      for (j=MM-1; j>i; j--)
      { k[j] = k[j-1]; p[j+1] = p[j];
      }
      k[i] = xnew; p[i+1] = tnew;
    }
    *y = k[M]; *n = M;
    *u = getnode(); (*u)->cnt = M;
    for (j=0; j < M-1; j++)
    { (*u)->key[j] = k[j+M+1];   (*u)->ptr[j] = p[j+M+1];
    }
    (*u)->ptr[M-1] = p[MM];   (*u)->key[M-1] = k_final;
    (*u)->ptr[M] = p_final;   return 0;
}


NODE *getnode()
{ NODE *p;
  char *malloc();
  p = (NODE *)malloc(sizeof(NODE));
  if (p == NULL) error("Not enough memory\n");
  return p;
}

error(str) char *str;
{ printf(str); exit(1);
}

NODE *delete(x, t) int x; NODE *t;
/* Driver function for node deletion, called only in the
   main program. Most of the work is delegated to 'del'.
*/
{ int code;
```

```
   NODE *newroot;
   code = del(x, t);
   if (code == 2) printf("%d not found\n", x);
   if (code) return t;
   /* 0 = underflow; 1 = success; 2 = key not found;   */
   /* If underflow, decrease the height of the tree:   */
   newroot = t->ptr[0]; free(t);
   return newroot;
}

int del(x, t) int x; NODE *t;
/* Delete item x in B-tree with root t.
   Returned value:
   0 = underflow, 1 = success, 2 = not found
*/
{ int i, j, *k, *n, *item, code,
    *nleft, *nright, *lkey, *rkey, borrowleft, nq, *addr;
  NODE **p, *left, *right, **lptr, **rptr, *q, *q1;
  if (t == NULL) return 2;
  n = & t->cnt; k = t->key; p=t->ptr;
  i = binsearch(x, k, *n);
  if (p[0] == NULL)    /*   *t is a leaf */
  { if (i == *n || x < k[i]) return 2;
    /* x is now equal to k[i], located in a leaf: */
    for (j=i+1; j < *n; j++)
    { k[j-1] = k[j]; p[j] = p[j+1];
    }
    --*n;
    return *n >= (t==root ? 1 : M);
  }
  /*   *t is an interior node (not a leaf):   */
  item = k+i; left = p[i]; nleft = & left->cnt;
  if (i < *n && x == *item)
  { /*   x found in interior node.  Go to left child     */
    /*   *p[i] and then follow a path all the way to     */
    /*   a leaf, using rightmost branches:               */
    q = p[i]; nq = q->cnt;
    while (q1 = q->ptr[nq], q1 != NULL)
    { q = q1; nq = q->cnt;
    }
    /* Exchange k[i] with the rightmost item in leaf:   */
    addr = q->key + nq - 1;
    *item = *addr; *addr = x;
  }
  /* Delete x in subtree with root  p[i]:               */
  code = del(x, left);
  if (code) return code;
  /* Underflow; borrow, and, if necessary, merge:       */
  borrowleft = i == *n;
  if (borrowleft)  /* p[i] is rightmost pointer in *p   */
  { item = k+i-1; left = p[i-1]; right = p[i];
    nleft = & left->cnt;
  } else right = p[i+1];
  nright = & right->cnt;
  lkey = left->key; rkey = right->key;
  lptr = left->ptr; rptr = right->ptr;
  if (borrowleft)  /* This is an exception */
  { rptr[*nright + 1] = rptr[*nright];
    for (j = *nright; j>0; j--)
    { rkey[j] = rkey[j-1];
```

```
      rptr[j] = rptr[j-1];
    }
    ++*nright;
    rkey[0] = *item; rptr[0] = lptr[*nleft];
    *item = lkey[*nleft - 1];
    if (--*nleft >= M) return 1;
  } else
  if (*nright > M)            /* Borrow from right sibling: */
  { lkey[M-1] = *item; lptr[M] = rptr[0]; *item = rkey[0];
    ++*nleft; --*nright;
    for (j=0; j < *nright; j++)
    { rptr[j] = rptr[j+1]; rkey[j] = rkey[j+1];
    }
    rptr[*nright] = rptr[*nright + 1];
    return 1;
  }
  /* Merge: */
  lkey[M-1] = *item; lptr[M] = rptr[0];
  for (j=0; j<M; j++)
  { lkey[M+j] = rkey[j]; lptr[M+j+1] = rptr[j+1];
  }
  *nleft = MM;
  free(right);
  for (j=i+1; j < *n; j++) {k[j-1] = k[j]; p[j] = p[j+1];}
  return --*n >= (t==root ? 1 : M);
}
```

We can use this program to demonstrate how a B-tree is built. The demonstration below builds the B-tree of Fig. 6.2(f). We can verify this by searching the tree for several items, as was done here for 1, 60, and 100. As will be discussed in the next section, we can in fact do more with this program, but here we restrict ourselves to tree insertion and tree search, which, incidentally, are the two most important operations.

```
Enter some integers, followed by the character /
60 20 80 10 15 30 70 22 12
18 19 4 5 6 2 3 1/

Delete (D), Insert (I), Search (S) or Quit (Q): s
Enter an integer: 1
Trace:
 15
 3 6
 1 2
Found in position 0 of node with contents:  1 2

Delete (D), Insert (I), Search (S) or Quit (Q): s
Enter an integer: 60
Trace:
 15
 20 60
Found in position 1 of node with contents:  20 60

Delete (D), Insert (I), Search (S) or Quit (Q): s
Enter an integer: 100
Trace:
 15
 20 60
 70 80
```

```
Item 100 not found

Delete (D), Insert (I), Search (S) or Quit (Q): q
```

6.2 DELETING NODES IN A B-TREE

Given a key, we now want to search our B-tree, and, if we find an item with this key we want to remove it from the tree. The basic characteristic concerning the number of items in each node must be maintained during the process of successive deletions. We shall use the same type of B-tree as in the previous section, with $M = 2$, so each node will contain at most four data items and five pointers. However, our implementation will again be more general, so that larger nodes can be obtained by a simple change of the named constant M (and MM, which means $2M$). In fact, our program BTREE.C already contains functions for deletion, so there is no need for another demonstration program in this section. Since tree deletion is a rather complex operation, let us not immediately turn to its implementation, but first consider an example.

If we are fortunate enough to find an item with the given key in a leaf that contains more than M items we can simply remove that item and shift any items to the right of it one position to the left. If that leaf contains precisely the minimum number of items, we still remove the item in question in the same way but the function call in which this occurs reports *underflow* on its return. In this case we try to borrow an item from a neighbouring sibling (that is, a brother or a sister). Figure 6.3 shows such a situation. Item 27 having been deleted, the node which contained it now contains only one remaining item, 25. In the program we detect this when we are dealing with the parent node (with items 20, 30, 40), after a recursive call to delete 27 in its child.

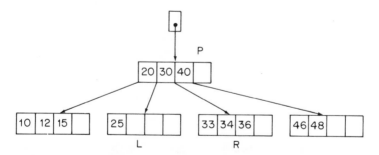

Fig. 6.3. Underflow after deleting item 27 in node L

Although the parent (P) contains three items we cannot simply use one of these (20 or 30) to fill the gap, since then there would remain two information items and four pointers, and, as we know, the number of pointers must be only one more than the number of information items. This is why we need a sibling. In this case, we can choose between a left and a right one. Let us, arbitrarily, always choose the right sibling if there is one (which would not be if we had removed 46 or 48; only in such cases will we borrow an item from the left sibling). Like the notation P for the parent, we shall use R for the right sibling and L for the node where underflow has occurred. We cannot just move 33 from R to L, since that would violate another rule, namely that all keys in children to the left of 30 must be less than 30, or, more precisely and in the terminology of the previous section, that all keys in the node pointed to by p_i must be less than k_i. (Here we have $k_0 = 20$, $k_1 = 30$, $k_2 = 40$, and p_1 pointing to node L.) So neither item 30 in node P nor item 33 in node R can help us, that is, by themselves. In combination, however, they can: we move 30 from P to L and then 33 from R to P. The resulting tree is shown in Fig. 6.4.

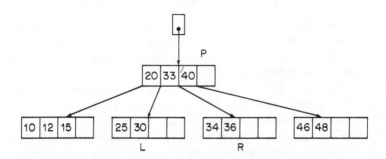

Fig. 6.4. Tree after borrowing an item from node R

Unfortunately, this method does not always work. Here it worked fine because in the original tree (Fig. 6.3) node R contained three items. If R had contained only two items (or, in general, M items) we would not have been able to borrow one of its items without causing underflow in R, which, of course, is as bad as underflow in L. In that case, we have to merge the two nodes L and R into one. Figure 6.5 shows a typical situation where this is necessary.

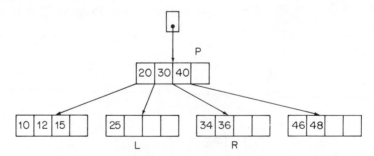

Fig. 6.5. Underflow after deleting item 27 in node L

Since node P has four pointers it seems that we have a problem, for after merging L and R there will be only three children. To get rid of a pointer in P we also have to reduce the number of information items in P by one, and, fortunately, we can achieve this by moving the very item 30, used above, to the node resulting from the merge. This is possible because we have exactly M items in R and, due to underflow, $M-1$ items in L. (After all, with more than M items in R we would have been able to borrow without merging.) Thus, if node L is $*p[i]$ and node R is $*p[i+1]$ we let item $k[i]$ participate in the merge operation, which means that the total number of items in the resulting node is

$$(M-1)+M+1 = 2M$$

Figure 6.6 shows the situation after this merge operation.

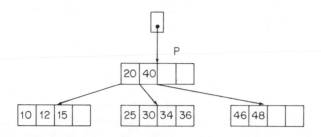

Fig. 6.6. Result after merging L and R

If underflow occurs in a child on the extreme right there is no right sibling to borrow an item from or to merge with. In this case we borrow an item from its left sibling and, in contrast to the normal case discussed above we do so even if that left sibling should contain only M items. In the latter situation the result of this borrow operation is that we obtain $M-1$ items in the left sibling and M items in the node under consideration, so if we call the former L and the latter R we have a situation similar to the one in Fig. 6.5, and we can apply the same program fragment for merging as before.

In the above discussion we have focused on the information items. Besides these, there are also pointer fields in the nodes, and it is time to see what happens with them in the borrow and merge operations. It is true that pointers in leaves are not very interesting because their values are *NULL*, but even with these we must not be inaccurate. More importantly, the above discussion about borrowing and merging applies not only to leaves but also to interior nodes, provided that the pointer fields are dealt with properly. To avoid any wordiness and inaccuracy let us recall that in each node we have information items k_i and pointers p_i in the following logical order:

$$p_0 \; k_0 \; p_1 \; k_1 \; \ldots \; p_{n-1} \; k_{n-1} \; p_n$$

If a node contains its minimum number of items we have $n = M$, and in the case of underflow we have $n = M-1$.

Let us now consider Fig. 6.3 once again, without the assumption that we are dealing with leaves. In node L we have $k_0 = 25$, and immediately to the right of k_0 we imagine pointer p_1, which, if L is an interior node, is the root of a subtree with items lying between 25 and 30. We can express this more briefly by saying that p_1 in node L *represents* such items. When we borrow an item from node R to obtain the tree of Fig. 6.4 we assign 30 to k_1 in node L, so p_1 in node L has just the correct pointer value. Returning to Fig. 6.3, we see that pointer p_0 in node R represents items lying between 30 and 33, so this is precisely the pointer we need as p_2 in node L (see Fig. 6.4).

Summarizing, when we remedy underflow in node L by borrowing an item from the right sibling R the pointer on the extreme left in R becomes the rightmost pointer in L. If, instead of borrowing an item, we have to merge two nodes we can again find out what to do with pointers by thinking of the range of items they represent. In Fig. 6.5 pointer p_0 in node R represents all items between 30 and 34, so this is the pointer we need as p_2 (or, in general, as p_M) in the resulting node, shown in Fig. 6.6. Obviously, pointers

p_0 and $p_1(p_0, \ldots p_{M-1})$ in the latter node are the same as those in the original node L. They involve no work at all, since we implement the merge operation by extending the contents of L and disposing of R. It will also be clear that we have to copy the pointers $p_1, \ldots, p_M$ of node R to use them as $p_{M+1}, \ldots, p_{2M}$ in the resulting node.

In the above discussion we suggested that borrowing and merging are to take place not only for leaves but also for interior nodes. Consider, for example, Fig. 6.2(f) in the previous section. The node that contains items 3 and 6 has exactly M items, and so have its three children. If we delete one item in such a child, say, 1 in the leftmost leaf, the two leaves on the left are to be merged into one. Item 3 in the parent node also participates in this merge, so after the merge only item 6 remains and we have underflow in this interior node. We now proceed in the same way as we did with underflow in leaves. If the interior node in question has a right sibling with more than M items we borrow an item from it. If not, as is the case in Fig. 6.2(f), we merge the two nodes, which means that we fetch an item from the parent of the two interior nodes. Again, underflow may occur in this parent, in which case we again either borrow or merge, and so on, until we are at the root. Here a special rule applies, namely that a root node is allowed to have less than M items, as long as it has at least one. In Fig. 6.2(f), the root node has only one item, 15, and when this participates in the merge of its two children the number of items in the root node becomes zero. This is the moment that we say there is underflow in the root node. We then remove the entire node, which decreases the height of the tree. We then obtain the tree of Fig. 6.2(e). Note that the reduction from Fig. 6.2(f) to Fig. 6.2(e) by deleting item 1 is exactly the reverse action from inserting 1 in the tree, which we did in Section 6.1.

So far, everything started with a deletion in a leaf, and we have seen that this may have far-reaching consequences with regard to the whole tree structure. We still have to consider a deletion which starts in an interior node. For example, let us again use Fig. 6.2(f) and try to delete the item 15 in the root node. We are now faced with a new problem, since a root node must always have at least one item, and we cannot simply borrow an item from its children. Fortunately, this problem can be reduced to deleting an item in a leaf. Recall that in Section 5.3, when dealing with binary search trees, we solved a similar problem by finding a key that was as great as possible but less than the key in the given node. We first went to the left child of that node and then followed the path all the way to a leaf, each time taking the right child. The same method is useful here. If in an interior node item k_i is to be deleted, we find the greatest item that is less than k_i. All items stored in the subtree with root p_i are less than k_i; to find the largest, we follow a path, starting in the node pointed to by p_i, and each time going to the rightmost child of the node where we are, until we have reached a leaf. The rightmost data item stored in this leaf is the one we are looking for. We may exchange it with the item k_i in the given node, without violating any rule for B-trees. In Fig. 6.2(f), this means that we can exchange items 15 and 12. Note that it would not have been correct if we had exchanged item 15 with item 6 in the left child of the root node, since then in that child the new position of item 15 would have been k_1, with p_2 pointing to the smaller items 10 and 12. After the correct exchange of items 15 and 12 we can delete item 15 in the usual way because it now resides in a leaf. Further details can be found in the functions *delete* and *del*, which have already been included in program BTREE.C, listed in Section 6.1. The program is useful to demonstrate how a B-tree grows and shrinks by insertions and deletions. After each operation that changes the tree we can search the tree for some given items. Such a search causes a complete search path to be shown, which enables us to examine the structure of the tree. The best way to learn how B-trees work is to build and modify them on paper or on a blackboard, inserting and deleting items ourselves; program BTREE.C then enables us to check our results step by step.

6.3 B-TREES ON DISK

In this section we shall use a B-tree which resides in a file on disk. For most computer systems this means that the tree can grow much larger than a tree in main storage. At any moment only a few nodes of the tree will be in memory, but with B-trees this does not imply that only a very limited amount of data should be in memory, since M, the minimum number of items per node, can be as large as we wish. The greater we choose M, the more memory will be used, but the faster the program will run because of less frequent disk access. The program to be developed in this section will enable us to investigate its efficiency experimentally. Though essentially an adaptation of program BTREE.C in Section 6.2, it will deal with one or two files. One file is essential because it accommodates the B-tree itself; the other is an optional input file, which contains integers to be stored in the B-tree. In this way we need no longer supply the input data only interactively but we can also prepare an input file containing integers in ASCII format, as required by the standard function *fscan*f. To create such a file any text-editor will do, but, instead, we can use the following program, GENNUM.C, which generates a number sequence using a random number generator.

```
/* GENNUM.C  Generation of an ASCII file with numbers,
     to be read by DISKTREE.C
*/
#include <stdio.h>
#include <time.h>

main()
{ long t;
  int i, n;
  char filnam[25];
  FILE *fp;
  printf("How many numbers are to be generated? ");
  scanf("%d", &n);
  printf("Name of output file: "); scanf("%s", filnam);
  fp = fopen(filnam, "w");
  time(&t);
  srand((int)t);
  /* Generate n integers, in lines of ten: */
  for (i=0; i<n; i++)
  if (fprintf(fp, "%c%d", i%10 ? ' ' : '\n', rand()) < 0)
  { printf("Unable to write on file\n"); exit(1);
  }
  fclose(fp);
}
```

With this program we can easily generate a file of, say, 10 000 integers, and our program DISKTREE.C, which we are developing, will be able to read them and insert them in the B-tree, in the same way as it does with integers entered one by one on the keyboard, which, incidentally, will still be possible. Program DISKTREE.C will inquire the names of the two files. The first is the name of the tree file. If it already exists, the B-tree stored in it will be updated, otherwise a new tree file with the given name will be created. The second is the input file discussed above; if it exists, the integers read from it are inserted in the tree, which, before this insertion, may or may not be empty, depending on whether or not a new tree file had to be created. If, instead of the name of an existing input file, we type something else (for example, NONE), no such input takes place, and we can start updating the (possibly empty) B-tree straightaway. The update operations will be the same as those in Section 6.2, so at this stage program DISKTREE.C will behave similarly to BTREE.C, and the user will hardly be aware that the tree resides on disk. However, after our entering the quit command, Q, the B-tree will not get lost this time but remain safely in the tree file for subsequent use. Thus the program will be somewhat similar to a text-editor, where we can also either begin with a new file or use an existing file. However, most editors perform a special SAVE operation at the end of a normal edit session, to store the workfile onto a permanent file; in contrast to this, program DISKTREE.C will be working with a permanent file all the time.

We now turn to the internal aspects of the program. It will be clear that in a file we cannot use normal pointers, since these have memory addresses as their values, and on disk we use positions, which are (long) integers denoting a byte number. Recall that in C we can write

```
fseek(fp, pos, 0);
fwrite(&buf, size, n, fp);
```

where *pos* is a long int value denoting the desired position relative to the beginning of the file. We have

$$pos \; = \; 0 \text{ for the first byte}$$
$$pos \; = \; 1 \text{ for the second}$$

and so on. In the above call of *fwrite* the first argument &*buf* is the begin address in memory from which data are to be written to the file with file pointer *fp*. The number of bytes to be transmitted is the product of *size* and *n*. Thus *pos*, the second argument of *fseek*, can now be used like a pointer; instead of

```
struct node {int cnt, key[MM]; struct node *ptr[MM+1];};
struct node *root, ...
```

we can now use

```
struct node {int cnt, key[MM]; long ptr[MM+1];};
long root, ...
```

Each element of *ptr* can contain a file position, and so can the variable *root*. We have now solved the problem of data representation, but there is still a more difficult question to be answered, namely how to find alternatives for the standard functions *malloc* and *free*. If new nodes are to be created, where shall we place them on disk, and if nodes are to be deleted, will there be portions of unused space in the file? To begin with the latter question, we shall consider such gaps acceptable, provided that they be reused as soon as any new nodes are to be inserted again. We shall therefore insert new nodes in such gaps, if any; otherwise we simply append the file with them. Thus we will not reserve a certain amount of space in advance, and, in principle, there is no limit to the number of nodes in the tree. We want the file to be a complete representation of the tree, which implies that, given only the file, we must be able to work out the position of the root node. We shall therefore store the root itself, that is, the position of the root node, before all other information in the file. Also, some information about any gaps as a result of deleted nodes must be stored in the file in order that we can start program execution with an existing file and fill the gaps when nodes are to be inserted. We shall therefore form a *linked list* of these gaps, using some pointer field, say *ptr*[0], to point to a next gap, if any. Note that we are now using the term *pointer* for long integers which denote positions or, in other words, byte numbers. Let us use $-1L$, and write this as *NIL*, instead of *NULL* used for real pointers in memory. A linked list of free locations is usually called a *free list*, and we shall use the long int variable *freelist* as a 'pointer' to the first element of this list. If the list is empty, *freelist* will have the value *NIL*. As long as the program is running, *root* and *freelist* are internal variables, but we reserve room for them at the beginning of the file, and, at the end of program execution, just before the file is closed, we write their two values in the file. Figure 6.7 shows the file contents for the B-tree of Fig. 6.2(b).

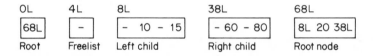

Fig. 6.7. *File representation of a B-tree with three nodes*

As in Section 6.2, we use $M = 2$, so, except for the root node, each node contains at least two and at most four items. For a B-tree on disk such a small value of M will not lead to a very fast program, but with only integer information items, the program will not be useful for real applications anyway; we will use it only for demonstration purposes, and it is instructive to see how fast or slow it is with $M = 2$. After all, we can then speed it up considerably in a very simple way, namely by choosing larger values for the named constants M and MM, for example $M = 1000$, $MM = 2000$. As Fig. 6.7 shows, the root node may not be the first node in the file. In fact the situation shown here with the root node at the end of the file will occur more frequently, which follows from the way a B-tree grows. As this root node will be needed quite often it will be worthwhile to have a copy of it available in main memory, although it must be said that this requirement complicates the program considerably. We shall use the function *readnode*, which normally reads a node from the file, but, instead, it uses the internal variable *rootnode* if the given pointer to the desired node happens to be equal to the variable *root*. Function *readnode* should not be confused with *getnode*; the latter is to return the position of a newly created node, so it plays the role of *malloc* in program BTREE.C. It first tries to obtain an element of the free list of gaps, mentioned above. If this free list is empty, then there are no such gaps, so we go to the end of the file and write a node there with no well-defined contents. This may seem odd, but we need it to reserve room, so that any subsequent call of *getnode* should not return the same location. Further details can be found in the program text itself; complex as it is, the program is easy to use, and it may be instructive to run it on various machines to see how it behaves. As mentioned above, we can speed it up considerably by increasing the values of M and MM (where MM stands for $2M$). There is one system-dependent element in the program, namely the second argument of *fopen*, as indicated by comment. The strings *"rb+"* and *"wb+"* can be used with Lattice C. The letter *b* in these strings causes the file to be opened in binary (untranslated) mode; without this *b*, the file would be opened in text (translated) mode, which implies a special treatment of the newline character, as required with text files.

```
/* DISKTREE.C:
      Demonstration program for a B-tree on disk.
      After building the tree by reading integers from a
      file, we can repeatedly search the tree for a
      given integer. Each time, a search path from root
      to leaf is displayed. We can also update the B-tree
      interactively.
*/
#include <stdio.h>
#include <ctype.h>
#define M 2
#define MM 4
#define NIL (-1L)
struct node { int cnt, key[MM]; long ptr[MM+1]; };
typedef struct node NODE;
NODE rootnode;
long start[2], root=NIL, freelist=NIL;
FILE *fptree;

main()
{ int x;
  char ch, inpfilnam[30], treefilnam[30];
  FILE *fpinp;

  printf("Enter name of (binary) file for the B-tree: ");
  scanf("%s", treefilnam);
  fptree = fopen(treefilnam, "rb+");    /* rb+ and wb+ */
  if (fptree == NULL)                   /* are system  */
  { fptree = fopen(treefilnam, "wb+");  /* dependent   */
    wrstart();
  } else rdstart();

  printf("Enter name of (ASCII) input file (or NONE): ");
  scanf("%s", inpfilnam);
  fpinp = fopen(inpfilnam, "r");
  if (fpinp != NULL)
  { while (fscanf(fpinp, "%d", &x) > 0) insert(x);
    fclose(fpinp);
  }

  while (1)
  { printf(
    "\nDelete (D), Insert (I), Search (S) or Quit (Q): ");
    do
    { ch = getchar(); ch = toupper(ch);
    } while (ch != 'D' && ch != 'I' &&
```

```
                    ch != 'S' && ch != 'Q');
        if (ch == 'Q') break;
        printf("Enter an integer: "); scanf("%d", &x);
        switch (ch)
        { case 'D': delete(x); break;
          case 'I': insert(x); break;
          case 'S': search(x); break;
        }
    }
    wrstart();
    fclose(fptree);
}

search(x) int x;
{ int i, j, *k, n;
  NODE nod;
  long t = root;
  printf("Trace:\n");
  while (t != NIL)
  { readnode(t, &nod);
    k = nod.key; n = nod.cnt;
    for (j=0; j < n; j++) printf(" %d", k[j]);
    printf("\n");
    i = binsearch(x, k, n);
    if (i < n && x == k[i]) { found(t, i); return; }
    t = nod.ptr[i];
  }
  notfound(x);
}

int binsearch(x, a, n) int x, *a, n;
/* Search array a[0], a[1], ..., a[n-1] for x.        */
/* Returned value:  0 if x <= a[0],  n if x > a[n-1], */
/*                  or r, where  a[r-1] < x <= a[r]   */
{ int i, left, right;
  if (x <= a[0]) return 0;
  if (x > a[n-1]) return n;
  left = 0; right = n-1;
  while (right - left > 1)
  { i = right + left  >> 1;
    if (x <= a[i]) right = i; else left = i;
  }
  return right;
}

found(t, i) long t; int i;
{ NODE nod;
  printf("Found in position %d ", i);
  printf("of node with contents: ");
  readnode(t, &nod);
  for (i=0; i < nod.cnt; i++) printf(" %d", nod.key[i]);
  printf("\n");
}

notfound(x) int x;
{ printf("Item %d not found\n", x);
}

insert(x) int x;
/* Driver function for node insertion, called only in the
```

```
       main program. Most of the work is delegated to 'ins'.
 */
 { long tnew, u, getnode();
   int xnew, code;
   code = ins(x, root, &xnew, &tnew);
   if (code == 2) printf("Duplicate key %d ignored\n", x);
   if (code) return;
   u = getnode();
   rootnode.cnt = 1; rootnode.key[0] = xnew;
   rootnode.ptr[0] = root; rootnode.ptr[1] = tnew;
   root = u;
   writenode(u, &rootnode);
 }


 int ins(x, t, y, u) int x, *y; long t, *u;
 /* Insert x in B-tree with root t. If not completely
    successful, the integer *y and the pointer *u
    remain to be inserted.
    Returned value:
        0 if insertion not completely successful,
        1 if insertion successful,
        2 if x is already present in B-tree.
 */
 { long tnew, getnode(), p_final, *p;
   int i, j, xnew, k_final, *n, *k, code;
   NODE nod, newnod;
   /* Examine whether t is a pointer field in a leaf:
   */
   if (t == NIL) { *u = NIL; *y = x; return 0; }

   readnode(t, &nod);
   n = & nod.cnt; k = nod.key; p = nod.ptr;

   /* Select pointer p[i] and try to insert x in
      the subtree of which p[i] is the root:
   */
   i = binsearch(x, k, *n);
   if (i < *n && x == k[i]) return 2; /* Duplicate key */
   code = ins(x, p[i], &xnew, &tnew);
   if (code) return code;

   /* Insertion in subtree did not completely succeed;
      try to insert xnew and tnew in the current node:
   */
   if (*n < MM)
   { i = binsearch(xnew, k, *n);
     for (j= *n; j>i; j--)
     { k[j] = k[j-1]; p[j+1] = p[j];
     }
     k[i] = xnew; p[i+1] = tnew; ++*n;
     writenode(t, &nod); return 1;
   }

   /* The current node was already full, so split it. Pass
      item k[M] in the middle of the augmented sequence
      back through parameter y, so that it can move
      upward in the tree. Also, pass a pointer to the newly
      created node back through u. Return 0, to report
      that insertion was not completed:
```

```
     */
     if (i == MM) { k_final = xnew; p_final = tnew; } else
     { k_final = k[MM-1]; p_final = p[MM];
       for (j=MM-1; j>i; j--)
       { k[j] = k[j-1]; p[j+1] = p[j];
       }
       k[i] = xnew; p[i+1] = tnew;
     }
     *y = k[M]; *n = M;

     *u = getnode(); newnod.cnt = M;
     for (j=0; j < M-1; j++)
     { newnod.key[j] = k[j+M+1];  newnod.ptr[j] = p[j+M+1];
     }
     newnod.ptr[M-1] = p[MM];  newnod.key[M-1] = k_final;
     newnod.ptr[M] = p_final;
     writenode(t, &nod); writenode(*u, &newnod); return 0;
}


long getnode()
{ long t;
  NODE nod;
  if (freelist == NIL)
  { if (fseek(fptree, 0L, 2)) error("fseek in getnode");
    t = ftell(fptree);
    writenode(t, &nod);        /* Reserve space on disk */
  } else
  { t = freelist;
    readnode(t, &nod);  /* To update freelist:          */
    freelist = nod.ptr[0];
  }
  return t;
}

freenode(t) long t;
{ NODE nod;
  readnode(t, &nod);
  nod.ptr[0] = freelist;
  freelist = t;
  writenode(t, &nod);
}

readnode(t, pnode) long t; NODE *pnode;
{ if (t == root) { *pnode = rootnode; return; }
  if (fseek(fptree, t, 0)) error("fseek in readnode");
  if (fread(pnode, sizeof(NODE), 1, fptree) == 0)
                   error("fread in readnode");
}

writenode(t, pnode) long t; NODE *pnode;
{ if (t == root) rootnode = *pnode;
  if (fseek(fptree, t, 0)) error("fseek in writenode");
  if (fwrite(pnode, sizeof(NODE), 1, fptree) == 0)
                   error("fwrite in writenode");
}

rdstart()
{ if (fseek(fptree, 0L, 0)) error("fseek in rdstart");
  if (fread(start, sizeof(long), 2, fptree) == 0)
```

```
     error("fread in rdstart");
   readnode(start[0], &rootnode);
   root = start[0]; freelist = start[1];
}

wrstart()
{ start[0] = root; start[1] = freelist;
   if (fseek(fptree, 0L, 0)) error("fseek in wrstart");
   if (fwrite(start, sizeof(long), 2, fptree) == 0)
     error("fwrite in wrstart");
   if (root != NIL) writenode(root, &rootnode);
}

error(str) char *str;
{ printf("\nError: %s\n", str);
   exit(1);
}

delete(x) int x;
/* Driver function for node deletion, called only in the
   main program. Most of the work is delegated to 'del'.
*/
{ int code;
   long newroot;
   code = del(x, root);
   if (code == 2) printf("%d not found\n", x);
   if (code) return;
   /* 0 = underflow; 1 = success; 2 = key not found;   */
   /* If underflow, decrease the height of the tree:   */
   newroot = rootnode.ptr[0]; freenode(root);
   if (newroot != NIL) readnode(newroot, &rootnode);
   root = newroot;
}

int del(x, t) int x; long t;
/* Delete item x in B-tree with root t.
   Returned value:
   0 = underflow, 1 = success, 2 = not found
*/
{ int i, j, *k, *n, *item, code,
     *nleft, *nright, *lkey, *rkey, borrowleft, nq, *addr;
   long *p, left, right, *lptr, *rptr, q, q1;
   NODE nod, nod1, nod2;
   if (t == NIL) return 2;
   readnode(t, &nod);
   n = & nod.cnt; k = nod.key; p=nod.ptr;
   i = binsearch(x, k, *n);
   if (p[0] == NIL)    /*   *t is a leaf */
   { if (i == *n !! x < k[i]) return 2;
     /* x is now equal to k[i], located in a leaf: */
     for (j=i+1; j < *n; j++)
     { k[j-1] = k[j]; p[j] = p[j+1];
     }
     --*n;
     writenode(t, &nod);
     return *n >= (t==root ? 1 : M);
   }
   /* *t is an interior node (not a leaf):   */
   item = k+i; left = p[i]; readnode(left, &nod1);
   nleft = & nod1.cnt;
```

```
    if (i < *n && x == *item)
    { /* x found in interior node.                              */
      /* Go to left child *p[i] and then follow a path          */
      /* all the way to a leaf, using rightmost branches:        */
      q = p[i]; readnode(q, &nod1); nq = nod1.cnt;
      while (q1 = nod1.ptr[nq], q1 != NIL)
      { q = q1; readnode(q, &nod1); nq = nod1.cnt;
      }
      /* Exchange k[i] with the rightmost item in
         that leaf:
      */
      addr = nod1.key + nq - 1;
      *item = *addr; *addr = x;
      writenode(t, &nod); writenode(q, &nod1);
    }
    /* Delete x in subtree with root  p[i]:                     */
    code = del(x, left);
    if (code) return code;
    /* Underflow; borrow, and, if necessary, merge:            */
    borrowleft =  i == *n;
    if (borrowleft)  /* p[i] is rightmost pointer in *p  */
    { item = k+i-1; left = p[i-1]; right = p[i];
      readnode(left, &nod1);
      nleft = & nod1.cnt;
    } else right = p[i+1];
    readnode(left, &nod1);
    readnode(right, &nod2);
    nright = & nod2.cnt;
    lkey = nod1.key; rkey = nod2.key;
    lptr = nod1.ptr; rptr = nod2.ptr;
    if (borrowleft)  /* This is an exception */
    { rptr[*nright + 1] = rptr[*nright];
      for (j = *nright; j>0; j--)
      { rkey[j] = rkey[j-1];
        rptr[j] = rptr[j-1];
      }
      ++*nright;
      rkey[0] = *item; rptr[0] = lptr[*nleft];
      *item = lkey[*nleft - 1];
      if (--*nleft >= M)
      { writenode(t, &nod); writenode(left, &nod1);
        writenode(right, &nod2);
        return 1;
      }
    } else
    if (*nright > M)            /* Borrow from right sibling: */
    { lkey[M-1] = *item; lptr[M] = rptr[0]; *item = rkey[0];
      ++*nleft; --*nright;
      for (j=0; j < *nright; j++)
      { rptr[j] = rptr[j+1]; rkey[j] = rkey[j+1];
      }
      rptr[*nright] = rptr[*nright + 1];
      writenode(t, &nod); writenode(left, &nod1);
      writenode(right, &nod2);
      return 1;
    }
    /* Merge: */
    lkey[M-1] = *item; lptr[M] = rptr[0];
    for (j=0; j<M; j++)
    { lkey[M+j] = rkey[j]; lptr[M+j+1] = rptr[j+1];
```

```
    }
    *nleft = MM;
    freenode(right);
    for (j=i+1; j < *n; j++) {k[j-1] = k[j]; p[j] = p[j+1];}
    --*n;
    writenode(t, &nod);
    writenode(left, &nod1);
    return *n >= (t==root ? 1 : M);
}
```

EXERCISES

In the following exercises the same node type as in Section 6.1 is to be used. Write a main program to show that each function works properly.

6.1 Write a function to count the number of information items stored in a B-tree.

6.2 Write a function to determine the height of a B-tree.

6.3 Write a function to delete an entire B-tree.

6.4 Write a function which takes a B-tree and builds a new one containing the same integers as the given B-tree, except for those which are a multiple of 3. For example, if the given B-tree contains the integers 1, 4, 6, 7, 12, 20, 23, 24, then the new one will contain only the integers 1, 4, 7, 20, 23.

CHAPTER 7

Tries

7.1 INTRODUCTION

In the trees of Chapters 5 and 6 each node contained one or more key values, and we have seen that this principle may require special measures to prevent those trees from becoming unbalanced or even degenerated. Obviously, if a tree is to be searched efficiently the nodes must contain certain values that enable us to decide which branch to take, and, up to now, we have taken it for granted that those values must be existing key values. However, this is not absolutely necessary. Instead of using the complete key in each comparison we can compare only a certain portion of it. This idea is the basis of a special type of tree, called a *trie*. This peculiar word is derived from the two words *tree* and *retrieval*, and, in spite of this derivation, *trie* is often pronounced as *try*, to distinguish it from *tree* in spoken language. To understand what a trie is about let us consider a not-unrealistic example.

Our keys will be character strings, consisting of capital letters only; for example:

A
ALE
ALLOW
AN
ANY
ANYTHING

We will use the individual characters of the string to determine how to branch. All interior nodes, called *branch nodes*, will have 27 pointer fields and an integer field to be discussed later. The leaves, also called *information nodes*, will consist of the complete information records; each of them contains a key and, possibly, some other information associated with the key. In the branch nodes there is a pointer field for each of the letters $A, \ldots, Z$. The main rule is that branching on the ith level in the trie is determined by the ith character of the key. Figure 7.1 shows the trie for the above six words.

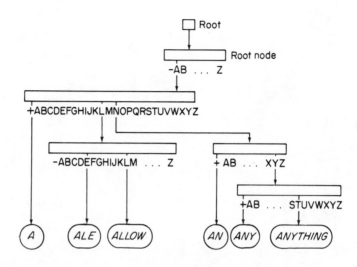

Fig. 7.1. A trie

If, for example, we search the trie for the word *ALE* we take the branch that corresponds to the letter *A* in the root node, then the branch corresponding to *L*, and, finally, the one corresponding to *E*. We find the key *ALLOW* similarly, but here we need only the first three letters, since there is no other key beginning with those letters. We say that *ALL* is a *prefix* of the key *ALLOW*, which, in contrast to the prefix *AL*, determines this key uniquely. Similarly, *ANYT* is a prefix that uniquely determines the key *ANYTHING*. The key *ANY* would also be a prefix of *ANYTHING* if we used only the visible characters of each key. Instead, we shall include the terminating null character in each key, which prevents any key from being a prefix of another key. Recall that this is in accordance with normal string-handling conventions in C. Thus, our keys should be read as

> *A\0*
> *ALE\0*
> *ALLOW\0*
> *AN\0*
> *ANY\0*
> *ANYTHING\0*

In every branch node we also reserve a pointer field that corresponds to this null character; in Fig. 7.1 these pointer fields are denoted by + if they contain a real pointer. This explains the pointers to the information nodes for the keys *A*, *AN*, *ANY*. If these pointer fields contain the null pointer this is denoted in Fig. 7.1 by −. In this example, one minus sign tells us that there is no key *AL*. Of course, we must be able to distinguish between branch keys and information keys. We will therefore include an integer field in each branch node; this field will be located at the very beginning of each branch node, and it will always contain the value 0. As for the information nodes, they represent variable-length strings, for which we shall allocate memory elsewhere, in the usual way.

Besides a pointer to such a character string we include a non-zero integer, to distinguish information nodes from branch nodes, and this integer will be the first field of each information node. Thus, we will be able to tell branch nodes from information nodes: the former begin with integer 0 and the latter with a non-zero integer. It may seem to be a waste of memory space to use an entire integer instead of only one bit for this; however, reserving only a single bit would result in allocating at least an entire byte on most machines. Furthermore, we shall use this integer for another purpose, namely as a count field, which says how many occurrences of the word have been read.

There is another little problem associated with using two distinct node types. Each pointer to an information node has a type different from the type of pointers to branch nodes. Since we want each pointer field in a branch node to be capable of containing pointers of either type we formally declare only pointers to branch nodes; we simply use a cast if the other pointer type is desired. Thus, we define the following type for branch nodes:

```
struct branchnode
   { int num; struct branchnode *ptr[27]; } *root;
struct infnode { int num; char *key; };
```

where the fields of a branch node have the following meaning:

num: 0 (to indicate that the node is a branch node)

$p[0]$: a pointer corresponding to '\0'

$p[1]$: a pointer corresponding to the letter A

. . .

$p[26]$: a pointer corresponding to the letter Z

7.2   A DEMONSTRATION PROGRAM

We shall now discuss program TRIE.C, which builds, prints, and searches a trie of the type we are discussing. The program will read words from a file and store them in a trie. Each information node will contain a word and a count field, the latter saying how many occurrences of the word have been read. So the value of each count field is at least 1, which makes it suitable as a means to distinguish information nodes from branch nodes. Internally, all names will consist of capital letters only: we will convert any lower-case letters to the corresponding capitals. The words are separated by sequences of any characters other than letters. After the trie has been built we shall print all words, just to show that we can easily traverse our trie and list the keys in alphabetic order. Finally, we will demonstrate searching the trie for keys entered on the keyboard; the special word *STOPSEARCH* will be interpreted as an end signal instead of being a key to be searched for. Since function *insert* in program TRIE.C is rather intricate, it is strongly recommended to study the functions *main*, *printtrie*, and *found* first.

```
/* TRIE.C: A demonstration program for tries
*/
#include <stdio.h>
#include <ctype.h>
struct branchnode
   { int num; struct branchnode *ptr[27]; };
struct infnode { int num; char *key; };
```

```
typedef struct branchnode *brptr;
typedef struct infnode *infptr;

main()
{ FILE *fp;
  char filnam[25], word[80], *malloc();
  brptr root;
  infptr q, found();
  printf("Input file: "); scanf("%s", filnam);
  fp = fopen(filnam, "r");
  if (fp == NULL) error("File not available");
  root = NULL;
  while (getword(fp, word) > 0) insert(&root, word, 0);
  fclose(fp);
  printf("\nContents of trie:\n");
  if (root != NULL) printtrie(root);
  while
  (printf("\nEnter a word, or type STOPSEARCH to stop: "),
   getword(stdin, word), strcmp(word, "STOPSEARCH"))
  { q = found(root, word);
    if (q == NULL) printf("Key not found\n"); else
      printf("Key found; count field = %d\n", q->num);
  }
}

printtrie(p) brptr p;
{ infptr ip;
  brptr q;
  int k;
  ip = (infptr) p;
  if (p->num)                    /* num > 0: Information node */
    printf("%5d %s\n", ip->num, ip->key); else
    for (k=0; k<27; k++)    /* num = 0: Branch node       */
      if (q = p->ptr[k], q != NULL) printtrie(q);
}

infptr found(p, word) brptr p; char *word;
{ int i=0, k;
  char ch;
  infptr ip;
  while (p != NULL && p->num == 0)
  { ch = word[i++]; k = (ch ? ch-'A'+1 : 0);
    if (k < 0 || k > 26) return NULL;
    p = p->ptr[k];
  }
  ip = (infptr)p;
  return (p == NULL ? NULL :
         strcmp(word, ip->key) == 0 ? ip : NULL);
}

insert(pp, word, i) brptr *pp; char *word; int i;
{ char ch, ch1;
  brptr p, p1, newbrnode(), newinfonode();
  infptr ip;
  int k, k1;
  p = *pp; ip = (infptr)p;
  if (p == NULL) {*pp = newinfonode(word); return;}
                           /* New info node created    */
  if (ip->num && strcmp(word, ip->key) == 0)
  { ip->num ++; return;        /* Word already in info node */
```

```
  }
  ch = word[i];                    /* num = 0: Branch node      */
  k = (ch ? ch-'A'+1 : 0);    /* num > 0: Information node */
  if (p->num == 0) {insert(& p->ptr[k], word, i+1); return;}
            /* Task completed if p points to branch node  */
  *pp = p1 = newbrnode();     /* Create new branch node    */
  ch1 = ip->key[i];                /* (p points to info node)   */
  k1 = (ch1 ? ch1-'A'+1 : 0);
  p1->ptr[k1] = p;                 /* Pointer to old info node  */
  insert(& p1->ptr[k], word, i+1);
}

brptr newbrnode()
{ char *malloc();
  brptr p;
  int k;
  p = (brptr)malloc(sizeof(struct branchnode));
  if (p == NULL) error("Not enough memory");
  p->num = 0;
  for (k=0; k<27; k++) p->ptr[k] = NULL;
  return p;
}

brptr newinfonode(word) char *word;
{ char *pch, *malloc();
  infptr ip;
  ip = (infptr)malloc(sizeof(struct infnode));
  pch = malloc(strlen(word)+1);
  if (ip == NULL ¦¦ pch == NULL)
    error("Not enough memory");
  strcpy(pch, word);
  ip->num = 1;
  ip->key = pch;
  return (brptr)ip;
}

int getword(fp, str) FILE *fp; char *str;
{ int ch, i=0;
  /* Skip non-alphabetic characters: */
  while (ch = getc(fp), ch != EOF && !isalpha(ch)) ;
  /* Read letters into str, if any: */
  while (isalpha(ch))
  { str[i++] = toupper(ch); ch = getc(fp);
  }
  str[i] = '\0';
  return i;
}

error(str) char *str;
{ printf("\nError: %s\n", str); exit(1);
}
```

There are many occurrences of the two pointer types *brptr* and *infptr* in this program. With

```
  brptr p;
  infptr ip;
```

the variables *p* and *ip* can be used as pointers to branch nodes and information nodes, respectively. Thus, we can use

```
p->num,    p->ptr,   ip->num,   ip->key,
```

but not *p—> key* or *ip—> ptr*. However, we can switch between these pointer types, using a cast. We need this facility, because when descending the tree from the root to a leaf we do not know in advance how many steps it takes to arrive at the leaf, that is, an information node. Each time, we use pointer *p* first, and check if *p—> num* is zero. As soon as that is not the case, we perform the statement

```
ip = (infptr) p;
```

and we then know that *ip* points to an information node. The functions *printtrie* and *found* should now be studied carefully, not only because they are interesting themselves but also as a preparation for the more difficult function *insert*. As the call

```
insert(&root, word, 0);
```

in the main program shows, the first argument of *insert* is the address of a pointer variable. This makes it possible for the function to assign a pointer value to that variable. Within the function we use the notation *pp* for the address of the pointer variable, so *pp is the pointer variable and **pp is the object pointed to by the latter variable. Instead of the expression *pp we use the local variables *p* and *ip* wherever possible. The second argument of *insert* is the word to be inserted, and the third denotes the next character position of this word, to be used in a comparison. There are many cases to consider, which is why this function is more complex than the rest of the program. If *p* is equal to *NULL* we create a new information node and assign its address to *pp. Notice that

```
*pp = ...
```

must not be replaced with

```
p = ...,
```

since that would mean that the new pointer value is assigned only to the local variable *p*. If *p—> num* is equal to 0 we know that *p* points to a branch node. We have already used the character *word*[*i*] to determine the value of *k*, so that we can go to the proper subtrie by using the recursive call

```
insert(& p->ptr[k], word, i+1)
```

which will then ensure that character *word*[*i*+1] is used for the next comparison. All that remains to be done is inserting the given word, using a pointer *ip* that points to an information node. If the word to be inserted is identical to the word in the information node we only have to increase the count field by one. Otherwise, we will need a new branch node, so we create this.

Let us assume that we are dealing with the trie of Fig. 7.1. We now distinguish between two cases, exemplified by the insertion of the new words *ALL* and *ALLOWANCE*,
respectively. In both cases *ip* will point to the information node containing *ALLOW*. To
reach this information node we have already used the three letters *A*, *L*, *L*, and we may
expect the insertion of *ALL* and *ALLOWANCE* to be essentially different. After all,
the new word *ALL* is a prefix of the existing word *ALLOW*, whereas with the new word
ALLOWANCE it is the other way round. However, recursion enables us to deal with
these two cases in the same way. Though not mentioned yet, we have already assigned
the address of the newly created branch node to the pointer field corresponding to *L* in
the parent node, using

```
*pp = p1 = newbrnode();
```

To fill in the newly created node, **p1*, we now use the fourth letter (*O*) of the word
ALLOW, and we make the pointer field corresponding to *O* point to the existing information node containing this word. This explains the statements

```
ch1 = ip->key[i];
k1 = (ch1 ? ch1-'A'+1 : 0);
p1->ptr[k1] = p;
```

We then perform the recursive call

```
insert(& p1->ptr[k], word, i+1);
```

Although in this call the pointer points to the same information node as before (the one
that contains *ALLOW*) we are one level deeper in the trie, thanks to the inserted branch
node, and the third argument is now one higher than it was last time. By inserting the
word *ALL* in the trie of Fig. 7.1 the information node containing *ALLOW* is replaced
with the trie fragment shown in Fig. 7.2. If, subsequently, we add *ALLOWANCE*, this
trie fragment is in turn replaced with Fig. 7.3.

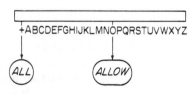

Fig. 7.2. Trie fragment replacing node ALLOW in Fig. 7.1, as a result of inserting ALL

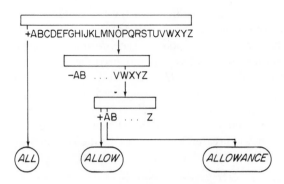

Fig. 7.3.   Trie fragment replacing node ALLOW in Fig. 7.1, as a result of inserting ALL and ALLOWANCE

It should be noted that tries are not economical with memory space. Besides the information nodes there are branch nodes, which use much space, especially in our type of trie with 27 pointer fields in each of them. Instead of using arrays with 27 elements we can use linked lists, but then each node of such a list must contain not only a pointer to a node of the tree but also both the character that corresponds to the latter pointer and a pointer to the next node of the linked list. Besides, searching such linked lists will take more time than selecting elements of our arrays. The type of trie we have been discussing is at least very efficient with respect to time. Tries are suitable data structures for spelling-checking programs. The information nodes would then contain the words of a dictionary. We could use only branch nodes (and no information nodes at all). This is possible, provided that, instead of a unique prefix, all letters of each word are used in the branching process. Unfortunately, we would then need many additional branch nodes, which may cost more than what we gained by abolishing the information nodes.

We have not discussed how trie nodes can be deleted. This can be done, and it is considerably simpler than deleting nodes in a B-tree, as we discussed in Section 6.2. If the option of deleting nodes is available we can use it in a spelling checker. We have just suggested that the trie should contain all words of a dictionary, so that we can search the trie for each word in the text that is to be checked. Alternatively, we can proceed the other way round: we can store each word of the text in question (only once) in a trie and then search it for each word in the dictionary. Each time a word is found, we delete it from the trie, so that the trie gradually shrinks. When all words of the dictionary have been searched for, any remaining words in the trie are just those which do not occur in the dictionary. Obviously, this method is feasible only if the dictionary is very limited in size. A curious point is that in this way we do not benefit from the alphabetic order of the dictionary. This observation suggests yet another method, namely, *traversing* the trie (rather than searching it), so that we encounter all words of our text in alphabetic order, and at the same time scanning the dictionary sequentially, each time comparing a word in the trie with a word in the dictionary.

There is another aspect of tries that deserves our attention, namely that a trie is a very suitable means of searching for all words with a given prefix. For example, we may want to enter COM to obtain the list:

COMMAND, COMPILER, COMPUTE, COMPUTER, COMPUTING

As a final remark, we can implement a trie on disk rather than in memory, as we did for B-trees in Section 6.3. This will slow down the search process considerably, but, provided that it is fast enough for our application, we may benefit from this method because of the large capacity of disks. Another favourable point is the permanent nature of disk files compared with the volatility of tries in main memory.

EXERCISES

7.1 In the tries in this chapter we used arrays of 27 pointer fields because we distinguished only the 26 capital letters. If, instead, we have to distinguish all printable ASCII characters we had better use linked lists instead of those arrays. Write a demonstration program for such a trie.

7.2 Write a demonstration program which manipulates a trie on disk.

7.3 Write an extension to program TRIE.C in Section 7.2, to delete words of a trie.

7.4 Write a program to traverse a trie, printing all words stored in it in alphabetic order.

7.5 Investigate the various ways of constructing a spelling checker by means of a trie, as suggested towards the end of this chapter. Examine analytically how running time will depend on:

(1) The size of the text to be checked;

(2) The number of distinct words in this text;

(3) The size of the dictionary.

Choose the method that seems best for your purposes and write a program for it.

7.6 Write a program to find all words in a trie which have a given prefix.

CHAPTER 8

Graphs

8.1 DIRECTED AND UNDIRECTED GRAPHS

The term *graph* is used for a set of *vertices* (or *nodes*) with a set of *edges*, each of which connects a pair of vertices. We may consider each edge between two vertices i and j to be the ordered pair $< i, j >$, and we then say that we have a *directed* graph. Alternatively, we may use only unordered pairs (i, j), in which case we are dealing with an *undirected* graph. We have in fact been dealing with directed graphs for a long time, since linked lists and trees are special cases of them. In a directed graph we usually represent each edge $< i, j >$ by an arrow, pointing from i to j. Obviously, for two distinct vertices i and j the pairs $< i, j >$ and $< j, i >$ represent two distinct edges. In an undirected graph the pairs (i, j) and (j, i) are two different notations for the same edge. (Incidentally, we can regard an undirected graph as a directed graph in which each edge $< i, j >$ is accompanied by an edge $< j, i >$; the notation (i, j) then represents this pair of edges.) In Fig. 8.1(a) we have a directed graph, with vertices labelled 1, 2, 3, 4, 5 and edges $< 1, 3 >$, $< 1, 4 >$, $< 3, 5 >$, $< 5, 2 >$, $< 2, 3 >$, $< 2, 1 >$. Figure 8.1(b) shows an undirected graph.

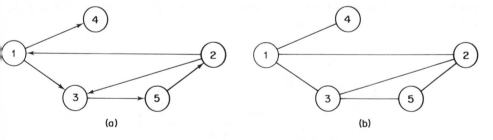

(a)   (b)

Fig. 8.1. (a) Directed graph; (b) undirected graph

A network of pipes through which water can flow in one direction is an example of a directed graph; the pipes are then drawn as arrows and the points of connection as vertices. If in each pipe the water can flow in both directions we have an undirected graph. Graph theory is an extensive branch of mathematics with many interesting theorems and useful applications. Also, there are good books on data structures, including those by Horowitz and Sahni (1977) and Aho *et al.* (1983), which discuss internal rep-

159

resentations of graphs and associated algorithms. Since in the present book we focus on programming in the C language we will select one application of graphs and work this out in a complete, efficient and possibly useful program. It is about *project planning* by means of a directed graph, also called an *activity network*. However, let us first see how we can represent directed graphs internally. From now on we will use the term *graph* for what actually is a directed graph.

8.2 GRAPH REPRESENTATIONS

An elegant but rather expensive means of representing a graph is a so-called *adjacency matrix*. For a graph with n vertices, numbered 1, 2, ..., n, the corresponding adjacency matrix has n rows and n columns. If $< i, j >$ is an edge in the graph the matrix element on the ith row and the jth column is 1, otherwise it is 0. For example, the adjacency matrix for the graph of Fig. 8.1(a) is:

$$
\begin{bmatrix}
0 & 0 & 1 & 1 & 0 \\
1 & 0 & 1 & 0 & 0 \\
0 & 0 & 0 & 0 & 1 \\
0 & 0 & 0 & 0 & 0 \\
0 & 1 & 0 & 0 & 0
\end{bmatrix}
$$

Since the given graph contains an edge from vertex 1 to vertex 3, the third element in the first row of the matrix is 1, and so on. Adjacency matrices in the form of two-dimensional arrays are not frequently used in practice, because for large graphs they use too much memory space and with many algorithms they lead to quadratic computing time. Matrices such as those under consideration, with a large proportion of zero elements, are called *sparse*. If they are large it may be advantageous to use dynamic data structures instead of two-dimensional arrays to represent them. Here we shall use linear lists, called *adjacency lists*, so that each row of the adjacency matrix corresponds to one list, and we shall place the starting pointers of these lists in an array. The elements of the lists contain at least a column number and a field for a pointer to the next list element. Figure 8.2 shows such adjacency lists for the graph of Fig. 8.1(a).

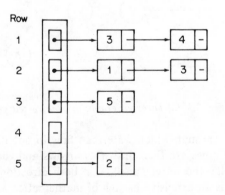

Fig. 8.2. Adjacency lists for the graph of Fig. 8.1(a)

Each element in an adjacency list represents an edge. Adjacency lists such as those shown in Fig. 8.2 are an excellent means of finding all immediate successors of a given vertex. For example, we find the edges $< 1, 3 >$ and $< 1, 4 >$ by traversing the first linear list. However, these lists do not provide an efficient way of finding all immediate predecessors of a given vertex. If, for example, we want to find all immediate predecessors of vertex 2 we would have to scan all linear lists to find the number 2 in the final one, as the only immediate successor of vertex 5. To find predecessors, we should use *inverted* adjacency lists. These contain the vertex numbers of immediate predecessors instead of immediate successors; all immediate predecessors of vertex 1 are in the first list, and so on. We shall use inverted adjacency lists in Section 8.4.

8.3 TOPOLOGICAL SORTING; DETECTING CYCLES

In Fig. 8.1(a), the edges $< 2, 3 >$, $< 3, 5 >$, $< 5, 2 >$ form a *cycle*: if we start in vertex 2 and we follow these three edges we arrive in vertex 2 again. In many applications we have to deal only with so-called *acyclic* graphs, which have no cycles. For acyclic graphs we can write the vertex numbers in a sequence, in such a way that for any edge $< i, j >$, vertex number i precedes vertex number j in this sequence. Such a sequence is called a *topological order*. Note that there may be several topological orders for the same graph. For example, each of the sequences

1, 2, 3, 4

and

1, 3, 2, 4

is a topological order for the graph shown in Fig. 8.3 (and there are no other topological orders for this graph).

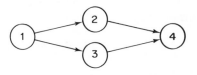

Fig. 8.3. An acyclic graph that has two topological orders

Usually, we do not need all topological orders; any will do. As a preparation for the next sections we shall now develop a program which may be applied to any (directed) graph; it will detect the occurrence of cycles, if any, and it will produce a topological order of the vertex numbers if the graph is acyclic. We shall use adjacency lists similar to Fig. 8.2, with one extension. The elements $a[i]$ of our array will be structures, each containing both a pointer $a[i].link$, pointing to an adjacency list, and a integer field $a[i].count$. The latter is intended primarily to indicate how many immediate predecessors the vertex corresponding to that array element has. That integer is called the *in-degree* of the vertex in question. The array and adjacency lists for the graph of Fig. 8.3 are shown in Fig. 8.4. The integers that denote in-degrees are surrounded by parentheses, to distinguish them from vertex numbers.

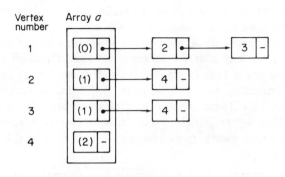

Fig. 8.4. Adjacency lists for the graph of Fig. 8.3

So far, we have paid hardly any attention to the way our vertices are numbered. If, for each edge $< i, j >$, we required number i to be less than number j our task would be very simple. First, this condition would exclude the possibility of cycles, and second, we would obtain a topological order simply by sorting all vertex numbers. However, we will not impose that requirement on our vertex numbering, because in practical applications alterations may be necessary, and the requirement $i < j$ might force us to renumber a great many vertices if one had to be inserted somewhere in the middle of the graph. Our vertex numbering will be almost completely free, the only restriction being that the range of numbers used should not be too large for the amount of memory that is available. After all, the range of these numbers will be the range of our subscripts and, depending on our computer system, we have to take into account certain limitations with respect to the maximum array size. Instead of a normal array we will use a pointer, pointing to some allocated area of memory which is just as large as we need. Thus, we again benefit from the well-known equivalence of arrays and pointers in the C language. Although we think in terms of array a, the variable a is actually a pointer, declared in:

```
struct edge { int num; struct edge *next; };
struct vertex { int count; struct edge *link; };
...
struct vertex *a;
```

Let us denote the user's vertex numbers by capital letters I and J. We will read them from a file, which enables us to scan them more than once. We first determine the least and the greatest value (*minim* and *maxim*) of all given vertex numbers. After this first scan, we compute

$$n = maxim - minim + 1$$

which is the number of array elements that we shall request to be allocated. Internally, we then use vertex numbers i, j, related to I, J as follows:

$$i = I - minim$$
$$j = J - minim$$

The least and the greatest internal vertex numbers are now 0 and $n-1$, respectively.

(Of course, in the output we reconstruct the user's vertex numbers I and J again by adding *minim* to i and j.)

For example, for the graph of Fig. 8.5 we have:

$$minim = 100$$
$$maxim = 130$$
$$n = 31$$

so the internal vertex numbers are 0, 10, 20, 30, and we allocate memory for $a[0]$, $a[1]$, ..., $a[30]$.

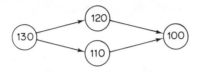

Fig. 8.5. Graph with large vertex numbers

Since a subset of the reserved array elements $a[0]$, ..., $a[n-1]$ may not be used we need a means of marking those elements by a code. Now we realize that each count field

$$a[i] \,.\, count$$

is primarily intended for the in-degree of vertex i, as mentioned above, and, as such, can have only a non-negative value. This opens the possibility of storing a negative value in this field as a code that indicates that there is no vertex i in the graph. Let us use -2 for this code (-1 having a different meaning, as we will see shortly). Thus, in the above example only the count fields of $a[0]$, $a[10]$, $a[20]$, and $a[30]$ are unequal to -2.

As for the topological order we want, we begin with all vertices with zero count fields. Their in-degree being zero, these vertices have no predecessors, so in a topological order they are to come first. Our algorithm works as follows. We begin with replacing these zero count fields with subscript values, in such a way that the array elements for all vertices without any predecessor form a linear list (to be distinguished from the adjacency lists). Note that this linear list does not require any additional memory space for the nodes; we use certain elements of array a as nodes and their subscript values as 'pointers'. An integer variable *start* will act as the start pointer of the list. It will be equal to the subscript of the first element of the list and the value -1 will denote a null pointer at the end of this linear list. For example, if we have

$$start = 34$$
$$a[34] \,.\, count = 87$$
$$a[87] \,.\, count = 22$$
$$a[22] \,.\, count = -1$$

then the vertices 34, 87, 22 have no predecessors. Note that our algorithm is destructive, since we actually alter the count fields. We even go a step further and gradually reduce the graph, each time deleting vertices that have no predecessors, until, in an acyclic graph, there are no vertices left. If, in this way, we do not get rid of all vertices, that is, if at some moment there are still vertices in the graph but each of them has at least one predecessor, the graph has a cycle. The list of vertices with no predecessors will be used as a stack: insertions and deletions occur only at the head of the list. This stack will grow and shrink all the time; when we are deleting a vertex, we place all its immediate successors on the stack, since these successors will be vertices without a predecessor after that deletion. Our program, TOPOL.C, reads a file containing number pairs $< I, J >$ for each edge of the graph. Its output consists of either all vertex numbers in a topological order or a message saying that there is a cycle.

```
/* TOPOL.C: Topological sorting; the presence of any
            cycles will be detected.
*/
#include <stdio.h>

struct edge { int num; struct edge *next; };
struct vertex { int count; struct edge *link; };

main()
{ FILE *fp;
  char filnam[25], *malloc();
  int n, i, j, k, I, J, start, first=1, minim, maxim,
      min1, max1, structsize = sizeof(struct vertex);
      /*    = sizeof(struct edge)    */
  struct vertex *a;
  struct edge *p, *p1;
  printf("Input file: "); scanf("%s", filnam);
  fp = fopen(filnam, "r");
  if (fp == NULL) error("File not available");

  /* Determine least and greatest vertex number: */
  while (fscanf(fp, "%d %d", &I, &J) == 2)
  { if (I < J) { min1 = I; max1 = J; }
         else { min1 = J; max1 = I; }
    if (first)
    { minim = min1; maxim = max1; first = 0;
    } else
    { if (min1 < minim) minim = min1;
      if (max1 > maxim) maxim = max1;
    }
  }
  fclose(fp);

  n = maxim - minim + 1;
  a = (struct vertex *)malloc(n * structsize);
  if (a == NULL) error("Vertex-number range too large");
  for (i=0; i<n; i++) {a[i].count = -2; a[i].link = NULL;}

  /* Build adjacency lists: */
  fp = fopen(filnam, "r");
  while (fscanf(fp, "%d %d", &I, &J) == 2)
  { i = I - minim; j = J - minim;
    if (a[i].count == -2) a[i].count = 0;
    if (a[j].count == -2) a[j].count = 0;
    p = (struct edge *)malloc(structsize);
    if (p == NULL) error("Not enough memory");
```

```
      p->num = j; p->next = a[i].link;
      a[i].link = p;
      a[j].count++;
  }
  fclose(fp);

  /* Form a linked stack of nodes that have no
     predecessor:
  */
  start = -1;
  for (i=0; i<n; i++)
    if (a[i].count==0)
    { a[i].count = start; start = i;
    }

  /* Print vertex numbers in topological order: */
  for (i=0; i<n; i++)
  { while (a[i].count == -2) i++;
    if (start == -1) error("There is a cycle");
    /* Take a vertex from the stack, print it,
       and decrease the in-degree of all its
       immediate successors by 1; as soon as the
       updated in-degree of a successor is zero,
       place it on the stack: and dispose of
       the (edge) node in the adjacency list.
    */
    j = start; start = a[j].count; p = a[j].link;
    J = minim + j;
    printf("%d ", J);
    while (p != NULL)
    { k = p->num;
      a[k].count--;
      if (a[k].count == 0)
      { a[k].count = start; start = k;
      }
      p1 = p->next;
      if (p1 == NULL) p = NULL; else {*p = *p1; free(p1);}
      /* In the adjacency list we have disposed of a node
         that we don't need any longer.
      */
    }
  }
}

error(str) char *str;
{ printf("Error: %s\n", str); exit(1);
}
```

Note the loop starting with

```
/* Print vertex numbers in topological order: */
for (i=0; i<n; i++)
{ while (a[i].count == -2) i++;
```

As a result of the inner (while) loop, the variable i will have only real vertex numbers as values in the program fragment that follows. However, the vertices are not dealt with in the order of these i-values. Instead, we always use the top of the linked stack containing all vertices that have no predecessor. Each time, we unstack the vertex that is to be deleted, but, at the same time, we stack its immediate successors if these, as a consequence of this deletion, no longer have any predecessors. If the linked stack should be empty before we have done this n times then we have a situation where there are still vertices left, each of which has a predecessor, which means that there is a cycle. If an input file contains the four lines

120	100
130	110
110	100
130	120

which correspond to the graph of Fig. 8.5, we obtain the following topological order as output:

130   110   120   100

Instead of this extremely simple example we could have used a very large graph without any problems as to computing time, because the algorithm that we have been using is very efficient. If the graph contains n vertices and e edges, then running time is $O(n+e)$; in other words, it is *linear* in the size of the problem. This is worth mentioning, since there are many graph problems where we can do no better than 'try all possibilities', which normally leads to exponential growth rate.

8.4   ACTIVITY NETWORKS; CRITICAL PATH METHOD

An important application of graphs is project planning and scheduling. Some well-known techniques in this area are *CPM* (Critical Path Method) and *PERT* (Performance Evaluation and Review Technique). Any project consists of a number of activities, some of which are related to one another. For example, when we are building a house it is obvious that the construction of its roof can take place only after the walls are ready. There are two possibilities to place activities in a graph, namely we can use either the vertices or the edges to denote them.

Let us choose the edges for this purpose. Besides the vertex pair $< i, j >$ each activity also has a given *duration*, which is an estimate of the time that activity will take, and a description, which, technically speaking, is a string of, say, at most 80 characters. In the framework of project planning we use the terms *activities* and *events* instead of *edges* and *vertices*, respectively. Figure 8.6 shows an *activity network* for a simple project. Two components A and B are involved in manufacturing a certain product; we only have to place an order to obtain component A, but it is estimated that the article will be delivered as many as 50 days after the order has gone out. Things are more complex for component B. We have to build it ourselves, which takes 20 days. Then we have to test it (25 days) and to correct the errors (15 days). Also, we have to write a user's guide (60 days), but the person who is to do this can start writing only after B has been built.

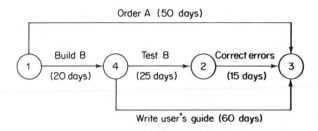

Fig. 8.6. *An activity network*

In Fig. 8.6 events 1 and 3 denote the start and the completion of the entire project, respectively. Note that this network includes two activities $< i, j >$ for which i is greater than j. Actually, there are real CPM programs that admit only activities $< i, j >$ for which i is less than j. This restriction would exclude any cycles; it would make the task of obtaining a topological order extremely easy, and would therefore simplify our program considerably. Instead, we will allow vertices to be numbered freely, but it is nevertheless a good idea from the planner's point of view to begin with a network with $i < j$ for all activities $< i, j >$, so the network shown in Fig. 8.6 is not a good example for project managers. However, when activities are to be inserted in a complex network the user of a more tolerant program like ours will appreciate that he need not worry about vertex numbers. Incidentally, the danger of introducing cycles should not be exaggerated: they can also be avoided simply by drawing all activities as arrows pointing more or less from left to right, as is usual in practice. If, in spite of this good advice, cycles should occur, then our program will detect them. (It would not be fair if we, as programmers, imposed the restriction $i < j$ on all activities $< i, j >$, using the argument about cycles as a pretext for our inability to solve an interesting programming problem!)

If all activities start as soon as possible, each event i occurs at its *earliest event* time, $ee(i)$. In our example, we have:

$$ee(1) = 0$$
$$ee(2) = 45$$
$$ee(3) = 80$$
$$ee(4) = 20$$

Note that even for this very simple project we have to be careful. We cannot take just any path from event 1 to event 3, but we have to work out the longest path, or, as we say, the *critical path*, which consists of activities $< 1, 4 >$ and $< 4, 3 >$.

In general, we have $ee(i) = 0$ for all events that have no predecessor. If event j has one or more predecessors its earliest event time $ee(j)$ is the maximum value of

$$ee(i) + \text{duration of } < i, j >$$

where all immediate predecessors i of event j are to be considered. To compute these values efficiently we traverse all events in a topological order (1, 4, 2, 3 in the example), using an algorithm similar to the one on which program TOPOL.C in Section 8.3 was based. We therefore also use similar data structures, that is, array a for the events and adjacency lists with a node for each activity (see Fig. 8.7).

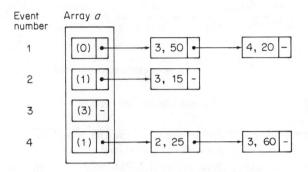

Fig. 8.7. Adjacency lists for the network of Fig. 8.6

For each activity its duration is stored in its node. (Remember that each activity, that is, each edge in the activity network, uniquely corresponds to a node of an adjacency list.) Again, the parenthesized integers in the array elements $a[i]$ denote the in-degree of vertex i, and are called $a[i].count$ in the program. Though not included in Fig. 8.7, the elements of array a are extended with two integer fields, $a[i].ee$ (earliest event) and $a[i].le$ (latest event, to be discussed shortly). Initially, all fields ee are set to zero. We now traverse the events in a topological order, using a linked stack and each time deleting events that have no predecessor. However, we do not destroy the fields ee and le as we are deleting events. When dealing with event i we update the earliest event times of all its successors j. Using the notation $ee(i)$ as an abbreviation for $a[i].ee$, we test, for each of these successors, if the sum

$$ee(i) + \text{duration of } <i, j>$$

is greater than the current value of $ee(j)$, and, if so, we assign that greater value to $ee(j)$. The greatest value of all earliest event times thus computed is the time needed for the entire project.

In the example of Fig. 8.6 we see that the activities $<1, 3>$, $<4, 2>$, $<2, 3>$ do not lie on the critical path (1, 4, 3). It is not absolutely necessary for them to begin as early as possible. For example, the activity $<2, 3>$ may begin as late as 15 days before the completion time (80) of the entire project, so instead of at time $ee(2) = 45$ we may start at time 65, without any danger of delaying the project (provided that all duration times are exact values instead of estimates). Again focusing on the events, rather than on the activities, we can compute their latest event times $le(i)$. The value of $le(i)$ is the minimum value of

$$le(j) - \text{duration of } <i, j>$$

where all immediate successors j of event i are to be considered. We compute the latest event times in a backward scan, which is analogous to the forward scan in which we computed the earliest event times. We therefore need *inverted adjacency lists*, as shown in Fig. 8.8.

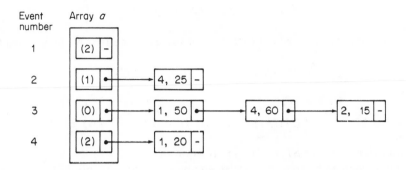

Fig. 8.8. Inverted adjacency lists for the network of Fig. 8.6

We will use the same array *a* as before. The nodes of the old adjacency lists were deleted when we were computing the earliest event times. (Recall that the earliest event times themselves are stored in array *a*, so we did not destroy them when we were deleting the adjacency lists.) We now build the inverted adjacency lists. In the new situation each array element *a*[*j*] contains the start pointer of a linear list in which the numbers of all predecessors *i* of event *j* are stored. Each node of the list starting at *a*[*j*].*link* corresponds to an activity $< i, j >$. A parenthesized integer *a*[*j*].*count* denotes the *out-degree* of vertex *j*, that is, the number of immediate successors of vertex *j*. Initially, we set all fields *le* to the time needed for the entire project, and we form a linked stack of all events that have no successor. Working with this stack in the same way as in the forward scan we deal with all events in a reverse topological order, and, when dealing with event *j*, we update the latest event time of all its predecessors *i* as follows.

If the difference

$$le(j) - \text{duration of } < i, j >$$

is less than the current value of $le(i)$ we assign that difference to $le(i)$. After this backward scan, we have computed both the earliest and the latest event times of all events, and we can find them in array *a*. However, in the program output we prefer to present these results in connection with the activities they are associated with rather that with the events. For every activity $< i, j >$, with duration *d*, we define its *earliest start time EST(i, j)*, its *earliest completion time ECT(i, j)*, its *latest start time LST*(i, j), and its *latest completion time LCT(i, j)* as follows:

$$EST(i, j) = ee(i)$$
$$ECT(i, j) = ee(i) + d$$
$$LST(i, j) = le(j) - d$$
$$LCT(i, j) = le(j)$$

The meaning of these quantities are as their names indicate. For example, *LST* denotes the latest time the activity may start without delaying the completion time of the entire project. If, for some activity, the earliest start time is equal to the latest start time, then that activity is said to lie on a *critical path*. We also define the (*free*) *slack* as

$$SLACK(i,\ j)\ =\ LST(i,\ j)-EST(i,\ j)$$

Thus, any activity on a critical path has zero slack. Note that we may instead define

$$SLACK(i,\ j)\ =\ LCT(i,\ j)-ECT(i,\ j),$$

since we have

$$LST(i,\ j)\ -\ EST(i,\ j)\ =\ \{le(j)-d\}-ee(i)$$

$$LCT(i,\ j)\ -\ ECT(i,\ j)\ =\ le(j)-\{ee(i)+d)\}$$

so both expressions for $SLACK(i, j)$ are equivalent.

We now want to write a program to compute all these quantities for a given project. For each activity of a project we will read the two relevant event numbers, the duration and a description, from a file. For example, this file may have the following contents for the network shown in Fig. 8.6:

```
1   3    50 Place order A
1   4    20 Build B
4   2    25 Test B
2   3    15 Fix errors
4   3    60 User's guide
```

With data in some file we want the program to inquire the name of this file and then to produce the following output:

I	J	DUR	EST	LST	ECT	LCT	SLACK		DESCRIPTION
1	3	50	0	30	50	80	30		Place order A
1	4	20	0	0	20	20	0	<--	Build B
4	2	25	20	40	45	65	20		Test B
2	3	15	45	65	60	80	20		Fix errors
4	3	60	20	20	80	80	0	<--	User's guide

Lines with an arrow pointing to a slack value 0 denote activities lying on a critical path. The order in which the activities are listed is based on the input file. We read this file in a third scan (after the two scans for the computation of ee and le), and we copy each line, extended with the computed items found in array a. In this way we need not store all descriptions in main memory: in the first and the second scan we simply skip them, and in the third scan we print each description immediately after reading it, which in case of a large project saves a good deal of memory space. In real critical path programs we can usually specify other orders as well, such as, for example, according to increasing slack; after our discussion of some sorting methods in Chapter 2, this should not be a difficult problem. The above output has actually been produced by program CPM.C, listed below.

```
/* CPM.C: Critical Path Method.
          The program asks for an input file, containing
          a line for each activity with two (integer)
          event numbers, a duration (integer), and an
          optional description. The range of the event
          numbers influences the amount of memory needed;
```

apart from this, there are no limitations
imposed on the number of events or on the way
they are numbered, nor are there any
restrictions to the number of activities or
their order in the input file, except for memory
limitations of the machine on which the program
runs. If the available amount of memory should
be exceeded, or if the network should contain a
cycle, the program gives an error message and
stops.

```c
*/
#include <stdio.h>
struct activity { int num, dur; struct activity *next; };
struct event
     { int count, ee, le; struct activity *link; };

main()
{ FILE *fp;
  char filnam[25], descript[80], *malloc();
  int n, i, j, k, I, J, t1, d, start, first=1, minim,
      maxim, min1, max1, tmax=0, est, lst, ect, lct,
      slack;
  struct event *a;
  struct activity *p, *p1;
  printf("Input file: "); scanf("%s", filnam);
  fp = fopen(filnam, "r");
  if (fp == NULL) error("File not available");

  /* Determine least and greatest event number: */
  while (fscanf(fp, "%d %d %d", &I, &J, &d) == 3)
  { fgets(descript, 80, fp); /* Skip text, if any */
    if (I < J) { min1 = I; max1 = J; }
           else { min1 = J; max1 = I; }
    if (first)
    { minim = min1; maxim = max1; first = 0;
    } else
    { if (min1 < minim) minim = min1;
      if (max1 > maxim) maxim = max1;
    }
  }
  fclose(fp);
  n = maxim - minim + 1;
  a = (struct event *)malloc(n * sizeof(struct event));
  if (a == NULL) error("Event-number range too large");
  for (i=0; i<n; i++)
  { a[i].count = -2; a[i].ee = 0;
    a[i].link = NULL;
  }

  /* Build adjacency lists: */
  fp = fopen(filnam, "r");
  while (fscanf(fp, "%d %d %d", &I, &J, &d) == 3)
  { fgets(descript, 80, fp); /* Skip text, if any */
    i = I - minim; j = J - minim;
    if (a[i].count == -2) a[i].count = 0;
    if (a[j].count == -2) a[j].count = 0;
    p =
    (struct activity *)malloc(sizeof(struct activity));
    if (p == NULL) error("Not enough memory");
    p->num = j; p->dur = d; p->next = a[i].link;
```

```
    a[i].link = p;
    a[j].count++;
  }
  fclose(fp);

  /* Form a linked stack of events that have no
     predecessors:
  */
  start = -1;
  for (i=0; i<n; i++)
    if (a[i].count==0)
    { a[i].count = start; start = i;
    }

  /* Compute earliest event time (ee) for each node: */
  for (i=0; i<n; i++)
  { while (a[i].count == -2) i++;
    if (start == -1) error("There is a cycle");
    j = start; start = a[j].count; p = a[j].link;
    while (p != NULL)
    { k = p->num;
      a[k].count--;
      t1 = a[j].ee + p->dur;
      if (t1 > a[k].ee) a[k].ee = t1;
      if (t1 > tmax) tmax = t1;
      if (a[k].count == 0)
      { a[k].count = start; start = k;
      }
      p1 = p->next;
      if (p1 == NULL) p = NULL; else {*p = *p1; free(p1);}
    }
  }

  /* Build inverted adjacency lists: */
  for (j=0; j<n; j++)
    if (a[j].count != -2)
    { a[j].le = tmax; a[j].count = 0; a[j].link = NULL;
    }
  fp = fopen(filnam, "r");
  while (fscanf(fp, "%d %d %d", &I, &J, &d) == 3)
  { fgets(descript, 80, fp); /* Skip text, if any */
    i = I - minim; j = J - minim;
    p =
    (struct activity *)malloc(sizeof(struct activity));

    if (p == NULL) error("Not enough memory");
    p->num = i; p->dur = d; p->next = a[j].link;
    a[j].link = p;
    a[i].count++;
  }
  fclose(fp);

  /* Form a linked stack of nodes that have no
     successors:
  */
  start = -1;
  for (j=0; j<n; j++)
    if (a[j].count == 0)
    { a[j].count = start; start = j;
    }
```

```
/* Compute latest event time (le) for each node: */
for (j=0; j<n; j++)
{ while (a[j].count == -2) i++;
  i = start; start = a[i].count; p = a[i].link;
  while (p != NULL)
  { k = p->num; a[k].count--;
    t1 = a[i].le - p->dur;
    if (t1 < a[k].le) a[k].le = t1;
    if (a[k].count == 0)
    { a[k].count = start; start = k;
    }
    p1 = p->next;
    if (p1 == NULL) p = NULL; else {*p = *p1; free(p1);}
  }
}

printf("Output:\n\n\n\n");
printf("%3s %3s %4s %5s %4s %5s %4s  %s\n\n",
  "I", "J", "DUR", "EST", "LST", "ECT", "LCT",
  "SLACK     DESCRIPTION");
fp = fopen(filnam, "r");
while (fscanf(fp, "%d %d %d", &I, &J, &d) == 3)
{ fgets(descript, 80, fp); /* Read text, if any */
  i = I - minim; j = J - minim;
  est = a[i].ee; lct = a[j].le;
  ect = est + d; lst = lct - d; slack = lst - est;
  printf("%3d %3d %4d %5d %4d %5d %4d %5d %3s %s",
       I, J, d, est, lst, ect, lct, slack,
       slack ? "   "  :  "<--", descript);
}
fclose(fp);
}

error(str) char *str;
{ printf("Error: %s\n", str); exit(1);
}
```

EXERCISES

8.1 If we require i to be less than j for all edges $< i, j >$ in a directed graph then the graph will have no cycles and we can easily find a topological order of all vertices. Write a program to demonstrate this. Do not use adjacency lists or an adjacency matrix.

8.2 Write a simple CPM program in the spirit of Exercise 8.1, allowing only activities $< i, j >$ with $i < j$.

8.3 Replace the tabular output of program CPM.C with graphical output in the form of line segments for the activities, each having a length proportional to its duration and placed in its proper position based on a horizontal time axis.

8.4 Extend program CPM.C, so that, in the case of a cycle, the vertex numbers of the cycle are printed.

8.5 Write a program which, for any directed graph, lists all vertices that are (not necessarily immediate) successors of a given vertex. The input data for this program consist of a file with a pair $< i, j >$ for each edge, as shown at the end of Section 8.3, along with a number entered on the keyboard, denoting the vertex whose successors are desired.

CHAPTER 9

Fundamentals of Interpreters and Compilers

This chapter deals with a well-defined infinite set of character strings that represent arithmetic expressions. In formal language theory such a set of strings (not necessarily consisting of arithmetic expressions) is called a *language*, so this word has a special technical meaning, to be distinguished from what we call a 'language' in everyday life. Whether or not a given string belongs to the language in question is determined by certain formation rules, also called *grammar* or *syntax rules*. For example, the C language can be defined as the set of all possible C programs. In this case, and for programming languages in general, there are also *semantic rules*, which define the actions to be performed when the programs are executed. We shall define a 'Very Simple Language' ourselves, and call it *VSL*. It is not just a language in the sense of formal language theory but each element of the language is a simple arithmetic expression with a very clear meaning, namely a computation in accordance with elementary arithmetic and resulting in an integer. Although it may be rather pretentious, we shall talk about VSL *programs*. Our goal will be to *implement* this new language, or, as we may say, we are interested in VSL *implementations*. As may be expected in this book, we shall present such implementations in the form of C programs. Depending on how they work, we call the latter programs either *interpreters* or *compilers*.

The present chapter is included in this book for two reasons. First, as we use real interpreters and compilers quite often, it is good to have an idea about how they work, and basic principles are always best explained by simple examples, hence our Very Simple Language. Second, there are computer applications where we want the user to enter some arithmetic expression, so that the program can read this character by character and subsequently either interpret it or convert it to some internal format. This chapter will be helpful in developing programs for such applications.

9.1 SYNTAX DIAGRAMS FOR A VERY SIMPLE LANGUAGE

The very simple language (VSL) that we will deal with consists of VSL programs, of which the following three expressions are examples:

{3 - 5}

```
{1 - 2 * ((9 - 5 + 1 - 2 * 3) - 2)}

{8}
```

A VSL program is written as an expression, as defined below, surrounded by a pair
of braces { } An expression consists of one or more terms separated by adding and
subtracting operators (+ and −). Similarly, each term consists of one or more factors,
separated by multiplication operators (*). Finally, each factor consists of either a one-
digit integer or an expression surrounded by parentheses. A verbal description like this
would do for VSL but not for a real programming language. We therefore normally use
a more formal means for syntactic definitions, such as a set of *syntax diagrams*. Figure
9.1 shows syntax diagrams for VSL.

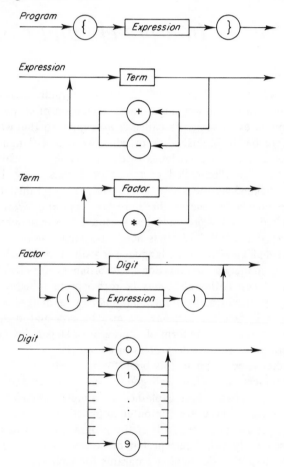

Fig. 9.1. Syntax diagrams for VSL

(It will be clear that in the last diagram we have used three dots to denote the remaining
seven digits 2, 3, 4, 5, 6, 7, 8.) The first diagram says that a program consists of three
components, namely an opening brace '{', an expression, and a closing brace '}', in that
order. Symbols such as '{' in

are *primitive* or *terminal symbols*: they may occur literally in a program, whereas names such as *expression* in

| Expression |

denote *syntactic categories*, also known as *non-terminal symbols*. In a complete set of syntax diagrams (such as Fig. 9.1) there is a syntax diagram for every non-terminal symbol that is used.

Although the language is very simple, VSL programs can be quite complex, such as, for example,

```
{((1 + 8 * (9 - 1) * 5 - (2 +( 3 * 4))) *
(7 - (3 - 1)) + 1) * 2}
```

This is so because of the recursive nature of the syntax diagrams: indirectly, we define an expression in terms of itself, since an expression contains a term, a term contains a factor, and a factor may again contain an expression. It is therefore quite natural to use recursive functions when we are writing a program to process expressions, as the next section will show. We have not explicitly discussed any precedence rules for the three operators +, −, *, but the above syntactic descriptions, both in words and in syntax diagrams, clearly suggest that * has higher precedence than + and −. After all, a term is composed of factors, not the other way round. For example, since each of the following two lines denotes a term:

```
2 * 4 * 1
7 * 5
```

and because terms are separated by + and −, the line

```
2 * 4 * 1 + 7 * 5
```

represents an expression consisting of two terms separated by +. This makes it clear that this expression is to be read as

```
(2 * 4 * 1) + (7 * 5),
```

not, for example, as

```
(2 * 4 * 1 + 7) * 5.
```

Incidentally, the latter form would be the correct interpretation if * and + had equal precedence.

We can represent our expressions as binary trees, as Fig. 9.2 shows. This tree clearly shows that the minus operator is to be applied to the terms 2 * 3 and 4 * 5.

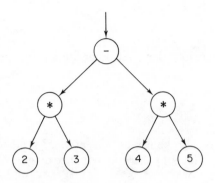

Fig. 9.2. Binary tree for 2 * 3 − 4 * 5

Note that we are using only *binary* operators, so

{2 * 3 − 4 * 5}

must not be written

{−4 * 5 + 2 * 3}

because we do not implement the *unary* operator −, used in the last line. Another point worth observing is that our operators are *left-associative*. This is relevant for operators with the same precedence, as + and − in our language VSL. For example, the expression

$$9-3+1$$

means

$$(9-3)+1,$$

not

$$9-(3+1).$$

We can see the difference between the second and the third of these three expressions very clearly by examining their binary trees. Since 9−3+1 and (9−3)+1 have exactly the same meaning, they correspond to the same binary tree, shown in Fig. 9.3(a). The tree for the expression 9−(3+1) is different, as Fig. 9.3(b) shows.

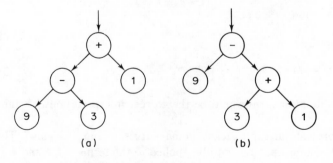

Fig. 9.3. Binary trees for (a) 9 − 3 + 1; (b) 9 − (3 + 1)

9.2   A SOURCE-TEXT INTERPRETER

When designing a programming language we have to define it not only *syntactically* but also *semantically*. The latter means that we must clearly say what each valid language construct means in terms of the operations to be performed. In our case the language is so simple that the meaning of every VSL program is rather obvious. We want the given expression to be evaluated according to the usual arithmetic rules and the resulting integer to be printed. For example, the program

    {9 - 2 * 4}

means that the product of 2 and 4 is to be subtracted from 9 and that the resulting value, 1, is to be printed.

In this section we shall write a C program which accepts any VSL program and performs the actions prescribed by it, so with the VSL program {9−2 * 4} as input the output of our C program will be 1. We shall call this C program an *interpreter*, and, more specifically, a *source-text* interpreter, since it will *immediately* interpret the given VSL program (which we call *source-text*, to distinguish it from any code derived from it). We shall write a function for each of the three syntactic categories *expression, term, factor*. Each of these functions has a well-defined task, which can be expressed in terms of its input data and its returned value. For example, the function *factor* is to read one factor from an input file, and it is to return the value of that factor. So it must be able to read not only a very simple factor, such as, for example, 5, but also a complex one, such as

    (3 - 4 * 5 - (3 + 6 * 2))

Because of the outermost parentheses this is really a factor, as defined in Section 9.1. Note that the function *factor* reads a sequence of characters but returns an integer. Thus, expressed in the C language, if, for example, it reads the factor consisting of only the character '5' then it returns the integer

$$\text{'5'} - \text{'0'} = 5$$

In case of the above more complex factor, it returns

$$3 - 20 - 15 = -32$$

Although in the input each integer consists only of one decimal digit the output can be any integer, such as -32 in the last example. If the input is incorrect, we shall print an error message and stop program execution. Blanks and newline characters will be allowed in the input, which enables us to write VSL programs of more than one line. It will be convenient to read one character ahead; for example, when function *term* is called, the first character of the term in question will already have been read and placed in the global variable *buf*. So the functions *expression, term,* and *factor* assume that the first character to be used is available in *buf*, and, before returning, they also place the next character in this global variable. Program INTERPR.C shows further details; it should be studied in connection with the syntax diagrams in Section 9.1.

```c
/* INTERPR.C: A source-text interpreter for VSL
*/
#include <stdio.h>
FILE *fp;
char buf;

main()
{ char filnam[25];
  int x;
  printf(
  "This program reads an input file, containing\n");
  printf(
  "a VSL program, such as, for example, {3-2*5}\n\n");
  printf("Name-of input file: "); scanf("%s", filnam);
  fp = fopen(filnam, "r");
  if (fp == NULL) error("File not available");
  printf("\nVSL program read from file:\n\n");
  if (nextchar() != '{') error("Open brace ({) expected");
  buf = nextchar();
  x = expression();
  printf("\n\nComputed value: %d\n", x);
  if (buf != '}') error("Close brace (}) expected");
  fclose(fp);
}

int nextchar()
{ int ch;
  do
  { ch = getc(fp);
    if (ch == EOF) error("End of file reached");
    putchar(ch);
  } while (ch == ' ' || ch == '\n');
  return ch;
}

error(str) char *str;
{ printf("\nError: %s\n", str); exit(1);
}

int expression()
{ int x, y;
  char optor;
  x = term();
  while (buf == '+' || buf == '-')
  { optor = buf; buf = nextchar(); y = term();
    if (optor == '+') x += y; else x -= y;
  }
  return x;
}

int term()
{ int x;
  x = factor();
  while (buf == '*')
  { buf = nextchar();
    x *= factor();
  }
  return x;
}
```

```
int factor()
{ int x;
  if (buf >= '0' && buf <= '9') x = buf - '0'; else
  if (buf == '(')
  { buf = nextchar();
    x = expression();
    if (buf != ')') error("')' expected");
  } else error("Digit or '(' expected");
  buf = nextchar();
  return x;
}
```

Program INTERPR.C reads a VSL program from a file prepared by the user, and it also prints each character read from this file, so in the following demonstration we need not list the contents of file TEST separately:

```
This program reads an input file, containing
a VSL program, such as, for example, {3-2*5}

Name of input file: TEST
VSL program read from file:

{ 2
  + 3 * 4 * (7 - 2 - 1)
  - (1 + 2)
}

Computed value: 47
```

9.3   CONVERSION FROM INFIX TO POSTFIX

We usually place a binary operator *between* its two operands, as, for example, in $8-3$, and we call this *infix* notation. Instead, we may place the same operator either before or after its operands, and we use the terms *prefix* and *postfix* for these notations. Thus we have:

$$
\begin{array}{lll}
- \ 8 \ 3 & \text{prefix} \\
8 \ - \ 3 & \text{infix} \\
8 \ 3 \ - & \text{postfix}
\end{array}
$$

The usual notation of functions with arguments is essentially prefix notation; for example, if we define the function *subtract* and write

$$subtract(8, 3)$$

to represent the difference $8-3 = 5$, we can regard the function name *subtract* as an operator, written before the operands 8 and 3. However, in the framework of compiler construction we are more interested in postfix notation, which, incidentally, is also known as *reverse Polish*. Postfix expressions can be evaluated very straightforwardly, as Section 9.4 will show. For the time being, let us assume that they are useful and that it therefore makes sense to perform automatic conversion from infix to postfix. If an infix expression is represented by a binary tree, as shown in Figs 9.2 and 9.3, we can find the corresponding postfix expression by traversing this tree (and its subtrees) as follows:

(1) Traverse the left subtree.
(2) Traverse the right subtree.
(3) Use the root node of the (sub-)tree.

For example, if we apply this to the left and the right subtrees in Fig. 9.2, we obtain 2 3 * and 4 5 *, respectively. Applying the method to the entire tree, we find the postfix expression

   2   3   *   4   5   *   −

Note that we do not need any parentheses in postfix notation. For example, Figs 9.3(a) and 9.3(b) lead to:

Infix	Postfix
9−3+ 1	9 3−1+
9−(3+1)	9 3 1+−

Fortunately, it will not be necessary to build a real binary tree because we do not need all information in the tree at the same time. However, we shall use recursion, which is closely related to trees, as we have seen in Section 1.5.

The basic idea of our method is quite simple. Let us focus on a term, which in infix has the form

$$f_1 * f_2 * f_3 * \ldots * f_n$$

where $f_1, \ldots, f_n$ are factors. To transform this into postfix, all we need is a function (to be called *term*) which reads this from an input file and writes the desired form

$$f_1 f_2 * f_3 * \ldots f_n *$$

to an output file. So first we have to copy factor f_1, which is always present. If an asterisk follows, we read it, but we postpone writing it until we have copied f_2; in other words, we read * f_2 and write f_2 *. Similarly, if an asterisk follows, we read * f_3 and we write f_3 *, and so on. If we again use a global variable *buf* (see program INTERPR.C in Section 9.2) and assume that *fpout* is the file pointer associated with the output file, we can write this function *term* as follows:

```
term()
{ factor();
  while (buf == '*')
  { buf = nextchar();
    factor(); putc('*', fpout);
  }
}
```

This function really does what we have said above, provided that function *factor*, used here, performs its copying task properly. If the factor to be copied is a only a digit, it is to be copied literally. For example, if the input is

```
3 * 8,
```

the digit 3 is copied by the first call of *factor*, before the while-loop is entered. In the inner part of the loop there is another call of *factor*, which copies 8. The important point to be noticed is that the asterisk is read before copying 8, but is written after it, so that the output is

```
3 8 *
```

In the case of more complex factors they must not be copied literally, but, instead, they must in turn be converted from infix to postfix. For example, if one of these factors is read as

```
(9 - 5)
```

it is to be written as

```
9 5 -
```

So we do not write the parentheses in the output, and we deal with the remaining infix expression 9−5 in a way that is similar to the way we would deal with 9 * 5. Program POSTFIX.C shows further details.

```
/* POSTFIX.C:
      Conversion from infix to postfix; the program
      reads a VSL program, which has the form

          { expression }

      The given expression is converted postfix, and
      written to another file. The names of both files
      are to be supplied by the user.
*/
#include <stdio.h>
FILE *fpin, *fpout;
char buf;

main()
{ char filnam[25];
   int ch;
   printf(
   "This program reads an input file, containing\n");
   printf(
   "a VSL program, such as, for example, {3-2*5}\n\n");
   printf("Name of input file:  "); scanf("%s", filnam);
   fpin = fopen(filnam, "r");
   if (fpin == NULL) error("File not available");
   printf("Name of output file: "); scanf("%s", filnam);
   fpout = fopen(filnam, "w");
   printf("\nVSL program read from file:\n\n");
```

```
    if (nextchar() != '{') error("Open brace ({) expected");
    buf = nextchar();
    expression();
    if (buf != '}') error("Close brace (}) expected");
    fclose(fpin); fclose(fpout);
    printf("\n\nContents of output file (postfix):\n");
    fpout = fopen(filnam, "r");
    while (ch = getc(fpout), ch > 0) putchar(ch);
    fclose(fpout);
}

int nextchar()
{ int ch;
  do
  { ch = getc(fpin);
    if (ch == EOF) error("End of file reached");
    putchar(ch);
  } while (ch == ' ' || ch == '\n');
  return ch;
}

error(str) char *str;
{ printf("\nError: %s\n", str); exit(1);
}

expression()
{ char optor;
  term();
  while (buf == '+' || buf == '-')
  { optor = buf; buf = nextchar();
    term(); putc(optor, fpout);
  }
}

term()
{ factor();
  while (buf == '*')
  { buf = nextchar();
    factor(); putc('*', fpout);
  }
}

factor()
{ if (buf >= '0' && buf <= '9') putc(buf, fpout); else
  if (buf == '(')
  { buf = nextchar();
    expression();
    if (buf != ')') error("')' expected");
  } else error("Digit or '(' expected");
  buf = nextchar();
}
```

The results are first placed in an output file, which we will use in Section 9.4. Then they are copied to the screen, so that we can immediately see what the result is. There are only digits and operators in the output file, no white-space characters. This causes no ambiguity at all because all integers in VSL consist of only one digit. Thus, in the following demonstration, 34 stands for the two integers 3 and 4:

This program reads an input file, containing
a VSL program, such as, for example, {3-2*5}

Name of input file: infix.txt
Name of output file: postfix.txt

VSL program read from file:

{ 3 * 4 - 5 * 6 - 7 * (4 + 2 + 2) }

Contents of output file (postfix):
34*56*-742+2+*-

9.4 A POSTFIX INTERPRETER

It is now time to see why postfix expressions are useful. In Section 9.3 we did not compute the integer values associated with the given infix expressions. Instead, we produced postfix expressions, and these might seem to be no good if we want the integer values, as computed in Section 9.2. We shall now discuss how to evaluate postfix expressions, and we will see that this can be done extremely simply. The main tool to be used is a *stack*. Scanning a given postfix expression from left to right, we place each operand (which, in our case, is a one-digit integer) on this stack, so that each time the stack height increases by 1. Whenever, during this scan, we encounter an operator, denoting some operation, we apply this operation to the two most recent operands on the stack, and the result of that operation will replace these two operands, so that the stack height decreases by 1. For example, with the VSL program

{5 - 3 - 4 - 7 * 3}

as input, program POSTFIX.C gives the postfix expression

53-4-73*-

as output, and this gives rise to the successive stack contents shown in Fig. 9.4.

						3		
	3		4		7	7	21	
5	5	2	2	-2	-2	-2	-2	-23

*Fig. 9.4. Successive stack contents, when evaluating 53 − 4 − 73 * −*

In each column we find the stack elements $s[0]$, $s[1]$, ..., from bottom to top. We begin with $s[0] = 5$, as shown in the first column. Then 3, the second character of the postfix expression, is placed in $s[1]$, as the second column shows. We now encounter the minus operator $(-)$ in the postfix expression, so we compute

$$5-3 = 2$$

and place the result in $s[0]$ (see the third column) so that it replaces the values 5 and 3. The important thing is that if we proceed in this way we end with $s[0] = -23$, which is just the value we want as the result of the given VSL program. Thus, if $s[t]$ is the next free stack location each integer i in the postfix expression will be pushed on the stack as follows:

```
s[t++] = i;
```

Also, each operator $+$, $-$, or $*$ performs an operation symbolically denoted by

```
t--; s[t-1] .= s[t];
```

where the dot (.) denotes one of the above three operators. In every (infix or postfix) expression with only binary operators the number of operators is one less than the number of operands. For example, in the above expression we have five operands and four operators. Each operand causes the stack pointer t to be increased by one and each operator causes it to be decreased by one. Altogether, this means that the final value of t is one higher than its initial value. So if initially we have $t = 0$, then we end with $t = 1$. The latter implies that $s[1]$ is the next free location, so the result is s[0]. We shall assume that there is a file with a correct postfix expression, produced by program POSTFIX.C. Then program POSTINT.C is a postfix interpreter, which reads the given file and computes the desired integer result.

```
/* POSTINT.C:
      A postfix interpreter, which interprets the
      postfix expression produced by POSTFIX.C.
*/
#include <stdio.h>
#define STACKSIZE 20
int t, s[STACKSIZE]; /*  Initially, t = 0  */

main()
{ FILE *fp;
  int ch;
  char filnam[25];
  printf("Name of input file (postfix): ");
  scanf("%s", filnam);
  fp = fopen(filnam, "r");
  if (fp == NULL) error("File not available");
  printf("The given postfix expression is:\n");
  while (ch = getc(fp), ch > 0)
  { putchar(ch);
    if (ch >= '0' && ch <= '9') push(ch-'0'); else
    if (ch == '+') add(); else
    if (ch == '-') subtract(); else
    if (ch == '*') multiply(); else break;
  }
  if (t != 1) error("Incorrect postfix expression");
  printf("\nComputed result: %d\n", s[0]);
  fclose(fp);
}

push(i) int i;
{ if (t == STACKSIZE)
    error(
    "STACKSIZE too small for this postfix expression");
    s[t++] = i;
```

```
}

add()
{ t--; s[t-1] += s[t];
}

subtract()
{ t--; s[t-1] -= s[t];
}

multiply()
{ t--; s[t-1] *= s[t];
}

error(str) char *str;
{ printf("\n\nError: %s\n", str); exit(1);
}
```

Let us use the last example of Section 9.3 to demonstrate this program. Recall that our VSL program was

```
{ 3 * 4 - 5 * 6 - 7 * (4 + 2 + 2) }
```

so we eventually have to compute:

$$12 - 30 - 7 * 8 = -74$$

Executing program POSTINT.C, and supplying the file POSTFIX.TXT, produced by program POSTFIX.C on the basis of this example, we obtain this desired result:

```
Name of input file (postfix): postfix.txt
The given postfix expression is:
34*56*-742+2+*-
Computed result: -74
```

It will be clear that we can combine the programs POSTFIX.C and POSTINT.C, and it is then not difficult to develop a program that we can use in the same way as IN-TERPR.C in Section 9.2. Program INTERPR.C interprets the source code immediately, whereas the combined new program uses a postfix expression as intermediate code. For a real programming language, the latter method is more efficient. Real interpreters usually first produce some intermediate code, which subsequently is interpreted. This has the advantage that in loops, where the same type of computation is done repeatedly, the relatively time-consuming task of processing the original source text and performing all kinds of syntactic checks is done only once; after this stage we have intermediate code available, which can be interpreted more rapidly than the source text. However, if we are not dealing with a complete programming language, but if, instead, we only have to interpret arithmetic expressions (even though these may be more realistic than those in VSL) it is not particularly advantageous to use postfix expressions as intermediate code, so direct interpreting the source text, in the spirit of Section 9.2, should be seriously considered.

9.5   OBJECT PROGRAM AND RUN-TIME SYSTEM

In the previous section we saw that there may be good reasons to separate the actual computation from the syntactic analysis, and to interpret intermediate code rather than the given source code. We can go a significant step further in this direction. Instead of generating intermediate code that has to be interpreted we can generate executable code, consisting of real program text. Traditionally, a real compiler translates a program from source text into machine code. However, some compilers produce programs in assembly language, which subsequently is converted into machine code by an assembler. Such an automatically generated assembly-language program is not the same as machine code, but its purpose is similar, and it is fundamentally different from intermediate code that is to be interpreted, as we did in Section 9.4. Although the task of converting it to machine code is delegated to an assembler (which relieves the task of the compiler), its eventual form will be an autonomous program, which has full control over the machine. Note that this is not the case when we are using an interpreter; the intermediate code then acts merely as input data; we do not transfer control to it. Thus, the distinction between an interpreter and a (code-generating) compiler can be summarized as follows.

An interpreter keeps control over the machine, and performs actions prescribed by its input data, which are either source text or intermediate code; a compiler, on the other hand, produces code that will eventually result in an independent program. Let us use the term *object program* for such code, even though it has not the form of machine code yet. Before writing a compiler to produce object programs we have to think about the structure of these object programs themselves. To keep our discussion machine-independent, we will not use real assembly language (let alone machine code), but instead, our object programs will consist of C text. This might seem odd, since C is a high-level language, and, indeed, it would be no good to transform a VSL program into a almost identical C program. However, our object program in C will have the structure of an assembly-language program. For example, the VSL program

```
{ 9 - 2 * 4 + 5 }
```

written in postfix notation as

```
9 2 4 * - 5 +
```

will be translated into the following object program:

```
/* OBJECT.C: Sample object program
*/
main()
{
  push(9);
  push(2);
  push(4);
  multiply();
  subtract();
  push(5);
  add();
  printresult();
}
```

Note the resemblance between this and the above postfix expression. This object program is in fact a syntactically correct C module, which can be compiled by any C compiler. So instead of making our VSL compiler produce assembly language to be processed by a standard assembler, we will make it produce C language, to be processed by a standard C compiler. An object module such as OBJECT.C has the same structure as an assembly-language module which consist only of subroutine calls, so with some imagination we may consider our object programs to be expressed in a machine-independent assembly language, which in turn is only a means of presenting machine code in a reasonably readable form. Thus, our object modules, though formally expressed in C for reasons of readability, are not essentially different from machine code.

To form a ready-to-run program we have to supply an additional program module, which we call a *run-time system*. We will express this in C, too, but again, we will be using only very simple and low-level language concepts, so, like object modules, run-time system RTS.C may be regarded as being expressed in a readable form of machine code:

```
/* RTS.C: A run-time system for VSL
*/

#define STACKSIZE 20
int t, s[STACKSIZE]; /*  Initially, t = 0  */

push(i) int i;
{ if (t == STACKSIZE)
    error(
    "STACKSIZE too small for this postfix expression");
    s[t++] = i;
}

add()
{ t--; s[t-1] += s[t];
}

subtract()
{ t--; s[t-1] -= s[t];
}

multiply()
{ t--; s[t-1] *= s[t];
}

error(str) char *str;
{ printf("\n\nError: %s\n", str); exit(1);
}

printresult()
{ if (t != 1) error("Incorrect object program");
    printf("Result: %d\n", s[0]);
}
```

If we compile object program OBJECT.C and we link it together with the compiled version of RTS.C, we obtain an executable program, which, when executed, gives the output:

```
Result: 6
```

It should be noted that our run-time system does not depend on the particular VSL program that we are dealing with. It need therefore be compiled only once, so its compiled version, say RTS.OBJ, is a constant component, whereas for each VSL program that we want to deal with we have to generate a program OBJECT.C, the variable component. The name we chose for the latter reflects that it is an object program generated by our VSL compiler, to be discussed in Section 9.6. (Formally speaking, the 'object program' OBJECT.C is a source program for the standard C compiler. This might seem confusing, but we should not forget that we are expressing our 'object programs' in C merely for reasons of readability. If, instead, we had been expressing them immediately in machine language then we would have avoided any confusion of this kind.)

9.6   A VSL COMPILER

There is only one thing that remains to be done, namely translating a given VSL program, such as

```
{ 9 - 2 * 4 + 5 }
```

into the corresponding object program, such as OBJECT.C in Section 9.5. Since this object program is essentially a postfix expression, such as

```
9 2 4 * - 5 +
```

in a different notation, and since in Section 9.3 we have already written program POST-FIX.C to produce postfix, our remaining task is extremely simple. All we have to do is to alter the code-generating parts of POSTFIX.C. In this way, we obtain:

```
/* COMPILER.C:
        This program reads a VSL program, and translates it
        into the VSL object program OBJECT.C. The latter is
        a C program with the structure of an assembly-
        language program. After compiling OBJECT.C by a
        standard C compiler, it is to be linked together
        with the compiled version of RTS.C, see Section 9.5.
        Program COMPILER.C has been derived from POSTFIX.C,
        discussed in Section 9.3.
*/
#include <stdio.h>
FILE *fpin, *fpout;
char buf;

main()
{ char filnam[25];
  int ch;
  printf(
  "This program reads an input file, containing\n");
  printf(
  "a VSL program, such as, for example, {3-2*5}\n\n");
  printf("Name of input file:   "); scanf("%s", filnam);
  fpin = fopen(filnam, "r");
  if (fpin == NULL) error("File not available");
  fpout = fopen("OBJECT.C", "w");
  fprintf(fpout, "main()\n{\n");
```

```
     printf("\nVSL program read from file:\n\n");
     if (nextchar() != '{') error("Open brace ({) expected");
     buf = nextchar();
     expression();
     fprintf(fpout, "  printresult();\n}\n");
     if (buf != '}') error("Close brace (}) expected");
     fclose(fpin); fclose(fpout);
     printf("\n\nContents of output file OBJECT.C:\n\n");
     fpout = fopen("OBJECT.C", "r");
     while (ch = getc(fpout), ch > 0) putchar(ch);
     fclose(fpout);
}

int nextchar()
{ int ch;
  do
  { ch = getc(fpin);
    if (ch == EOF) error("End of file reached");
    putchar(ch);
  } while (ch == ' ' || ch == '\n');
  return ch;
}

error(str) char *str;
{ printf("\nError: %s\n", str); exit(1);
}

expression()
{ char optor;
  term();
  while (buf == '+' || buf == '-')
  { optor = buf; buf = nextchar();
    term();
    fprintf(fpout, "  %s();\n",
      optor == '+' ? "add" : "subtract");
  }
}

term()
{ factor();
  while (buf == '*')
  { buf = nextchar();
    factor();
    fprintf(fpout, "  multiply();\n");
  }
}

factor()
{ if (buf >= '0' && buf <= '9')
    fprintf(fpout, "  push(%c);\n", buf); else
  if (buf == '(')
  { buf = nextchar();
    expression();
    if (buf != ')') error("')' expected");
  } else error("Digit or '(' expected");
  buf = nextchar();
}
```

For a demonstration let us use the same file INFIX.TXT as in Sections 9.3 and

9.4, where we computed the value −74 by using the programs POSTFIX.C and POSTINT.C. Here, we also need two steps to obtain this value. We first run the above compiler, to obtain:

```
This program reads an input file, containing
a VSL program, such as, for example, {3-2*5}

Name of input file:   infix.txt
VSL program read from file:

{ 3 * 4 − 5 * 6 − 7 * (4 + 2 + 2) }

Contents of output file OBJECT.C:

main()
{
  push(3);
  push(4);
  multiply();
  push(5);
  push(6);
  multiply();
  subtract();
  push(7);
  push(4);
  push(2);
  add();
  push(2);
  add();
  multiply();
  subtract();
  printresult();
}
```

After compiling this and linking the result together with the translated version of RTS.C (see Section 9.5) we obtain an executable program which (when executed) gives the following output:

```
Result: −74
```

EXERCISES

In each of the following exercises a new set of syntax diagrams is to be drawn. Then the language in question may be implemented in three ways:

(1) By a source-text interpreter (see Section 9.2);
(2) By both a conversion from infix to postfix and a postfix interpreter (see Sections 9.3 and 9.4);
(3) By both a compiler producing an object program and a run-time system (see Sections 9.5 and 9.6).

Since each of the methods (1)–(3) is applicable to each of the following four exercises, there are in fact twelve distinct exercises.

9.1 Extend the language VSL to admit also integers of more than one decimal digit, and implement the extended language.

9.2 Extend VSL with the binary operators / and %, which, respectively, yield the quotient and the remainder of an integer division. Implement the extended language.

9.3 Extend VSL with the unary minus operator. Since we have

$$(-a) * b = -(a * b)$$

you may regard the expression

$$-a * b$$

either as the product of $-a$ and b or as the negated product of a and b (where a and b stand for decimal digits). This means that the new operator may be applied either to a factor or to a term, whichever you prefer. If you apply it to a factor (and define the result to be a factor as well), you will admit constructions as, for example:

$$3 * ---(4 * 5)$$

which would not be admitted in the other case. (Note that there is a distinction between C and Pascal in this regard.) In postfix output a unary operator will follow its operand. For example, if in the postfix output we denote the unary minus operator by a dollar sign ($) to distinguish it from the binary minus operator ($-$), the postfix result in the above example $-a * b$ is either

$$a\$b*$$

or

$$a * b\$$$

depending on your choice mentioned above. Implement the extended language.

9.4 Define and implement the 'Very Logical Language' *VLL*.
Every expression in VLL may contain:

(1) The values 0 and 1 (to be regarded as *false* and *true*, respectively);
(2) The operators !, &, |, with the same meaning and precedence as in the C language;
(3) Parentheses, with their usual meaning.

APPENDIX A

Some Pitfalls for Beginning C Programmers

Though an excellent language in the long run, C has some well-known pitfalls or stumbling blocks for beginners. This appendix lists the most notorious among them for the benefit of those with little or no C experience. It covers only a few aspects of C, so the reader is referred to a book on this language for more information.

A1 THE EQUAL SIGN

A single equal sign (=) denotes assignment, and a double equal sign (==) is used in comparisons. Thus, to test if x is equal to a, we must write

```
if (x == a) ...
```

Writing = instead of == would cause the value of a to be assigned to x. In the case of such a mistake the compiler will find no error, because in C the character '=' (used for assignment) is really an operator, so it may occur in any expression, just like any other operator. There is no 'Boolean' or 'logical' type in C, but the integer value 0 means *false*, and, normally, 1 denotes *true*. Also, any other non-zero value will be interpreted as *true*, so if we write

```
if (x = a) ...
```

then the statement denoted by the three dots will be executed if the value of a is non-zero.

A2 THE OPERATOR &

With the declaration

```
int n, a[3];
```

the four expressions $\&n$, a (not preceded by &), $a+1$, $a+2$ denote addresses, so we can write

195

```
scanf("%d %d %d %d", &n, a, a+1, a+2);
```

if we want to read four integers and to assign them to *n*, *a*[0], *a*[1], *a*[2], in that order. Omitting & in &*n* is a very common mistake; its consequence is that the *value* of the variable *n* is interpreted as an address to store the value that has been read. If our system provides for memory protection, some technical error message such as '*Memory access violation*' may follow. We are worse off on most microcomputers, since without memory protection the contents of some memory location may be destroyed, which may cause the system to crash or produce all kinds of unpredictable results.

A3   VALUES RETURNED BY FUNCTIONS

If a function is not declared before it is used the compiler will assume the returned value to be of type *int*. For example, in Section 1.6 we discussed the function *factorial*, which returns a double-precision floating-point value. In a main program such as

```
main()
{ double factorial();
  printf("%f", factorial(10));
}
```

we must not forget to declare *factorial* as was done here on the second line, even if the function text itself follows immediately in the same file. In the latter case, most compilers will give at least a warning, but we very frequently call functions that are not defined in the same file. Such functions must be declared, as in the above example, unless they return a value of type *int* (or no value at all). This is particularly relevant for mathematical standard functions. In this case, the declarations we need are included in the header file *math.h*. For example, instead of declaring

```
double cos();
```

ourselves, we normally write

```
#include <math.h>
```

If we used neither this line nor our own declaration of *cos*, a call of this function would lead to wrong results. Again, we should not blame the C compiler for not giving an error message, since in C it is quite normal to use external functions; the compiler will not miss any definitions or declarations of functions, but assume

(1) That those functions will be present in some object module or library offered to the linker; and
(2) That they will return an integer value.

In our example, (1) is correct but (2) is not, so the compiler will generate incorrect object code.

In the case of a *macro* we may have a problem with assumption (1). For example, if we do not include the header file *stdio.h* by writing

```
#include <stdio.h>
```

and we use *getchar*, then the compiler will not know that this is a macro (defined in that header file) and therefore mistake it for a function. Again, we will not get any error message, but, after compilation, the linker will not find it, so in this case we may expect an error message from the linker.

A4   TYPES OF ARGUMENTS AND FORMAL PARAMETERS

Since functions are frequently defined in files other than those in which they are used the compiler does not always know the specified types of formal parameters and will therefore not perform any checking as to the type of arguments. Nor will it perform any automatic conversion from *int* to *double*, as far as arguments of functions are concerned. For example, we can compute the value of the mathematical constant π as follows:

```
#include <math.h>
double pi;
. . .
pi = 4.0 * atan(1.0);
```

If in the last line we had written *atan*(1) instead of *atan*(1.0) the compiler would have generated incorrect object code because it does not know that the function *atan* expects a floating-point argument.

We also obtain incorrect object code in a case such as

```
int n;
. . .
printf("%f". n):
```

since the integer argument *n* will not automatically be converted to a floating)point value, required here because of "%f".

APPENDIX B

Program Index by Chapter

For quick reference, here is a summary of some useful (or, at least, interesting) programs and functions, in the same order as they occur in this book. Page numbers are given in parentheses. Most modules mentioned below are complete, ready-to-run programs. If not, the description will indicate this.

CHAPTER 1: PROGRAMMING STYLE, ITERATION AND RECURSION

TIME.C — Measure the time used by both a recursive and a non-recursive function to compute $n!$ (14–15)

EUCLID.C — Function to compute the greatest common divisor of two integers, using Euclid's algorithm (17)

READINT.C — Function to read an integer, including a test for integer overflow (21)

PRINTINT.C — Function to print an integer with a field width given as an argument (22)

POWER6.C — Function to compute x^n efficiently (27)

CHAPTER 2: ARRAY AND FILE MANIPULATION

SORT1.C — Straight selection sort (function) (32)

SORT2.C — Straight selection sort (function), applied to fixed-length strings (33)

SORT3.C — Shaker sort (function) (34)

QSORT1.C — Quicksort (function) (35)

QSORT3.C — Quicksort (function) with limited recursion depth (38)

STRQSORT.C — Quicksort, applied to variable-length strings (40–41)

MERGE.C — Merge two files containing integers (43–44)

NMSORT.C — Natural merge sort, applied to floating-point numbers in a file (44–46)

FQSORT.C   External quicksort, applied to floating-point numbers in a file
                  (47–49)
BINSEARCH.C   Function for binary search (52)
HASH1.C   Hashing with linear probing (55–56)
HASH2.C   Double hashing (57–58)

CHAPTER 3:   SOME COMBINATORIAL ALGORITHMS

NESTED.C   A variable number of nested loops (62–63)
PERM.C   Generate permutations in natural order (67–68)
COMB.C   Generate combinations (70–71)
KNAPSACK.C   Solve the (simplified) knapsack problem (72–73)
DYNPRO.C   Use dynamic programming to form a given sum in the shortest
                  way that is possible, using only integers out of a given set (75–76)

CHAPTER 4:   LINEAR LISTS

LIST.C   Build a linear list (80)
INFSYS1.C   An information system based on a linear list (86–88)
QUEUE.C   Demonstration of a queue (91–92)

CHAPTER 5:   BINARY TREES

BINTREE.C   Build and search a binary search tree, and print its contents
                  (103–105)
PERFBAL.C   Build a perfectly balanced binary search tree (108)
INFSYS2.C   An information system based on a perfectly balanced binary
                  search tree (111–113)
PTREE.C   Delete nodes and subtrees from a binary search tree, using point-
                  ers to pointers (119–120)

CHAPTER 6:   B-TREES

BTREE.C   Build and update a B-tree in main memory (130–134)
GENNUM.C   Generate an ASCII file with numbers, to be read by DISK-
                  TREE.C (139)
DISKTREE.C   Build and update a B-tree on disk (142–148)

CHAPTER 7:   TRIES

TRIE.C   Build and search a trie (151–153)

CHAPTER 8:   GRAPHS

TOPOL.C   Topological sorting (164–165)
CPM.C   Critical Path Method for project planning (170–173)

CHAPTER 9: FUNDAMENTALS OF INTERPRETERS AND COMPILERS

INTERPR.C   A source-text interpreter for VSL (180–181)

POSTFIX.C   Conversion from infix to postfix (183–184)

POSTINT.C   A postfix interpreter, which interprets postfix expressions pro-
                  duced by POSTFIX.C (186–187)

OBJECT.C   Sample object program, generated by COMPILER.C, and to be
                  linked together with RTS.C (188)

RTS.C   Run-time system to be used in connection with object programs
                  such as OBJECT.C (189)

COMPILER.C   VSL compiler, generating object programs (190–191)

Bibliography

Aho, A. V., J. E. Hopcroft, and J. D. Ullman (1974). *The Design and Analysis of Computer Algorithms*, Reading, Mass.: Addison-Wesley.

Aho, A. V., J. E. Hopcroft, and J. D. Ullman (1983). *Data Structures and Algorithms*, Reading, Mass.: Addison-Wesley.

Ammeraal, L. (1986). *Programming Principles in Computer Graphics*, Chichester: John Wiley.

Ammeraal, L. (1986). *C for Programmers*, Chichester: John Wiley.

Ammeraal, L. (1987). *Computer Graphics for the IBM PC*, Chichester: John Wiley.

Atkinson, L. V. (1980). *Pascal Programming*, Chichester: John Wiley.

Bellman, R. E. (1957). *Dynamic Programming*, Princeton, NJ: Princeton University Press.

Berge, C. (1958). *The Theory of Graphs and its Applications*, New York, NY: John Wiley.

Feuer, A., and N. Gehani (eds) (1984). *Comparing and Assessing Programming Languages Ada C Pascal*, Englewood Cliffs, NJ: Prentice-Hall.

Gonnet, G. H. (1984). *Handbook of Algorithms and Data Structures*, London: Addison-Wesley.

Harbison, S. P., and G. L. Steele Jr (1984). *C A Reference Manual*, Englewood Cliffs, NJ: Prentice-Hall.

Horowitz, E., and S. Sahni (1977). *Fundamentals of Data Structures*, London: Pitman.

Kernighan, B. W., and D. M. Ritchie (1978). *The C Programming Language*, Englewood Cliffs, NJ: Prentice-Hall.

Knuth, D. E. (1968). *The Art of Computer Programming Vol. I: Fundamental Algorithms*, Reading, Mass.: Addison-Wesley.

Knuth, D. E. (1969). *The Art of Computer Programming Vol. II: Seminumerical Algorithms*, Reading, Mass.: Addison-Wesley.

Knuth, D. E. (1973). *The Art of Computer Programming Vol. III: Sorting and Searching*, Reading, Mass.: Addison-Wesley.

Tondo, C. L., and S. E. Gimpel (1985). *The C Answer Book*, Englewood Cliffs, NJ: Prentice-Hall.

Wirth, N. (1976). *Algorithms + Data Structures = Programs*, Englewood Cliffs, NJ: Prentice-Hall.

Index

activity, 166
activity network, 160
acyclic graph, 161
adjacency matrix, 160
ASCII file, 42
AVL-tree, 107

B-tree, 123
balanced binary tree, 106
binary file, 42
binary operator, 178
binary search, 51, 101
binary search tree, 102
binary tree, 101
bitwise AND, 24
bottom-up, 10, 75
bubble sort, 34

C language, 80, 195
changing money, 74
child, 101
circular list, 92
closed hashing, 57
coins, 74
collision, 54
combination, 69
compiler, 175
complexity, 2
conversion (of radix), 19
CPM, 166
critical path, 167, 169
critical path method, 166
cycle, 161

direct access, 47
directed graph, 159
disk, 123, 139
double hashing, 57
doubly-linked list, 93
dummy header node, 93
dynamic programming, 75

earliest event time, 167
edge, 159
empty list, 93
Euclid's algorithm, 17
event, 166
expression, 176
external sort, 41

factor, 176
factorial, 13
feof, 47
file, 139
fopen, 142
free, 84
fseek, 47, 140
ftell, 47
fwrite, 140

gcd, 15
genuinely recursive, 11
global variable, 6
grammar, 175
graph, 159
graphics, 9
greatest common divisor, 15
greedy algorithm, 74
growth rate, 2

hashing, 54
head of a list, 79
height-balanced, 107
height, 101, 107
Horner's rule, 17

implementation, 175
in-degree, 161
infix notation, 181
interpreter, 175, 179
inverted adjacency list, 161
inverted adjacency list, 168

Josephus problem, 98

key, 31
knapsack problem, 71

language, 175
left-associative, 178
level, 101
linear list, 79
linear probing, 54
linear search, 3, 51
linked list, 79
linked stack, 91
list, 79

malloc, 80
merging, 43

natural merge sort, 42
nested loops, 61
node, 79
non-terminal symbol, 177
NULL, 79

object program, 188
open hashing, 57, 99
ordered list, 82,83
out-degree, 169

parent, 101
perfectly balanced, 106
performance, 49
permutation, 65
PERT, 166
pointer, 32, 79, 115
postfix notation, 181
power, 22
prefix, 150,156
prefix notation, 181
primitive symbol, 177
project planning, 160, 166

queue, 91
quicksort, 35

radix, 19
ramdisk, 49
random access, 42, 47
random number, 139
realloc, 90
record, 54, 79
recursion, 10
recursion depth, 12

reverse Polish, 181
root, 101
root node, 101
run-time system, 189
run, 44

secondary storage, 123
semantic rule, 175
sentinel, 3, 80, 93
sequential access, 47
shaker sort, 34
shift right, 24
side-effect, 8
sorting, 31
source-text, 179
sparse matrix, 160
spelling checker, 156,157
stable sorting, 50
stack, 89
stack overflow, 12, 89
static variable, 8
straight selection, 32
strcmp, 33
strcpy, 33
string, 32
structure, 79
syntactic category, 177
syntax rule, 175

tail of a list, 79
tail recursion, 12
term, 176
terminal symbol, 177
text editor, 95
time complexity, 2, 32
top-down, 10
topological order, 161
tree, 10, 101
treesort, 107
trie, 141

unary operator, 178
undirected graph, 159
unformatted I/O, 42
user-interface, 110

vertex, 159
virtual disk, 49

word processor, 95
workfile, 95, 110